SPELLING WORKOUT

Phillip K. Trocki

Modern Curriculum Press

EXECUTIVE EDITOR   Wendy Whitnah

PROJECT EDITOR   Diane Dzamtovski

EDITORIAL DEVELOPMENT
DESIGN AND PRODUCTION   The Hampton-Brown Company

ILLUSTRATORS   Anthony Accardo, Peter Bianco, Roberta Collier-Morales, Mike Eagle,
Meryl Henderson, Jane McCreary, Masami Miyamoto, Rik Olson, Rod Thomas,
John Sandford, Joyce Zarins.

PHOTO CREDITS   8, Frank Siteman/The Picture Cube; 10, Frank Siteman/The Picture Cube;
12, Robert W. Ginn/The Picture Cube; 18, Okapia/Photo Researchers;
20, Bil Plummer/Image Bank; 28, Sharon Bazarian/The Picture Cube;
30, Jeffrey Dunn/Jeffrey Dunn Studios; 36, Jeffrey Dunn/Jeffrey Dunn Studios;
40, Palmer & Brilliant/Andrew Brilliant-Carol Palmer Photography;
44, Palmer & Brilliant/Andrew Brilliant-Carol Palmer Photography;
52, Carl Purcell/Photo Researchers; 66, Palmer & Brilliant/Andrew Brilliant-
Carol Palmer Photography; 80, Andrew Brilliant/Andrew Brilliant-
Carol Palmer Photography; 91, Lionel Brown/Image Bank;
95, Paula M. Lerner/The Picture Cube; 100, David S. Strickler/The Picture Cube;
110, The Multiple Mirror Telescope is a joint project of the Smithsonian Institute and
the University of Arizona. Photo courtesy of the Smithsonian Astrophysical
Observatory; 112, Comstock; 114, Jaye R. Phillips/The Picture Cube;
116, Uniphoto/Pictor; 126, NASA (National Aeronautics and Space Administration);
138, William A. Todd, Jr./The Picture Cube; 140, David Young-Wolff/Photo Edit;
142, Jeffrey Dunn/Jeffrey Dunn Studios; 144, Culver Pictures.

COVER DESIGN   The Hampton-Brown Company
COVER PHOTO   Peter Miller/Image Bank

Typefaces for the cursive type in this book were provided
by Zaner-Bloser, Inc., Columbus, Ohio, copyright, 1993.

Game Plan
You may find it easier to spell a word that contains double consonants if you first divide the word into syllables. Pronounce each syllable of the following words and listen for the sounds of the consonants.

ne/ces/si/ty   with/hold/ing

Warm Up

Vocabulary Development

Write the List Word that matches each synonym.

1. restraining _withholding_
2. ruin _corrupt_
3. graciously _succulent_
4. enormous _immense_
5. need _assistance_
6. agreement _boycott_
7. juicy _drizzle_
8. squash _oppress_
9. call _summon_
10. ownership _possession_

Dictionary Skills

Write the List Word that comes between each pair of dictionary guide words.

1. succeed/succinct _____
2. immerse/immortal _____
3. denounce/drain _____
4. access/assurance _____
5. breeze/coral _____
6. detour/drum _____
7. polka/position _____
8. neck/policy _____
9. white/width _____
10. astute/canary _____

1. acceptance
2. corrupt
3. immigration
4. boycott
5. summon
6. assistance
7. depression
8. necessity
9. pollen
10. suppress
11. cancellation
12. drizzle
13. possession
14. succulent
15. wholly
16. cordially
17. immense
18. oppress
19. successive
20. withholding

Practice

Word Analysis

Write List Words to answer the following questions.

Which words contain the following suffixes?

ance	**sion**	**ly**

1. _____   3. _____   5. _____

2. _____   4. _____   6. _____

Which words contain the prefix **im**?

7. _____   8. _____

Proofreading

Use the proofreading marks to correct the mistakes in the sentences. Then write misspelled List Words correctly.

Proofreading Marks
- ⬭ spelling mistake
- ⊙ add period
- ? add question mark
- ! add exclamation mark
- ≡ capital letter
- ∧ add comma
- ∨ add apostrophe

Did you know?

Around 1880, a man named Captain Charles Boycott acted as a rent collector for wealthy land-owners in Ireland. Captain Boycott charged farmers extremely high rent for the land they worked. As a result, the farmers got together and refused to pay. Their tactics worked, and the rents were lowered. Soon, the term **boycott** became part of our language, meaning "a strike against unfair practices."

1. During the mayors acceptance speech, a light drizle began to fall _____

2. The police department is witholding facts about the case _____

3. What a surprise it was to see that imennse bear in our campsite _____

4. Dans offer of assisstence was cordialy accepted. _____ _____

5. We wholy support the boycot unless the employer guarantees higher wages.

_____ _____

6. Will the Federal Imigration bureau summon Nikko to take an oath of allegiance

_____

7. There is polen in the air, so I can't suppres a sneeze. _____ _____

8. Because of the cancilation, the championship games will be played on two sucessive weekends.

_____ _____

9. If your steak is tasty and juicy you are eating suculant steak. _____

List Words

acceptance	assistance	cancellation	cordially
corrupt	depression	drizzle	immense
immigration	necessity	possession	oppress
boycott	pollen	succulent	successive
summon	suppress	wholly	withholding

Puzzle

Use the List Words to complete the crossword puzzle.

ACROSS

2. holding something by ownership
6. very large
8. the act of doing away with
9. deeply felt; sincere
10. the entire amount or degree
11. to refuse to buy, sell, or use
13. change from good to bad
14. yellow powder found on the stamen of flowers
15. coming in regular order without a break
16. help; aid
17. to put down by force; crush

DOWN

1. to rain lightly in fine drops
3. to call together
4. something necessary or needed
5. sadness; gloominess
6. the act of moving to a foreign country
7. taking willingly; responding in the affirmative
10. to keep from giving or granting
12. to trouble the mind of; worry
15. full of juice; juicy

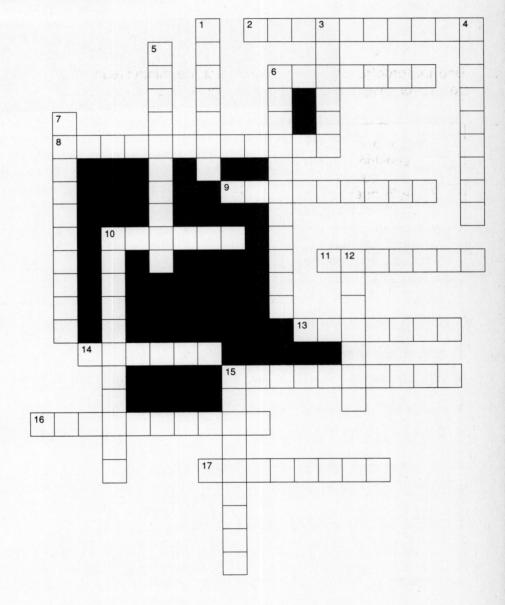

Test Yourself

In each pair of List Words, underline the
misspelled List Word and write it correctly
on the line.

1. immense, posession   _____

2. pollen, imigration   _____

3. opress, necessity   _____

4. boycott, witholding   _____

5. succesive, summon   _____

6. supress, drizzle   _____

7. depression, aceptance   _____

8. asistance, corrupt   _____

Express Yourself

Reporters for both television and newspapers often interview public figures to
discover current news and information. They usually prepare their interview
questions in advance. Pretend you are a television reporter who intends to
interview the mayor of your city about the plan to clean up the city streets.
Prepare at least five questions to ask the mayor. Proofread and revise your
questions. With a partner, role play the interview of the mayor by the reporter.

Bonus Words: Government Offices

commissioner	magistrate	ambassador	attorney general	supervisor
treasurer	superintendent	secretary	coroner	vice-president

Write the Bonus Word that matches each clue given.

1. title of some members of the president's cabinet _____

2. representative of one country to another country _____

3. minor official, such as a justice of the peace _____

4. country's top law official _____

5. official next in rank to the president _____

6. officer in charge of funds or finances _____

7. official who determines causes of death _____

8. official who heads a government department, such as fire or police _____

9. manager or director of a department or group _____

10. person in charge of a department or institution, such as a school _____

Game Plan

The /ər/ sound that you hear at the end of <u>murmur</u>, <u>linear</u>, <u>alligator</u>, and <u>glacier</u> can be spelled many different ways. When you hear this sound in a word, pay close attention to how it is spelled. Remember, when the sound comes at the end of a word that names a person who does something, the sound is often spelled with **or**, as in <u>conqueror</u>.

1. alligator
2. junior
3. incubator
4. murmur
5. reflector
6. ancestors
7. glacier
8. investor
9. particular
10. anchor
11. angular
12. gladiator
13. linear
14. perpendicular
15. tweezers
16. conqueror
17. impostor
18. moderator
19. professor
20. vinegar

Warm Up

Vocabulary Development

Write the List Word that matches each synonym.

1. straight _____
2. crocodile _____
3. winner _____
4. faker _____
5. younger _____
6. whisper _____
7. forebears _____
8. warrior _____
9. pincers _____
10. teacher _____
11. vertical _____
12. specific _____

Dictionary Skills

Write the List Word that matches each sound-spelling.

1. (käng´ kər ər) _____
2. (an´ ses tərs) _____
3. (mäd´ ə rāt ər) _____
4. (ing´ kyə bāt´ ər) _____
5. (ang´ gyə lər) _____

6. (ri flek´ tər) _____
7. (vin´ i gər) _____
8. (in vest´ ər) _____
9. (glā´ shər) _____
10. (ang´ kər) _____

Practice

Word Analysis

Write the List Words in which /ər/ is spelled **ar**.

1. _____
2. _____
3. _____
4. _____
5. _____

Wriite the List Words in which /ər/ is spelled **er**.

6. _____
7. _____
8. _____
9. _____

Write the List Word in which /ər/ is spelled **ur**.

10. _____

Write the List Words containing these double Letters:

11. ee _____
12. ss _____
13. ll _____

> **Did you know?**
>
> **Tweezers** comes from an old French word, now no longer used, that means "a set of surgical instruments." That word came in turn from *etuis*, plural of a word for a small case used to hold needles or other small implements.

Word Application

Replace the underlined word or words in each sentence with a List Word. Write the List Word on the line.

1. The two lines are <u>at right angles</u> to each other. _____

2. The recipe calls for just a dash <u>of a sour liquid</u>. _____

3. We are looking for an <u>exact</u> kind of mustard. _____

4. The trek will begin at the base of the <u>mountain of ice</u>. _____

5. Although the artist's people were rounded, the buildings had a <u>narrow, uniform</u> appearance.

_____

6. Mrs. Greenbaum, a wealthy stockbroker, discussed the methods she used to become a

successful <u>person who uses money for a business to gain a profit</u>. _____

7. Mr. Olson moved the hen's eggs into the <u>place that is kept warm for hatching eggs</u>.

_____

8. Captain Martinez ordered the sailors to drop the <u>heavy object that is put in water to keep a ship

from drifting</u>. _____

List Words

alligator	ancestors	angular	conqueror
junior	glacier	gladiator	impostor
incubator	investor	linear	moderator
murmur	particular	perpendicular	professor
reflector	anchor	tweezers	vinegar

Puzzle

Use the List Words to complete the crossword puzzle.

ACROSS

1. at right angles
6. a sour liquid
7. person in charge of conducting a debate
9. surface that reflects
11. large mass of snow and ice
12. in a line
14. small pincers for holding small items
16. having sharp corners
18. warm container for hatching eggs

DOWN

2. person who invests
3. distinct, not general
4. one who cheats or tricks people
5. one who overcomes another
8. teacher at college
10. people who came before others in a family line
11. ancient Roman fighter
13. large lizard-like animal
15. low, steady sound
17. a younger person
19. heavy object that holds boat in place

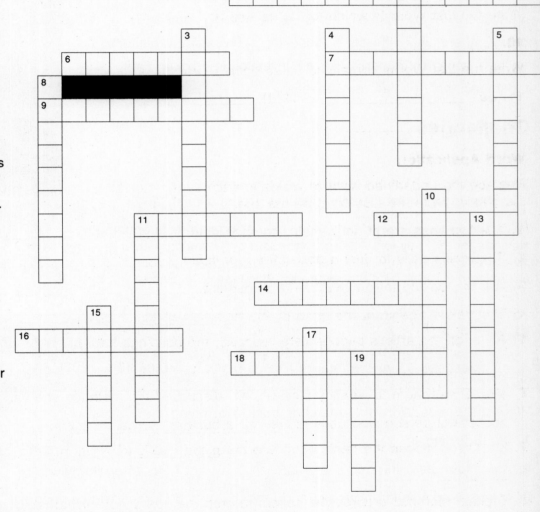

Proofreading

Use the proofreading marks to correct the mistakes in the letter to the editor. Then write the misspelled List Words on the lines.

Proofreading Marks		
⬭ spelling mistake	ⱱ	add apostrophe
! add exclamation mark	⌃	add comma

     Its a terrible shame! Did you know that people are no longer allowed to walk their dogs in Pocket Park? The town never heard a mumer from me when the leash law went into effect. However Im upset about this partikular move. I hadnt noticed any problem before yet problems were just what the modorator of last weeks town meeting mentioned. In my opinion, he is an imposter. I don't believe there was any study done by a university profesor on dog behavior in parks. As an investtor in Pocket Park, I demand that the law be repealed

1. _____

2. _____

3. _____

4. _____

5. _____

6. _____

Challenges

Express Yourself

Write a paragraph on this topic:
    Should dogs roam freely or should there be a leash law?

First, state your opinion clearly. Then give at least three supporting reasons for that opinion. After proofreading and revising your paragraph, meet with your classmates and compare opinions. Organize a class debate that presents two sides of this issue.

Bonus Words: Law

petition	property	warrant	judicial	mandate
trespass	misdemeanor	indictment	subpoena	judgment

Write the Bonus Word that matches each clue given.

1. legal decision _____

2. order to appear in court _____

3. a formal accusation from a grand jury

    _____

4. written order to arrest _____

5. order from higher court _____

6. something that is owned _____

7. to enter illegally _____

8. formal written request _____

9. related to judges _____

10. minor offense _____

Doubling Final Consonants

Game Plan

When a short-vowel word or syllable ends in a single consonant, usually double the final consonant before adding an ending that begins with a vowel.

unforget + **able** = <u>unforgettable</u>   **defer** + **ed** = <u>deferred</u>

overlap + **ing** = <u>overlapping</u>   **propel** + **er** = <u>propeller</u>

When adding **ly** to a word that ends in **l**, keep both **l**'s.

usual + **ly** = <u>usually</u>

Warm Up

1. *controller*
2. *patrolled*
3. *forbidden*
4. *conferred*
5. *preferred*
6. *unforgettable*
7. *deferred*
8. *expelled*
9. *transmitting*
10. *deterring*
11. *occasionally*
12. *occurring*
13. *incurred*
14. *propeller*
15. *admitting*
16. *omitted*
17. *permitted*
18. *acquitted*
19. *overlapping*
20. *handicapped*

Vocabulary Development

Write the List Word from column B that matches the definition in column A.

A		B
1. stopping	_____	permitted
2. came together	_____	omitted
3. memorable	_____	deferred
4. cast out	_____	deterring
5. cleared one's name	_____	conferred
6. chose a certain one	_____	unforgettable
7. postponed	_____	expelled
8. once in a while	_____	acquitted
9. allowed to act	_____	occasionally
10. left out	_____	preferred

Dictionary Skills

Rewrite each of the following List Words to show how they are divided into syllables.

1. handicapped _____		6. controller _____
2. patrolled _____		7. occurring _____
3. forbidden _____		8. incurred _____
4. transmitting _____		9. propeller _____
5. overlapping _____		10. admitting _____

Practice

Word Analysis

Write the List Word formed by adding one of the following endings to each of the words given: **er**, **ed**, **en**, **ing**, **ly**.

1. admit _____
2. confer _____
3. omit _____
4. forbid _____
5. permit _____
6. defer _____
7. patrol _____
8. control _____
9. occur _____

10. occasional _____
11. propel _____
12. handicap _____
13. incur _____
14. overlap _____
15. prefer _____
16. acquit _____
17. expel _____
18. deter _____

Word Application

Write a List Word to complete each sentence.

1. The directors of the manufacturing firm _____ about ways to increase production.

2. Unfortunately, Ian _____ his name from his project.

3. Lois was _____ from the program because she broke the rules.

4. The breathtaking view from the top of Mt. Washington was _____ .

5. A new local television station will begin _____ programs next week.

6. Mrs. Chase is the air-traffic _____ who will be guiding the disabled jet through the landing.

7. The guard dogs are doing a fine job of _____ trespassers.

8. After weeks of testimony, the jury _____ the defendant.

9. A solar eclipse will be _____ at the beginning of next month.

10. Any bills that have been _____ during your stay will be paid by the company.

11. Although Jon enjoyed skiing, he really _____ summer sports.

12. Since their vacations are _____ , they plan to spend some time together at the beach.

13. State troopers _____ the highway in unmarked cars.

List Words

controller	unforgettable	occasionally	omitted
patrolled	deferred	occurring	permitted
forbidden	expelled	incurred	acquitted
conferred	transmitting	propeller	overlapping
preferred	deterring	admitting	handicapped

Puzzle

Write the List Word that is a synonym for each word given to complete the crossword puzzle.

ACROSS

1. disabled
5. director
7. policed
8. ejected
10. postponed
14. sending
16. confessing
17. allowed
18. preventing

DOWN

2. cleared
3. outlawed
4. rotor blades
6. happening
9. favored
11. eliminated
12. memorable
13. consulted
15. acquired

Did you know?

There is a game that dates back to the 1300s in which two players would put money into a hat, and bet on the values of different items. An umpire would make the decision who came closest to the actual value. It eventually came to be called "hand in the cap," and later known as **handicap**. Today the word not only applies to a disadvantage in a sporting event, like golf or bowling, but is used to describe physical and mental disabilities.

Proofreading

Use the proofreading marks to correct the mistakes in the play review below. Then write the misspelled List Words on the lines.

Proofreading Marks	
⬭ spelling mistake	⊙ add period
≡ capital letter	⌄⌄ add quotation marks

The premiere performance of *Three cheers* at the harrison Theater was unforgetable The cast from Indy high School are true comedians. they ocassionaly made mistakes, but when the lead omited key words and said, now the propeler has expired, the result was very funny

1. _____

2. _____

3. _____

4. _____

Express Yourself

In a story, **dialogue** helps reveal the character's personality to the reader. Think about a conversation that you have had recently with someone. In a few paragraphs, write that conversation. Use realistic language and speech patterns in your dialogue. Proofread and revise your dialogue. Then work with a partner to read your dialogues aloud for the class.

Bonus Words: Grammar

adverb	interjection	nominative	singular	auxiliary verb
adjective	possessive	objective	interrogative	clause

Write the Bonus Word that the underlined word or words exemplify.

1. <u>They</u> arrived in time to see the opening ceremonies. _____

2. We read in the paper that <u>Raymond's</u> brother joined the Peace Corps. _____

3. Tina drove <u>cautiously</u> on the icy road. _____

4. <u>Wow</u>! What a surprise it is to see you again! _____

5. <u>Because it was raining</u>, the game was postponed. _____

6. We <u>will</u> help Mom fix dinner. _____

7. You have to read this <u>marvelous</u> book. _____

8. <u>Are you listening carefully to the directions</u>? _____

9. Miss Lewis assigned <u>him</u> the role of Caesar in the play. _____

10. In the box, there were magazines, postcards, stamps, and one <u>pencil</u>. _____

Game Plan

Dividing words into syllables can help you spell them. Usually, you can divide between a root word and a prefix or suffix, as in re/act. You can divide between two consonants that come between two vowels, as in col/lect. When only one consonant comes between two vowels, divide after the first vowel if it is long, as in pro/tect, and after the consonant if the vowel is short, as in sat/is/fy. A vowel can also form its own syllable, as in vi/o/lent.

Pay particular attention to the spelling of word endings. Words ending with **al**, such as fiscal, may sound as if they end with **le** or **el**. The /ər/ sound you hear at the end of junior can be spelled many ways, as in murmur, grammar, humor, and super.

Pay attention to words that have endings beginning with vowels. These may have had their final consonants doubled if the vowel before the consonant is short, as in trotting and permitted.

Practice

Write a List Word to complete each sentence.

Lesson **1**

affidavit
appetite
commemorate
tendency
voluntary
resurrect
dominate
guardian
saturate
installation

_____

_____

1. Tomatoes have a _____ to grow best during hot, sunny weather.

2. An _____ is a written statement.

3. Your idea didn't work last year, but let's _____ it and see if we have better luck this year.

4. A sprinkler is the easiest way to _____ the grass.

5. A child's _____ is an adult who is authorized to make decisions for the child.

6. We would like everyone to make a _____ contribution to this worthy cause.

7. The _____ of an antenna will improve TV reception.

8. A water tower that large will _____ the landscape.

9. My parents will plant a tree to _____ my sister's birth.

10. After a workout, it takes a lot more than one sandwich to satisfy my _____ .

Write a List Word to complete each analogy.

1. Huge is to small as _____ is to tiny.

2. Cold is to hot as arctic is to _____.

3. Careful is to thoughtless as _____ is to irrational.

4. Death is to burial as rebirth is to _____.

5. Serenity is to disorganization as tranquil is to

_____ .

6. Genuine is to authentic as _____ is to unnatural.

7. Eternity is to momentary as _____ is to temporary.

8. Honorable is to dishonorable as legal is to

_____ .

9. Purposeful is to scheduled as _____ is to unscheduled.

10. Photography is to artistic as chemistry is to

_____ .

Lesson 2

artificial	tropical
criminal	logical
experimental	perpetual
hysterical	colossal
revival	accidental

_____

_____

Write List Words to answer the questions.

Which words contain double **m**?

1. _____

2. _____

3. _____

Which words contain double **s**?

4. _____

5. _____

6. _____

7. _____   8. _____

Which words end in **ance**?

9. _____   10. _____

Which words end in **ation**?

11. _____   12. _____

Which words end in **sion**?

13. _____   14. _____

Lesson 3

possession	assistance
summon	depression
cancellation	immense
successive	necessity
acceptance	immigration

_____

_____

Write the List Word that matches each clue.

1. found in a cold place _____

2. a gentle sound _____

3. shines light back at you _____

4. someone with money to loan _____

5. not rounded _____

6. not slanted _____

7. ingredient in salad dressing _____

8. great-grandparents, for instance _____

9. a winner _____

10. separate or special _____

Lesson **4**

ancestors	murmur
investor	vinegar
particular	glacier
perpendicular	conqueror
reflector	angular

_____

_____

Unscramble the List Words to complete the crossword puzzle.

ACROSS
2. INROCRUCG
4. LYANSOACLOCI
7. REPFREDER
8. UCRINDRE
9. FRONDRECE

DOWN
1. LABEFUNGETORT
2. TOMIDET
3. REFEDDER
5. ENPAIDDPACH
6. INTAMGTID

Lesson **5**

admitting	conferred
deferred	handicapped
incurred	occurring
omitted	occasionally
preferred	unforgettable

_____

_____

summon	guardian	depression
saturate	assistance	appetite
investor	tropical	murmur
particular	occasionally	accidental
unforgettable	colossal	omitted

Mixed Practice

Write a List Word to complete each series.

1. memorable, outstanding, _____

2. sometimes, periodically, _____

3. command, invite, _____

4. financier, depositor, _____

5. individual, certain, _____

6. unintended, unexpected, _____

7. sweltering, steamy, _____

8. protector, defender, _____

9. forgot, erased, _____

10. help, support, _____

11. soak, drench, _____

12. ditch, hollow, _____

13. hunger, desire, _____

14. whisper, mumble, _____

15. mammoth, vast, _____

Test Yourself

In each of the following groups of words, one word is misspelled. Fill in the circle that appears before the word.

1. o posession
o summon
o necessity
o cancellation

2. o successive
o arteficial
o revival
o affidavit

3. o immense
o tropical
o assistance
o depresion

4. o immagration
o acceptance
o criminal
o appetite

5. o hysterical
o comemmorate
o tendency
o deferred

6. o voluntary
o admitting
o incured
o logical

7. o perpetual
o handicapped
o ancesters
o murmur

8. o colossel
o accidental
o dominate
o saturate

9. o gaurdian
o installation
o resurrect
o occasionally

10. o resurrect
o investor
o particular
o reflecter

11. o preferred
o vinegar
o ommited
o unforgettable

12. o glacier
o conferred
o perpendiculer
o occurring

Game Plan

Prefixes with Greek or Latin roots can indicate "how much." Some examples follow.

Prefix	Origin	Meaning	Prefix	Origin	Meaning
milli–	Latin	one-thousandth	**duo–**	Latin	two
centi–	Latin	one-hundredth	**deca–**	Latin	ten
deci–	Latin	one-tenth	**kilo–**	Greek	one thousand
semi–	Latin	half	**myria–**	Greek	countless
mono–	Greek	one			

1. centigrade
2. decimal
3. kiloliter
4. monolith
5. monarch
6. centimeter
7. deciliter
8. kilowatt
9. monopoly
10. myriad
11. decade
12. duet
13. milligram
14. monotone
15. semiannual
16. decimeter
17. duplex
18. milliliter
19. monologue
20. semiprecious

Warm Up

Vocabulary Development

Write the List Word that matches each definition.

1. music for two people _____

2. speech by one person _____

3. on one tone _____

4. 1,000 watts _____

5. not of high value _____

6. total control _____

7. 0.1 liter _____

8. 0.01 meter _____

9. 0.001 liter _____

10. large stone block _____

11. ten years _____

12. king or queen _____

Dictionary Skills

Write the List Word that matches each sound-spelling.

1. (sem´ i an´ yōō wəl) _____

2. (des´ ə mēt´ ər) _____

3. (sen´ tə grād) _____

4. (män´ ə lôg) _____

5. (mil´ ə gram) _____

6. (kil´ ə let´ ər) _____

7. (des´ ə m'l) _____

8. (mir´ ē əd) _____

9. (dōō´ pleks) _____

10. (män´ ərk) _____

Practice

Word Analysis

Write the List Word derived from the Greek or Latin root given.

1. Greek **polein** ("to sell") _____

2. Greek **plax** ("surface") _____

3. Greek **lithos** ("stone") _____

4. Latin **annus** ("year") _____

5. Greek **tonos** ("tone") _____

6. Greek **archein** ("to rule") _____

7. Latin **gradus** ("degree") _____

8. Greek **legein** ("to speak") _____

9. Latin **gramma** ("small weight") _____

10. Latin **pretium** ("price") _____

Write each List Word under the correct category.

Words with Two Syllables

11. _____
12. _____
13. _____
14. _____

Words with Three Syllables

15. _____
16. _____
17. _____
18. _____
19. _____
20. _____
21. _____
22. _____

Words with Four Syllables

23. _____
24. _____
25. _____
26. _____
27. _____
28. _____
29. _____

Words with Five Syllables

30. _____

Word Application

Write each List Word that is a unit of measurement under the correct category.

Measures Electric Power

1. _____

Measures Weight

2. _____

Measures Length

3. _____
4. _____

Measures Volume of Liquid

5. _____
6. _____
7. _____

Classification

Write a List Word to complete each series.

1. Fahrenheit, Celsius, _____

2. weekly, monthly, _____

3. solo, _____ , trio

4. home, apartment, _____

5. year, _____ , century

6. _____ , gram, metric ton

List Words

centigrade	centimeter	decade	decimeter
decimal	deciliter	duet	duplex
kiloliter	kilowatt	milligram	milliliter
monolith	monopoly	monotone	monologue
monarch	myriad	semiannual	semiprecious

Alphabetical Order

On the lines below, write in alphabetical order the List Words
that contain the prefix meaning "one."

1. _____   **3.** _____   **5.** _____

2. _____   **4.** _____

Puzzle

Use the List Words to complete the crossword puzzle.

ACROSS

1. period of ten years
3. large block of stone
7. owned or controlled by one person or group
8. maintaining the same tone or pitch
9. one-thousandth of a gram
10. having two units or parts
14. thermometer based on 0° as the freezing point of water
16. one-tenth of a meter
17. large, indefinite number or variety
18. one thousand liters
19. one-thousandth of a liter

DOWN

1. fraction with a denominator of ten
2. long speech by one person
4. king, queen, or emperor
5. happening twice a year
6. not highly valuable
11. one-tenth of a liter
12. one-hundredth of a meter
13. one thousand watts
15. music for two voices

Proofreading

Use the proofreading marks to correct the mistakes in the article below. Then write the misspelled List Words on the lines.

Proofreading Marks	
⬭ spelling mistake	? add question mark
⊙ add period	︿ add comma

Have you wondered what it would be like to talk to famous people from history Yesterday students played the roles of a miriad of well-known figures in a dramatized television talk show Who were the interviewees They included a French monark an artist who built a monoolith and a pair of well-known musicians who played a dyuet

1. _____

2. _____

3. _____

4. _____

Express Yourself

You are to be interviewed by a television news reporter. To prepare her questions, the reporter has asked you to submit a one-page autobiographical sketch. Include such information as your birthdate, place of birth, residences, and your interests, accomplishments, and plans. After proofreading and revising your autobiographical sketch, rewrite it neatly and, if you wish to do so, include it with yourclassmates' writing in a class book.

Bonus Words: Biology

genetics	reproduction	pregnancy	fetus	identical
heredity	fertilization	embryo	umbilical cord	fraternal

Write a Bonus Word to complete each sentence.

1. Twins from the same egg are _____ .

2. _____ twins come from two different eggs and do not look identical.

3. The branch of biology that deals with heredity and variation in living things is

   _____ .

4. The _____ is the source of nourishment for a fetal mammal.

5. The transmission of traits from parent to offspring is called _____ .

6. Animals create new members of the species through the process of _____ .

7. _____ is the state of a female animal as she carries her unborn child.

8. Through _____ , the female's egg begins to develop into offspring.

9. The _____ stage is the earliest stage of development of the fertilized egg.

10. In its later stages of development, the unborn offspring is called the _____ .

Game Plan

The prefixes **ante**, **epi**, **pre**, and **pro** may refer to time or place. An understanding of these prefixes can help you spell many words. Look at the chart below.

Prefix	Meaning	Example	Meaning
ante	before, in front of	**anteroom**	entrance room
epi	on the outside, over	**epidermis**	outer layer
pre	in front, earlier	**premature**	happening early
pro	forward, ahead	**protrude**	to stick out

1. antecedent
2. epilogue
3. episode
4. premier
5. protrude
6. anterior
7. premonition
8. preamble
9. prejudice
10. procession
11. epitaph
12. anteroom
13. presuppose
14. premature
15. prophet
16. epistle
17. epidermis
18. prelude
19. proposal
20. protocol

Warm Up

Vocabulary Development

Write the List Word that matches each synonym.

1. event _____
2. first _____
3. letter _____
4. assume _____
5. early _____
6. overhang _____
7. foreseer _____
8. parade _____
9. skin _____
10. forerunner _____
11. forward _____
12. forewarning _____

Dictionary Skills

Rewrite each of the following words to show how they are divided into syllables.

1. protocol _____
2. presuppose _____
3. prelude _____
4. epitaph _____
5. anteroom _____
6. proposal _____
7. premonition _____
8. epilogue _____
9. anterior _____
10. prejudice _____

Practice

Word Analysis

Write the missing prefixes to form List Words that complete the definitions.

1. _____ **dermis**, the outer layer of skin

2. _____ **monition**, a preconceived notion

3. _____ **trude**, to stick out

4. _____ **suppose**, to suppose beforehand

5. _____ **tocol**, a code of proper behavior

6. _____ **room**, an outside chamber

7. _____ **posal**, a suggestion

8. _____ **judice**, judging beforehand

9. _____ **logue**, a speech at the end of a play

10. _____ **taph**, words engraved on a tombstone

11. _____ **mature**, before the proper or usual time

12. _____ **lude**, a preliminary part

Word Application

Replace the underlined words in each sentence with List Words.
Write the List Words on the lines.

1. As we entered the <u>front part</u> of the courtyard, we saw a long <u>parade</u> of dignitaries being

   received by the Queen. _____ _____

2. During his life, he was considered a great <u>seer</u>, which is why the <u>inscription</u> on his gravestone

   refers to him as a man of wisdom and faith. _____ _____

3. If it weren't for the unpleasant <u>event</u> with the doorman, no one would have known that our

   arrival was <u>too early</u>. _____ _____

4. <u>Correct behavior</u> dictates that we must wait in the <u>outer room</u> before all the elders have

   taken their seats. _____ _____

5. The <u>beginning</u> or opening paragraph of the Constitution is a kind of <u>introduction</u> for the rest of

   the document. _____ _____

6. It is of <u>the first</u> importance that this <u>letter</u> be sent immediately!

   _____ _____

List Words

antecedent	anterior	epitaph	epistle
epilogue	premonition	anteroom	epidermis
episode	preamble	presuppose	prelude
premier	prejudice	premature	proposal
protrude	procession	prophet	protocol

Puzzle

This is a crossword puzzle without clues. Use the length and the spelling of each List Word to complete the puzzle.

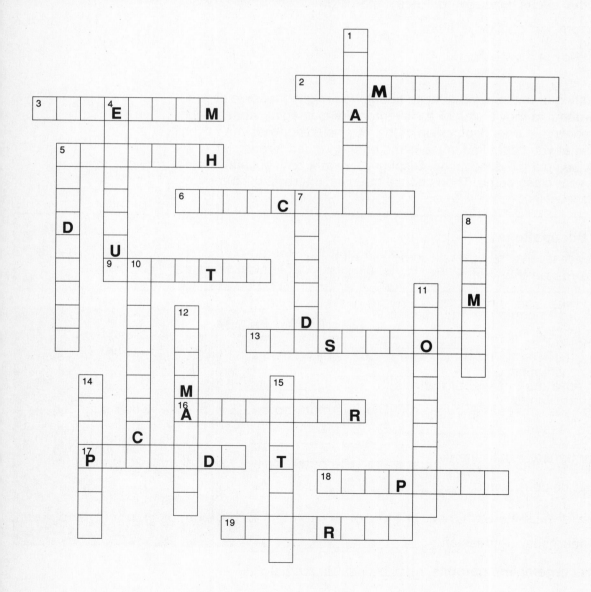

Proofreading

Use the proofreading marks to correct the mistakes in the want ad below. Then write the misspelled List Words on the lines.

A Recent propozal hascreated new new Positions in the Cary Circus. Clowns must must beable to to marchin a procesion and Follow protocol. All applications must be returned to the antiroom of the office. Interviews will take place with the circus Manager onFriday morning.

1. _____

2. _____

3. _____

4. _____

Challenges

Express Yourself

Think of an interesting or unusual job to write about. You might choose a circus performer, an astronaut, a movie star, or an inventor. Try to imagine what the job would be like. Then write a brief description of the job, including what you might like about it, and what you might find unpleasant, boring, or dangerous. Proofread and revise your job description. Display your work on a bulletin board along with that of your classmates. Then choose the most interesting job for you.

Bonus Words: Occupations

chiropractor	horticulturist	psychiatrist	meteorologist	dental hygienist
dietitian	mathematician	metallurgist	physical therapist	musician

Write a Bonus Word to complete each series.

1. ores, smelting, mines, _____

2. food, nutrition, vitamins, _____

3. weather, clouds, winds, _____

4. teeth, dentist, X-rays, _____

5. songs, performances, instruments, _____

6. nerves, spinal column, joints, _____

7. numbers, formulas, equations, _____

8. psychoses, neuroses, depression, _____

9. trees, shrubs, vegetables, gardens, _____

10. hydrotherapy, exercises, massage, _____

Prefixes **ab, af, ag, an, anti**

LESSON
9

Game Plan

When added to base words derived from Latin roots, the prefix **ab** usually means <u>away</u>, <u>from</u>, or <u>down</u>. The prefixes **af, ag,** and **an** usually mean <u>to</u>, <u>at</u>, or <u>toward</u>. The prefix **anti** means <u>against</u>.

Latin Root	Meaning	English Word with Prefix	Meaning
horrere	to shudder	**abhor** (verb)	to dislike intently
filius	son	**affiliate** (verb)	to connect with
gravis	heavy	**aggravate** (verb)	to make something worse
nihil	nothing	**annihilate** (verb)	to destroy completely
socius	companion	**antisocial** (adj.)	unfriendly

1. abhor
2. abstain
3. affirmative
4. announcement
5. annul
6. abolish
7. absolve
8. affiliate
9. annotate
10. antibiotic
11. absurd
12. affable
13. aggravate
14. annihilate
15. antihistamine
16. abstract
17. affluent
18. aggressive
19. annex
20. antisocial

Warm Up

Vocabulary Development

Write the List Word that matches each synonym or definition.

1. wealthy _____
2. friendly _____
3. ridiculous _____
4. to add notes _____
5. positive _____
6. to refrain, willingly _____
7. to free from guilt _____
8. something added on _____
9. ready to argue _____
10. declaration _____

Dictionary Skills

Write the List Words beginning with **ab** in alphabetical order.

1. _____ 3. _____ 5. _____
2. _____ 4. _____ 6. _____

Write the List Words beginning with **af** and **ag** in alphabetical order.

7. _____ 9. _____ 11. _____
8. _____ 10. _____ 12. _____

Write the List Words beginning with **an** in alphabetical order.

13. _____ 16. _____ 19. _____
14. _____ 17. _____ 20. _____
15. _____ 18. _____

Practice

Word Analysis

Write the List Word derived from the Latin root given.

1. **notare** ("to mark") _____
2. **fluere** ("to flow") _____
3. **nectare** ("to tie") _____
4. **nullum** ("nothing") _____
5. **biosis** ("life") _____

6. **solvere** ("to release") _____
7. **firmare** ("to make firm") _____
8. **abolere** ("to destroy") _____
9. **nuntiare** ("to report") _____
10. **surdus** ("dull; insensible") _____

Analogies

Write a List Word to complete each analogy.

1. Up is to down as love is to _____ .
2. Dessert is to meal as _____ is to building.
3. Artistic is to painter as _____ is to companion.
4. Performance is to play as _____ is to news.
5. Feed is to hunger as _____ is to guilt.
6. _____ is to allergy as rain is to drought.
7. Fast is to slow as specific is to _____ .
8. "Yes, please" is to accept as "No, thank you" is to _____ .

> **Did you know?**
>
> **Aggravate** comes from a Latin word which means "to make heavier" and is related to the word *gravity*. When a problem is *aggravated*, it is made heavier or greater than it was.

Word Application

Select a List Word from the choices in parentheses to complete each sentence. Write your answer on the line.

1. Many nations _____ with the United Nations. (affiliate, annul, aggravate)
2. Jim took his _____ dog to obedience school. (antibiotic, abstract, aggressive)
3. People on low-fat diets _____ from eating rich foods. (absolve, abstain, aggravate)
4. This storm will _____ the river's floodlike conditions. (abhor, aggravate, annul)
5. I don't mean to be _____ , but I'd like to be alone. (affluent, affable, antisocial)
6. We _____ termites, or they will ruin the house. (absolve, annihilate, annex)
7. With an _____ vote, he approved the new law. (affiliate, affirmative, absurd)
8. Both parties voted to _____ the unsatisfactory agreement. (annul, absolve, abstract)
9. An _____ family donated funds for the hospital wing. (antibiotic, affluent, annex)

List Words			
abhor	abolish	absurd	abstract
abstain	absolve	affable	affluent
affirmative	affiliate	aggravate	aggressive
announcement	annotate	annihilate	annex
annul	antibiotic	antihistamine	antisocial

Syllables

Write List Words under the correct categories.

Words with Two Syllables

1. _____
2. _____
3. _____
4. _____
5. _____
6. _____
7. _____

Words with Three Syllables

8. _____
9. _____
10. _____
11. _____
12. _____
13. _____
14. _____

Words with Four Syllables

15. _____
16. _____
17. _____
18. _____

Words with Five Syllables

19. _____
20. _____

Definitions

Write a List Word to solve each definition clue.

1. medicine to reduce allergy symptoms _____

2. bold; positive _____

3. ready to argue or fight _____

4. medicine to kill bacteria _____

5. theoretical; nonspecific _____

6. to destroy _____

7. to choose to do without _____

8. to provide explanatory notes _____

9. not liking to be with other people _____

Proofreading

Use the proofreading marks to correct the mistakes in the article. Then write the misspelled List Words on the lines.

Proofreading Marks	
⬭ spelling mistake	ⱱ add apostrophe
⊙ add period	¶ new paragraph

Karse was just discovered by astronomers a few months ago. The planet is covered with afable and abzurd Kamimsham trees, which thrive in the planets tropical climate

    Samples of sap have been gathered from the afluant groves The saps rare composition can be used in producing an effective antebiotic. An anouncment will be made pending approval of the new drug.

1. _____
2. _____
3. _____
4. _____
5. _____

Challenges

Express Yourself

In two paragraphs, describe one of your favorite places. Tell about the sights, sounds, smells, and feelings you experience there. Be imaginative! Use figurative language and vivid images. Avoid such trite words as *wonderful, beautiful,* and *nice.* Proofread and revise your description. Then read it aloud to a group and discuss the effectiveness of your words.

Bonus Words: Language

cliché	obsolete	slang	superfluous	verbose
jargon	colloquial	trite	redundant	vernacular

Write a Bonus Word to match each etymology.

1. Greek **tryein** ("to wear away") _____

2. Latin **ob** ("toward") + **exolescere** ("out of use") _____

3. Latin **super** ("above") + **fluctus** ("wave") _____

4. Latin **verna** ("native population") _____

5. German **klitsch** ("clump of clay") _____

6. Latin **com** ("together") + **loqui** ("to speak") _____

7. Latin **verbum** ("word") _____

8. Latin **re** ("again") + **undare** ("to swell") _____

Write a Bonus Word to define each example.

9. His input should impact the meeting. _____

10. Those wheels will run you about ten grand. _____

Game Plan

The prefixes **mal**, **de**, and **dis** have Latin roots. The prefix **mal** usually means <u>bad</u>. The prefix **de** often means <u>away</u> from or <u>undo</u>. The prefix **dis** often means <u>not</u> or <u>apart</u>. The prefix **meta** has Greek roots. It can mean <u>with</u>, <u>beyond</u>, <u>among</u>, or <u>over</u>.

Root	Meaning	English Word with Prefix	Meaning
functio	to perform	**malfunction**	to function incorrectly
morphé	form; shape	**metamorphosis**	a change in form
cedere	to go forward	**deceased**	dead
solvere	to free	**dissolve**	to break apart in liquid

1. malfunction
2. detour
3. metaphor
4. disadvantage
5. decompose
6. malevolent
7. dissatisfaction
8. metamorphosis
9. distort
10. decanter
11. metabolism
12. dissolve
13. decline
14. maladjusted
15. dispute
16. descendant
17. malice
18. deception
19. deplete
20. deceased

Warm Up

Vocabulary Development

Write the List Word that matches each definition clue.

1. argument _____

2. twist; deform _____

3. displeasure _____

4. drawback; minus _____

5. alternate route _____

6. untruth; fraud _____

7. break apart in liquid _____

Dictionary Skills

Under each category, write the List Words in alphabetical order.

Words with Prefix **de**

1. _____
2. _____
3. _____
4. _____
5. _____
6. _____
7. _____
8. _____

Words with Prefix **mal**

9. _____
10. _____
11. _____
12. _____

Words with Prefix **meta**

13. _____
14. _____
15. _____

Practice

Word Analysis

Write the List Word derived from the Latin root given.

1. clinare ("to bend") _____

2. deplere ("to empty") _____

3. satis ("enough") _____

4. torquere ("to twist") _____

5. volens ("to wish") _____

6. functio ("to perform") _____

7. componer ("to put together") _____

8. scandere ("to climb") _____

9. cedere ("to go forward") _____

10. justus ("just") _____

> ### Did you know?
> We often use the word **metamorphosis** to describe the transformation of a caterpillar into a butterfly. *Metamorphosis* literally means "a change," but the origin of the word is based on the name Morpheus, the Greek god of dreams. The usage of the word most likely evolved from the fact that when insects change form, they are usually in a dream-like state.

Antonyms

Write the List Word that matches each antonym.

1. satisfaction _____

2. truth _____

3. accept _____

4. agreement _____

5. ancestor _____

6. kind _____

7. goodwill _____

8. alive _____

9. constancy; permanence _____

10. benefit; asset _____

Word Application

Select a List Word from the choices in parentheses to complete each sentence. Write your answer on the line.

1. Through _____ , the body regulates its flow of energy. (metaphor, metabolism, malice)

2. The crystal _____ was filled with cold water. (decanter, deplete, maladjusted)

3. The sugar will _____ in water as you stir the mixture. (metamorphosis, metaphor, dissolve)

4. Fallen trees will eventually _____ and enrich the forest soil. (dispute, decompose, distort)

5. The _____ around the construction site is clearly marked. (dispute, deplete, detour)

6. "Life is just a bowl of cherries" is a _____ . (decanter, metaphor, malice)

7. Food may spoil if refrigerators _____ . (detour, distort, malfunction)

List Words			
malfunction	malevolent	metabolism	descendant
detour	dissatisfaction	dissolve	malice
metaphor	metamorphosis	decline	deception
disadvantage	distort	maladjusted	deplete
decompose	decanter	dispute	deceased

Puzzle

Each of the following clues is an example, or illustration, of a
List Word. Write the associated List Words in the answer
spaces. Then transfer the numbered letters to the spaces below
to answer the question.

1. "No, thank you." __ __ __ __ __ __ __
                          7   23

2. Traffic is diverted. __ __ __ __ __ __
                             14   5

3. grandchild __ __ __ __ __ __ __ __ __ __
                   24   2

4. "Truth is beauty." __ __ __ __ __ __ __ __
                           1   20

5. Flowers wither. __ __ __ __ __ __ __
                                12 19

6. "I'm not pleased." __ __ __ __ __ __ __ __ __ __ __ __ __ __ __
                                          8   4

7. false advertising claims __ __ __ __ __ __ __ __ __
                                                    17 6

8. Stir sugar in water. __ __ __ __ __ __ __ __
                                      22   3

9. revenge __ __ __ __ __ __
               16   9

10. Exaggerate the facts. __ __ __ __ __ __
                                         10 18

11. cemetery occupants __ __ __ __ __ __ __ __
                           13   15

12. fairy tale dragon __ __ __ __ __ __ __ __ __
                                      21   11

RIDDLE: How did the caterpillar turn into an elephant?

ANSWER: through a __ __ __ __ __ __ __ __ __ __ __ of
                      1 2 3 4 5 6 7 8 9 10 11

__ __ __ __ __ __ __ __ __ __ __ __ __
12 13 14 15 16 17 18 19 20 21 22 23 24

Proofreading

Use the proofreading marks to correct the mistakes in the following paragraph. Then write the misspelled List Words on the lines.

Proofreading Marks
⬭ spelling mistake   ⌃ add comma
? add question mark   / small letter

For whom do architects design buildings Architects design buildings for clients. If the client spots a malfunktion in the plans the Architect must redraw them. A Building can be beautiful, but occupants may express disatisfaction if it is not practical to work in. Any despute between architect and client must be worked out before construction begins. During construction a structure undergoes a metamorfosis as it goes from foundation and frame to finished building.

1. _____

2. _____

3. _____

4. _____

Challenges

Express Yourself

The year is 2100, and you're an architect. Use a ruler, compass, and graph paper to design a building of your choice. Write a description of the materials you used and the architectural details you included. Proofread and revise your description and display it with your design in the classroom.

Bonus Words: Architecture

arcade	façade	geodesic	Doric	colonnade
buttress	frieze	Corinthian	Ionic	gargoyle

Write the Bonus Word that matches each definition clue.

1. ornamental "creature" _____

2. with a gridlike frame _____

3. projecting support structure _____

4. row of columns _____

5. band of sculpture _____

6. front of building _____

7. arched building _____

Write a List Word to label each type of column.

8. _____   9. _____   10. _____

Game Plan

Some Greek and Latin prefixes can be added to roots and root words to indicate time, place, direction, or value. Here are some examples.

Prefix	Meaning	English Word	Meaning
ab	away, from, down	**abhor**	to dislike intently
af, **ag**, **an**	at, toward	**affiliate**	to join with
ante	before, in front	**anterior**	toward the front
anti	against	**antisocial**	unfriendly
bene, **beni**	good	**benefit**	advantage
coll, **com**	with, together	**commerce**	business, trade
contra	against	**contradict**	disagree, dispute
de	apart, undo	**detour**	alternative route
dis	apart, not	**dissatisfied**	not satisfied
epi	outside, over	**epidermis**	outside skin layer
eu	good	**eulogy**	funeral tribute
mal	bad	**malevolent**	evil
meta	with, beyond	**metaphor**	exaggerated comparison
pre	before, forward	**preview**	glimpse of future event
pro	before, forward	**protrude**	stick out in front

Other Greek and Latin prefixes, such as **duo** and **deca**, indicate number. A _duet_ is music for two voices. A _decade_ is ten years.

Practice

Write prefixes and List Words to complete this chart.

	Prefix	English Word	Meaning
1.	_____	_____	ten years
2.	_____	_____	one-tenth of a liter
3.	_____	_____	an extreme amount
4.	_____	_____	one-thousandth of a gram
5.	_____	_____	one thousand watts
6.	_____	_____	occurring twice a year
7.	_____	_____	one-hundredth of a meter
8.	_____	_____	having two units
9.	_____	_____	speech by one person
10.	_____	_____	not of the highest value

Lesson 7

centimeter
monologue
semiprecious
decade
myriad
kilowatt
semiannual
deciliter
milligram
duplex

_____
_____

Write a List Word to complete
each sentence.

1. In the _____ , the author explained what
   happened to the explorers following their discovery.

2. The humorous poet Dorothy Parker once suggested this

   _____ for her own tombstone: "Excuse My Dust."

3. As the maid of honor, I led the bridal _____ .

4. The _____ of the U.S. Constitution begins, "We
   the people of the United States. . . ."

5. In an _____ to his editor, the author F. Scott
   Fitzgerald introduced a writer named Ernest Hemingway.

6. A pronoun must agree in number with its _____ .

7. The _____ lobe is in the front part of the brain.

8. _____ can cause people to dislike strangers.

9. Sunburn is an inflammation of the _____ .

10. Wheat and corn are two of the _____ agricultural
    products of America's midwestern states.

Lesson 8

antecedent	preamble
epilogue	premier
epidermis	epistle
prejudice	anterior
procession	epitaph

_____

_____

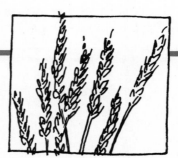

Write a List Word to
answer each definition
clue.

Lesson 9

abhor	antihistamine
affiliate	affirmative
absurd	aggressive
antisocial	announcement
annihilate	aggravate

_____

_____

1. medicine to relieve
   allergy symptoms   _____

2. silly or foolish   _____

3. unfriendly   _____

4. ready to argue or fight   _____

5. to become a member   _____

6. to destroy completely   _____

7. a public message   _____

8. positive or bold   _____

9. dislike intently   _____

10. to make worse or to annoy _____

Each of these sentences contains the wrong List Word. Cross out the word and write the correct List Word on the line.

1. A kind eulogy donated funds. _____

2. The contrary damaged my car. _____

3. The two writers agreed to contradict on a book. _____

4. Doctors must be both intelligent scientists and contrast listeners. _____

5. At the memorial, an eloquent commencement was delivered. _____

6. Compare and collaborate the music of Mozart and Bach. _____

7. After the benefactor ceremony, the graduates shook hands. _____

8. Your collision, or associate, left this message for you. _____

9. In the debate, Frank used established facts to colleague the position of his opponent. _____

10. Although we're friends, Jim and I have benign ideas on many subjects. _____

Lesson **10**

contrast	contradict
collision	benefactor
eulogy	commencement
contrary	collaborate
benign	colleague

_____

_____

Use the List Words to complete the crossword puzzle.

ACROSS
1. to rot or erode
4. to twist or bend
5. active ill will; spite
7. to use up a supply
8. evil or mean

DOWN
1. child of future generation
2. dramatic change in form
3. fraud or falsehood
4. to break apart in liquid
6. figurative comparison

Lesson **11**

deception	descendant
deplete	metamorphosis
dissolve	decompose
malice	malevolent
distort	metaphor

_____

_____

monologue	epistle	benign
semiprecious	annihilate	colleague
deciliter	absurd	malevolent
epidermis	abhor	metaphor
epilogue	contradict	descendant

Mixed Practice

Write List Words to answer the questions.

Which words are verbs?

1. _____ 2. _____ 3. _____

Which words are nouns?

4. _____ 7. _____ 10. _____

5. _____ 8. _____ 11. _____

6. _____ 9. _____

Which words are adjectives?

12. _____ 14. _____

13. _____ 15. _____

Test Yourself

In each of the following groups of words, one word is misspelled. Fill in the circle that appears before that word.

1. o procession
   o benefacter
   o duplex
   o deception

5. o deplete
   o antihistimine
   o myriad
   o metamorphosis

2. o afilliate
   o dissolve
   o monologue
   o collision

6. o decompose
   o affirmative
   o anterior
   o commencment

3. o semiprecious
   o descendant
   o prejudice
   o agressive

7. o colleage
   o semiannual
   o antisocial
   o epilogue

9. o decade
   o abhor
   o contradict
   o epitauph

11. o centimeter
    o epistle
    o eulougy
    o announcement

4. o aggravate
   o deciliter
   o premier
   o benine

8. o malice
   o anticedent
   o contrary
   o malevolent

10. o kilowatt
    o epedermis
    o distort
    o collaborate

12. o metaphor
    o annilate
    o milligram
    o preamble

Game Plan

A **root** is a word part that gives the word its basic meaning. Here are some English words that are based on Latin roots.

Latin Roots (meaning)	English Word (meaning)
aqua (water)	**aquatic** (growing or living in water)
hosp, **host** (house, guest)	**hostel** (inn)
lat (side)	**lateral** (toward the side)
mort (death)	**mortal** (that which will die)
sim (like, same)	**simultaneous** (occurring at once)
liber (free)	**liberate** (to set free)

1. aquarium
2. hostel
3. lateral
4. mortuary
5. simultaneous
6. dissimilar
7. hostage
8. aquatic
9. mortgage
10. simulate
11. hospitalize
12. hostile
13. liberal
14. mortician
15. unilateral
16. hospice
17. mortal
18. aquamarine
19. quadrilateral
20. liberate

Warm Up

Word Analysis

Write List Words with the same Latin root as the word given.

latitude   1. _____   3. _____

2. _____

mortality   4. _____   6. _____

5. _____   7. _____

simile   8. _____   10. _____

9. _____

liberty   11. _____   12. _____

Dictionary Skills

Write the List Words that come between each pair of dictionary guide words. Write the words in alphabetical order.

apt/arid

1. _____

2. _____

3. _____

hose/hot

4. _____

5. _____

6. _____

7. _____

8. _____

Practice

Word Analysis

Write List Words to answer the following questions.
Which words contain the Latin root that means <u>to free</u>?

1. _____ 2. _____

Which words contain the Latin root that means <u>death</u>?

3. _____ 5. _____

4. _____ 6. _____

Which words contain the Latin root that means <u>water</u>?

7. _____ 8. _____ 9. _____

Which words contain the Latin root that means <u>like</u> or <u>same</u>?

10. _____ 11. _____ 12. _____

Which words contain the Latin root that means <u>house</u> or <u>guest</u>?

13. _____ 16. _____

14. _____ 17. _____

15. _____

Which words contain the Latin root that means <u>to the side</u>?

18. _____ 20. _____

19. _____

> ### Did you know?
> **Mortgage** comes from two words in old French *mort* and *gage* that meant "dead" and "pledge." The pledge would be "dead" to the lender if the borrower paid the debt and kept the property that had been pledged. And the pledge would be "dead" to the borrower if he or she failed to pay the debt and lost the property.

Analogies

Write a List Word to complete each analogy.

1. <u>Three sides</u> are to a <u>triangle</u> as <u>four sides</u> are to a _____ .

2. <u>Loan</u> is to <u>automobile</u> as _____ is to <u>house</u>.

3. <u>Free</u> is to _____ as <u>imprison</u> is to <u>enslave</u>.

4. <u>Beautician</u> is to <u>salon</u> as _____ is to <u>funeral parlor</u>.

5. <u>Belligerent</u> is to _____ as <u>neighborly</u> is to <u>friendly</u>.

6. <u>Bluff</u> is to <u>fake</u> as <u>imitate</u> is to _____ .

7. <u>Different</u> is to _____ as <u>same</u> is to <u>similar</u>.

8. <u>Vertical</u> is to <u>up and down</u> as _____ is to <u>sideways</u>.

9. <u>Democrat</u> is to <u>Republican</u> as _____ is to <u>conservative</u>.

10. <u>Plants</u> are to <u>terrarium</u> as <u>fish</u> are to _____ .

List Words

aquarium	dissimilar	hospitalize	hospice
hostel	hostage	hostile	mortal
lateral	aquatic	liberal	aquamarine
mortuary	mortgage	mortician	quadrilateral
simultaneous	simulate	unilateral	liberate

Puzzle

Use the List Words to complete the crossword puzzle.

ACROSS

1. growing or living in water
6. happening at the same time
9. to admit to a medical care facility
10. bluish-green color
12. a prisoner taken by an enemy
13. in a sideward direction
14. a health-care facility with home-like feeling
15. free-thinking; generous
18. an overnight shelter used by hikers and other travelers
19. place where corpses are kept before funeral

DOWN

2. a figure with four sides and four angles
3. to pretend; to act like
4. a person who prepares bodies for burial
5. a long term loan on a piece of property
7. to set free
8. not alike; different
11. one-sided
12. warlike; unfriendly
16. a place where fish are exhibited
17. that which will die

Proofreading

Use the proofreading marks to correct the mistakes in the article below. Then write the misspelled List Words on the lines.

Proofreading Marks

◯ spelling mistake   ⌒ add space

⌄ add apostrophe   ¶ new paragraph

The newly remodeled akuarium hired an agency to handle their advertisingcampaign. The campaign was designed to release simultanious printand media ads.

   The newspaper and magazine ads were not dissimmular—both featured photos of the aquariums acuamarine life. The television ad was able to simmulate an underwater dive where viewers saw a coral reef. The advertising agencys production department outdid itself and created a great campaign, which generated increased ticket sales in a matter of weeks.

1. _____

2. _____

3. _____

4. _____

5. _____

Challenges

Express Yourself

Invent a new product and write a script for a television commercial promoting it. Include a description of the set and the characters, dialogue for the characters and an announcer, and directions to the camera operator. After proofreading and revising your script, work with a group to present your commercial to the class.

Bonus Words: Television

telecast	ad-libbed	broadcasting	technological	frequencies
audition	videotape	amplifier	closed circuit	production

Write the Bonus Word that matches each clue given.

1. cable TV program _____

2. TV transmission _____

3. technical progress _____

4. transmitted TV signals _____

5. a TV presentation _____

6. spoken without preparation _____

7. to broadcast by TV _____

8. device to increase sound _____

9. a prerecorded TV program _____

10. to try out for a TV show _____

Game Plan

Recognizing Latin roots in words can help you determine the meaning of unfamiliar words. Here are some examples.

Latin Roots (meaning)	English Word (meaning)
plic, **plex** (fold)	**complication** (something that confuses)
rupt (break)	**interrupt** (break in upon)
pend (hang)	**suspended** (hanging down)
struct (build)	**structural** (suitable for building)

Look for Latin roots in the List Words.

1. abrupt
2. complex
3. implicate
4. inexplicable
5. structural
6. applicable
7. disrupt
8. independently
9. pendulum
10. suspended
11. bankrupt
12. duplicate
13. instruction
14. pendant
15. suspense
16. complication
17. impending
18. interrupt
19. destruction
20. perplexing

Warm Up

Vocabulary Development

Write the List Word from column B that matches the synonym in column A.

A		B
1. puzzling	_____	implicate
2. disturb	_____	bankrupt
3. individually	_____	impending
4. involve	_____	duplicate
5. unexplainable	_____	destruction
6. sudden	_____	perplexing
7. impoverished	_____	independently
8. threatening	_____	inexplicable
9. copy	_____	disrupt
10. wreckage	_____	abrupt

Dictionary Skills

Write the List Word that matches each sound-spelling.

1. (pen´ jōō ləm) _____

2. (sə spend´ ed) _____

3. (in struk´ shən) _____

4. (ap´ li kə b'l) _____

5. (käm´ plə kā´ shən) _____

6. (struk´ chər əl) _____

7. (sə spens´) _____

8. (pen´ dənt) _____

9. (kəm pleks´) _____

10. (in tə rupt´) _____

Practice

Word Analysis

Write List Words to answer the following questions.

Which words contain the Latin root that means <u>hang</u>?

1. _____ 3. _____ 5. _____

2. _____ 4. _____ 6. _____

Which words contain the Latin root that means <u>build</u>?

7. _____ 8. _____ 9. _____

Which words contain the Latin root that means <u>break</u>?

10. _____ 12. _____

11. _____ 13. _____

Which words contain the Latin root that means <u>fold</u>?

14. _____ 17. _____ 20. _____

15. _____ 18. _____

16. _____ 19. _____

Proofreading

Use the proofreading marks to correct the mistakes in the letter. Then write the misspelled List Words correctly on the lines.

Agnes Wilson
Monogram corporation
5520 Lodge Highway
Huntsville Nebraska 98755

Dear Mrs. Wilson:

We have a purplexing problem regarding your account Due to an unknown complecation, our computer has suspendid any activity to your file. According to the computer, your company is bankrupt! we know that this is not possible, but there seems to be an inexplecable bug in the system that we cannot locate. We are in the process of trying to duplicate your records and make any aplicable changes. We will interupt your service for a few days but hope that this does not desrupt your business in any way. We are very sorry for the inconvenience, but we would like to avoid any impinding problems. Thanks for your cooperation in this complix matter.

Sincerely

Ted Pierce, district Manager

Proofreading Marks

⬭	spelling mistake
⊙	add period
?	add question mark
!	add exclamation mark
≣	capital letter
⋀	add comma
⁋	new paragraph

1. _____

2. _____

3. _____

4. _____

5. _____

6. _____

7. _____

8. _____

9. _____

10. _____

| **List Words** |
abrupt	applicable	bankrupt	complication
complex	disrupt	duplicate	impending
implicate	independently	instruction	interrupt
inexplicable	pendulum	pendant	destruction
structural	suspended	suspense	perplexing

Puzzle

Use the List Words to complete the crossword puzzle.

ACROSS

3. something that is taught
7. an object hung from a fixed point so as to swing freely
9. uncertain, doubtful, confusing
13. an exact copy or reproduction
16. the act or process of being destroyed
17. relevant; appropriate
18. to break into or in upon a discussion
19. hanging from a support

DOWN

1. to disturb the orderly course of a meeting or other social affair
2. financially broke
4. not simple; complicated
5. used in or suitable for building
6. state of anxious uncertainty
8. involve in a crime
10. freely; without influence or assistance
11. about to happen
12. not able to be explained or understood
14. a hanging ornamental object
15. something that is hard to solve or untangle
17. unexpected

59

Test Yourself

In each pair of words, underline the correctly spelled List Word.

1. pendent, pendant
2. structural, structeral
3. suspinded, suspended
4. duplicate, duplicite
5. implicate, implacate
6. indipendantly, independently
7. complecation, complication
8. inexplicable, inixplecable
9. interupt, interrupt
10. applicable, aplicable
11. pendulum, pandulum
12. distruction, destruction
13. suspanse, suspense
14. perplexing, purplexing
15. impending, empending
16. instrction, instruction

> **Did you know?**
>
> **Bankrupt** comes from two Italian words meaning "broken bench." Moneylenders used to carry on their business at a bench or table. They would be put out of business if the bench were broken, just as nowadays people are put out of business if they cannot pay their debts.

Challenges

Express Yourself

Pretend that you are a playwright. You are writing a drama that takes place in a mysterious old house. One of your first tasks is to describe the house so that set designers can build a realistic stage set. Write a one-paragraph description of the house. Include suggestions about the furniture, windows, entrances, and exits. Provide as many details as possible. After you proofread and revise your description, read it to a partner and have your partner try to illustrate the house.

Bonus Words: Interior Decorating

chandelier	pedestal	parquet	mahogany	canopy
draperies	ottoman	upholstery	veneer	davenport

Write the Bonus Word that matches each definition clue.

1. thin surface layer of
   fine wood _____

2. large couch or sofa _____

3. curtains of heavy
   material _____

4. a lighting fixture
   hanging from ceiling _____

5. a roof-like covering
   over a bed _____

6. a column-like stand
   for displaying art _____

7. dark, reddish-
   brown wood _____

8. inlaid wood flooring _____

9. materials used to cover
   furniture _____

10. low cushioned seat
    without back or arms _____

Game Plan

Here are some common Latin roots and their meanings.

Latin Roots (meaning)	English Word (meaning)
voc, **vok** (voice)	**vocalize** (speak or sing)
var (different)	**variety** (number of different things)
vag (wander)	**vagabond** (wanderer)
centr (center)	**centralize** (to bring to the center)
term (end or limit)	**terminal** (at the end)
terr (land)	**territory** (large tract of land)

1. advocate
2. centralize
3. terrain
4. vagabond
5. variety
6. concentric
7. exterminate
8. terrace
9. vague
10. various
11. determine
12. provoke
13. territory
14. vagrant
15. vocation
16. eccentric
17. revoke
18. terminal
19. variation
20. vocalize

Warm Up

Vocabulary Development

Write the List Word from column B that matches the synonym in column A.

A		B
1. unclear	_____	vagabond
2. assortment	_____	eccentric
3. annoy	_____	terrace
4. tramp	_____	terrain
5. destroy	_____	provoke
6. odd	_____	exterminate
7. land	_____	determine
8. patio	_____	vocalize
9. sing	_____	variety
10. conclude	_____	vague

Dictionary Skills

Write the List Word that matches each sound-spelling.

1. (ver´ ē ā´ shən) _____
2. (ver´ ē əs) _____
3. (kən sen´ trik) _____
4. (ri vōk´) _____
5. (sen´ trə liz) _____
6. (prə vōk´) _____
7. (vā´ grənt) _____
8. (ad´ və kāt´) _____
9. (ter´ ə tôr´ ē) _____
10. (tʉr´ mə n'l) _____

Practice

Word Analysis

Write List Words to answer the following questions.

Which words contain the Latin root that means <u>wander</u>?

1. _____ **2.** _____ **3.** _____

Which words contain the Latin root that means <u>voice</u>?

4. _____ **6.** _____ **8.** _____

5. _____ **7.** _____

Which words contain the Latin root that means <u>center</u>?

9. _____ **10.** _____ **11.** _____

Which words contain the Latin root that means <u>different</u>?

12. _____ **13.** _____ **14.** _____

Which words contain the Latin root that means <u>end</u> or <u>limit</u>?

15. _____ **16.** _____ **17.** _____

Which words contain the Latin root that means <u>land</u>?

18. _____ **19.** _____ **20.** _____

Word Application

Replace the underlined word or words in each phrase with a List Word. Write the List Word on the line.

1. an <u>odd or unusual</u> person _____

2. a <u>generous selection</u>
of fruits and vegetables _____

3. a religious <u>profession</u> _____

4. the northwest <u>border country</u> _____

5. hilly <u>ground</u> _____

6. <u>with the same center</u> circles _____

7. a <u>change</u> of a familiar theme _____

8. a consumer <u>rights speaker</u> _____

9. <u>take back</u> a driver's licence _____

10. the bus <u>station</u> _____

LETTUCE .48 ea   ORANGES 10 ea   POTATOES 10/2.00

CORN 3/1.00

List Words

advocate	concentric	determine	eccentric
centralize	exterminate	provoke	revoke
terrain	terrace	territory	terminal
vagabond	vague	vagrant	variation
variety	various	vocation	vocalize

Puzzle

Use the List Words to complete the crossword puzzle.

ACROSS

2. the main station of a railroad
5. person with no obvious means of support
6. to anger or irritate
7. a paved area near a house
8. ground or area of land
12. not definite or distinct
13. several or many
14. to speak or sing
17. person who wanders from place to place
18. to find out exactly
19. one's profession or occupation
20. the land ruled by a nation or state

DOWN

1. to gather together
3. to kill or destroy
4. sharing the same center
9. to speak or write in support of something
10. change in form or appearance
11. to take back or put an end to
15. not usual or normal
16. number of different things

Proofreading

Use the proofreading marks to correct the mistakes in the paragraph below. Then write the misspelled List Words on the lines.

Satellite photos reveal that the newly-discovered planet has a vairiety of terran. In in various areas there are small craters that appear to be caused by meteors. Because the entire physical make-up of the planet is still vage researchers advokate further study

1. _____

2. _____

3. _____

4. _____

Challenges

Express Yourself

Continue the following short adventure story:

I'd been wandering for hours, trying to find my way out of the jungle. Darkness was descending. I had the vague impression that I had passed these trees before. Was I walking in circles? Suddenly, I heard a rustling from the bushes behind me.

After you proofread and revise your story, read it aloud to a partner.

Bonus Words: Adventure

escapade	confrontation	courier	treacherous	intrepid
sojourn	bivouac	harrowing	dauntless	desperation

Write the Bonus Word that matches each definition clue.

1. recklessness resulting from a loss of hope _____

2. a brief or temporary stay or visit _____

3. used to describe an experience that causes mental distress _____

4. a reckless adventure or prank _____

5. the act of facing someone boldly or defiantly _____

6. used to describe someone or something that is untrustworthy _____

7. messenger sent with an urgent message _____

8. temporary encampment in the open with tents _____

Write the Bonus Words that are synonyms for <u>fearless</u>.

9. _____

10. _____

Game Plan

These common Latin roots can help you determine the meanings of many English words.

Latin Roots (meaning)	English Word (meaning)
spec (see)	**perspective** (a particular view)
spir (breathe)	**expire** (to come to an end)
clu, **clud** (shut)	**exclude** (keep out)
mater, **matri** (mother)	**maternal** (motherly)

Study the Latin roots to determine the meanings of the List Words.

1. conspiracy
2. expire
3. inspiration
4. matrimony
5. spectacle
6. disrespect
7. expectation
8. maternity
9. perspective
10. speculate
11. exclusive
12. including
13. matron
14. preclude
15. spiritual
16. exclude
17. inspection
18. maternal
19. seclusion
20. transpired

Warm Up

Vocabulary Development

Write the List Word that matches each definition.

1. to make impossible _____
2. a grand event _____
3. privacy; isolation _____
4. critical examination _____
5. a stimulation to do something creative _____
6. an unlawful plot _____
7. of the soul rather than the body _____
8. to think about _____
9. happened _____
10. making a part of a whole _____

Dictionary Skills

Write the List Words that come between each pair of dictionary guide words. Write the words in alphabetical order.

conspire/external	mate/precious
1. _____	6. _____
2. _____	7. _____
3. _____	8. _____
4. _____	9. _____
5. _____	10. _____

Practice

Word Analysis

Write List Words to answer the following questions.

Which words contain the Latin root that means <u>breathe</u>?

1. _____   **3.** _____   **5.** _____

2. _____   **4.** _____

Which words contain the Latin root that means <u>see</u>?

6. _____   **8.** _____   **10.** _____

7. _____   **9.** _____   **11.** _____

Which words contain the Latin root that means <u>shut</u>?

12. _____   **14.** _____   **16.** _____

13. _____   **15.** _____

Which words contain the Latin root that means <u>mother</u>?

17. _____   **19.** _____

18. _____   **20.** _____

Analogies

Write a List Word to complete each analogy.

1. <u>Fatherhood</u> is to <u>paternity</u> as <u>motherhood</u> is to

_____ .

2. <u>Guess</u> is to <u>predict</u> as <u>think</u> is to _____ .

3. <u>Allow</u> is to <u>forbid</u> as <u>permit</u> is to _____ .

4. <u>Body</u> is to <u>soul</u> as <u>physical</u> is to _____ .

5. <u>Ordinary</u> is to <u>common</u> as <u>unique</u> is to _____ .

Word Application

Replace the underlined word or words in the paragraph with List Words. Write the words on the lines.

    The <u>privacy</u> of the hillside cabin allowed Martin to change his <u>view</u> on life. He found that the solitude of the mountains served as an <u>uplifting experience</u> and helped him to reaffirm his <u>religious</u> beliefs. A dramatic change had <u>occurred</u> within him.

> ### Did you know?
> **Spectacle, spectacular, spectator, spector, spectroscope,** and **spectrum** all come from the Latin word *spectare,* meaning "to behold." All of these words have to do with someone seeing or with something seen or used in seeing.

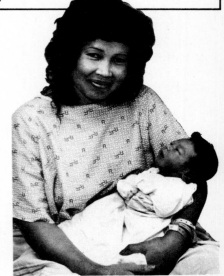

1. _____

2. _____

3. _____

4. _____

5. _____

List Words			
conspiracy	disrespect	exclusive	exclude
expire	expectation	including	inspection
inspiration	maternity	matron	maternal
matrimony	perspective	preclude	seclusion
spectacle	speculate	spiritual	transpired

Puzzle

Unscramble the List Words to complete the crossword puzzle.

ACROSS

1. NPRTADEISR
6. CSUVIEELX
8. PCUSALETE
9. OYISCPNARC
12. REUEPCLD
15. LANEMTRA
16. ESLSUNCIO
17. NIEPSNCITO
18. IEDTRSEPSC
19. NLIDCGUIN

DOWN

2. UPIIRLSTA
3. RXIEPE
4. ECPTSLEAC
5. RPPVEECSETI
6. EEUXLCD
7. TNRPNISIAIO
10. YENAMTRIT
11. PECXTENTAIO
13. RNAMTO
14. ROYTAIMMN

Proofreading

Use the proofreading marks to correct the mistakes in the letter below. Then write the misspelled List Words on the lines.

<table>
<tr><td colspan="2" align="center">**Proofreading Marks**</td></tr>
<tr><td>⬭ spelling mistake</td><td>ⱽ add apostrophe</td></tr>
<tr><td>? question mark</td><td>/ small letter</td></tr>
</table>

Dear Jackie,

    Weve been Pen pals for so long, I can't believe we'll actually be meeting soon. I often spekulate on what it'll be like. Do you wonder, too I also look forward to a different perzpective from a new country. I have heard theres a winter carnival in Quebec City in February. Would it be possible for us to see this spectacel and tour your city My family will be leaving on Saturday, inclooding my sister and her friend. My expictation is that this will be a great trip.

See you Soon,
Chen

1. _____

2. _____

3. _____

4. _____

5. _____

Challenges

Express Yourself

Imagine that you have a pen pal from a foreign country. Write a friendly letter to your pen pal, introducing yourself. Include information about your family, your school, and the subjects that you are studying. Tell about your favorite sports and activities you enjoy. Think about what you would like to know about your pen pal. Include those questions. Proofread and revise your letter. Then share it with a friend or talk to your teacher about sending it to an actual pen pal.

Bonus Words: Countries

| Guatemala | Chile | Yugoslavia | Pakistan | Zimbabwe |
| El Salvador | Portugal | Morocco | Indonesia | Sierra Leone |

Write the Bonus Words that match each geographical location given.

Africa   **1.** _____   **2.** _____   **3.** _____

Asia   **4.** _____   **5.** _____

Europe   **6.** _____   **7.** _____

Central America   **8.** _____   **9.** _____

South America   **10.** _____

Game Plan

Some words are especially difficult to spell because they contain sounds that can be spelled by different letters. For example, the soft **c** sound in <u>fallacy</u> sounds very similar to the **s** sound in <u>defenseless</u>. In other "hurdle words," letters may stand for unusual sounds. For example, in <u>especially</u> the **c** stands for /sh/. Memorize the spellings of the List Words so that you aren't fooled by their subtle "tricks."

Warm Up

Vocabulary

Write the List Word that matches each synonym or definition.

1. anxiety
2. customer
3. diminish
4. entirely
5. expenses
6. controversial
7. customary
8. eloquent
9. equally
10. fallacy
11. courtesy
12. decision
13. eminent
14. excitable
15. source
16. cruel
17. defenseless
18. sophomore
19. excess
20. especially

1. costs _____
2. totally _____
3. client _____
4. traditional _____
5. lessen _____
6. unmerciful _____
7. polite behavior _____
8. easily provoked _____
9. worry or fear _____
10. particularly _____

Dictionary Skills

Write the List Word that comes between each pair of dictionary guide words.

1. entrance/equation _____
2. sorrow/south _____
3. deal/defeat _____
4. common/count _____
5. ember/empty _____
6. sole/soup _____
7. examine/exchange _____
8. decoy/dill _____
9. either/emigrate _____
10. fabulous/fame _____

Practice

Word Analysis

Write List Words to answer the following questions.

Which words contain the double consonant **ll**?

1. _____   3. _____

2. _____

Which words contain the letter **x**?

4. _____   6. _____

5. _____   7. _____

Which words contain the letter **q**?

8. _____   9. _____

Which words contain no more than two syllables?

10. _____   12. _____

11. _____

Word Application

Complete each of the following phrases by writing a List Word to replace the word or words in parentheses.

1. an (famous) author   _____

2. (origin) of the problem   _____

3. common (polite behavior) _____

4. (too much) baggage   _____

5. (completely) correct   _____

6. a (helpless) animal   _____

7. the (expressive) poet   _____

8. travel (costs)   _____

9. a difficult (choice)   _____

10. (student class) dance   _____

Analogies

Write a List Word to complete each analogy.

1. <u>Fat</u> is to <u>thin</u> as <u>increase</u> is to _____ .

2. <u>Kind</u> is to <u>happiness</u> as _____ is to <u>sorrow</u>.

3. <u>Calm</u> is to <u>still</u> as _____ is to <u>active</u>.

4. <u>Two</u> is to <u>three</u> as _____ is to <u>junior</u>.

5. <u>Disagree</u> is to _____ as <u>agree</u> is to <u>acceptable</u>.

6. <u>Profits</u> are to <u>in</u> as _____ are to <u>out</u>.

7. <u>Contentment</u> is to <u>happy</u> as _____ is to <u>worried</u>.

List Words

anxiety	controversial	courtesy	cruel
customer	customary	decision	defenseless
diminish	eloquent	eminent	sophomore
entirely	equally	excitable	excess
expenses	fallacy	source	especially

Puzzle

Use the List Words to complete the crossword puzzle.

ACROSS

2. easily provoked or excited

4. polite behavior

5. second year of high school or college

7. to lessen

9. helpless; unable to stand up for oneself

10. starting point; origin

12. totally

14. false or mistaken idea

15. mean; unmerciful

17. client or purchaser of goods or services

18. extreme concern, worry, or fear

DOWN

1. settlement, conclusion, or choice

2. costs; money spent

3. debatable; subject to divided opinions

6. distinguished; famous; above others in rank

8. following tradition, custom, or usual routine

11. in identical portions, sizes, or values

12. particularly

13. well-spoken; expressive; poetic

16. too much; more than enough

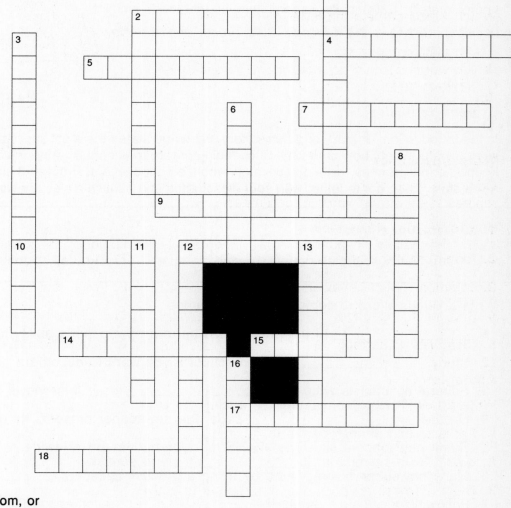

Proofreading

Use the proofreading marks to correct the mistakes in the article below. Then write the misspelled List Words on the lines.

Proofreading Marks	
⬯ spelling mistake	🖾 add space
≡ capital letter	⊙ add period

the first newspapers appeared inancient rome. At that time, it was custumary to post the "newssheets," espesially in places where the public gathered Germany had the first regularly published newspaper in europe in 1609. the first U.S. newspaper was published in Boston in the American Colonies in 1690. Today the U.S. has approximately 1,800 daily papers, two of the most eminint newspapers being the *Chicago Sun Times* and the *New York Times.*

1. _____

2. _____

3. _____

Challenges

Express Yourself

In the introduction, or **lead**, of a news story, the writer states the most important facts—who, what, where, when, how, and why. Succeeding paragraphs contain supportive details. Following this process, write a news story about a school event. Proofread and revise your news story. Then get together with your classmates and publish a class newspaper.

Bonus Words: Newspapers

journalism	editorial	lithography	libelous	censorship
obituary	distribution	investigative	muckrake	commentaries

Write a Bonus Word to complete each sentence.

1. _____ of the press could harm a newspaper's ability to publish important facts.

2. Study _____ in school if you want to become a newspaper reporter.

3. Several columnists write _____ to air their views on newsworthy issues.

4. On the _____ page, the newspaper presents its opinions on current issues.

5. Some newspapers, like *The Wall Street Journal*, have worldwide _____ .

6. Many newspapers are printed by using a process called _____ .

7. Following a person's death, the _____ summarizes the events of his or her life.

8. _____ reporters aim to find the facts behind a mystery or unsolved crime.

9. A story may be judged _____ if it unfairly injures or ridicules an individual.

10. To _____ is to write a news story to expose corruption in business or politics.

Game Plan

You know that Latin roots can help you determine the meanings of unfamiliar words. Knowing the way a Latin root is spelled can also help you figure out how to spell a difficult word. Here are some examples:

Latin Root (Meaning)	English Word	Latin Root (Meaning)	English Word
aqua (water)	**aquatic**	**voc/vok** (voice)	**vocalize**
later (side)	**unilateral**	**var** (different)	**variety**
sim (like)	**simulate**	**vag** (wander)	**vagrant**
liber (free)	**liberal**	**centr** (center)	**centralize**
host/hosp (house)	**hostel**	**term** (end)	**terminal**
mort (death)	**mortal**	**terr** (land)	**terrace**
plic/plex (fold)	**complex**	**spec** (see)	**inspection**
rupt (break)	**abrupt**	**spir** (breathe)	**spiritual**
pend (hang)	**pendant**	**clu/clud** (shut)	**preclude**
struct (build)	**construct**	**mater** (mother)	**maternity**

Words that do not follow ordinary spelling rules present a challenge. Memorize and practice spelling such tricky hurdle words as these.

<u>customer</u>   <u>eloquent</u>   <u>eminent</u>

Practice

Write List Words to answer the questions.

Lesson **13**
aquarium   mortgage
lateral   hospitalize
hostile   simultaneous
dissimilar   quadrilateral
hostage   liberate

_____

_____

Which List Words contain the Latin root **host** or **hosp** that mean <u>house</u>?

1. _____   3. _____

2. _____

Which List Word contains the Latin root **aqua** that means <u>water</u>?

4. _____

Which List Word contains the Latin root **mort** that means <u>death</u>?

5. _____

Which List Words contain the Latin roots **sim** that means <u>like</u>?

6. _____   7. _____

Which List Words contain the Latin root **later** that means <u>side</u>?

8. _____   9. _____

Which List Word contains the Latin root **liber** that means <u>free</u>?

10. _____

Write a List Word to complete each sentence.

1. If you do a project without a partner, you work

   _____ .

2. If you see something you can't explain, it is

   _____ .

3. If you read mystery stories, you enjoy _____ .

4. If a tornado whips through town, it causes

   _____ .

5. If a remark is off the subject, it is not _____ .

6. An identical copy of a contract is called a _____ .

7. If a building collapses, it probably has _____ deficiencies.

8. A balloon flying high is _____ in the air.

9. If you break into a conversation, you _____ .

10. To learn how to play the violin, you look for

    _____ .

Lesson **14**	
inexplicable	duplicate
instruction	structural
destruction	suspense
independently	interrupt
suspended	applicable

_____

_____

VIOLIN LESSONS
INQUIRE WITHIN

Write a List Word to match each clue.

Lesson **15**	
advocate	various
terrain	determine
concentric	eccentric
exterminate	territory
vague	variation

_____

_____

1. circles _____
2. a change _____
3. destroy _____
4. unclear _____
5. different _____
6. a region _____
7. odd _____
8. supporter _____
9. land _____
10. figure out _____

Fill in the puzzle by writing a
List Word to match each
synonym.

ACROSS
2. keep out
7. privacy
8. view
9. display
10. marriage

DOWN
1. conjecture
3. plot
4. rudeness
5. encouragement
6. motherly

Lesson **16**

conspiracy	maternal
inspiration	perspective
matrimony	speculate
spectacle	speculate
spectacle	exclude
disrespect	seclusion

_____

_____

Write the List Words that
come between each pair of
dictionary guide words. Write
the words in alphabetical
order.

answer/deal

1. _____

2. _____

3. _____

4. _____

5. _____

debt/fawn

6. _____

7. _____

8. _____

9. _____

10. _____

Lesson **17**

anxiety	decision
cruel	excitable
customary	controversial
fallacy	defenseless
courtesy	especially

_____

_____

dissimilar	advocate	exclude
hostile	vague	customary
liberate	eccentric	fallacy
applicable	inspiration	excitable
independently	disrespect	defenseless

Mixed Practice

Write the List Word that is an antonym for the word given.

1. truth _____

2. friendly _____

3. discouragement _____

4. calm _____

5. imprison _____

6. ordinary _____

7. cooperatively _____

8. alike _____

9. courtesy _____

10. armed _____

11. unrelated _____

12. clear _____

13. unusual _____

14. critic _____

15. include _____

Test Yourself

In each of the following groups of words, one word is misspelled. Fill in the circle that appears before that word.

1. o fallacy
   o exclude
   o eccentric
   o prespective

2. o decision
   o spectacle
   o teritory
   o disrespect

3. o destruction
   o suspended
   o applicable
   o structeral

4. o customary
   o espescially
   o matrimony
   o speculate

5. o determine
   o terrain
   o conspiricy
   o maternal

6. o inexplicible
   o interrupt
   o liberate
   o hospitalize

7. o hostile
   o instruction
   o morgage
   o concentric

8. o advocate
   o controversial
   o crule
   o various

9. o exterminate
   o simaltaneous
   o independently
   o dissimilar

10. o aquarium
    o duplicate
    o quadralateral
    o inspiration

11. o vague
    o anxiety
    o hostage
    o suspence

12. o lateral
    o seclusion
    o vareation
    o courtesy

Game Plan

The prefixes **co** and **syn** mean <u>together</u>. However, the prefix **syn** changes its spelling to **syl** when it is used before words beginning with **l**; it changes to **sym** when it is used before words beginning with **b**, **m**, or **p**. Notice the spelling of these example words.

<u>co</u>author	<u>syn</u>theses	<u>syl</u>lable
<u>sym</u>bolize	<u>sym</u>metry	<u>sym</u>ptom

Warm Up

Vocabulary Development

Write the List Word that matches each definition.

1. balance _____

2. sentence structure _____

3. a temple _____

4. to be identical or in accord _____

5. live together _____

6. understandable _____

7. musical _____

8. a medical indicator _____

9. an outline of a course of study _____

10. bring together _____

11. word part _____

12. guaranteed by property _____

Dictionary Skills

Write the List Word that matches each sound-spelling.

1. (kō′ pī lət) _____   6. (sim pō′ zē əm) _____

2. (sim′ b'l īz) _____   7. (sin′ thə sis) _____

3. (kō′ in sīd′) _____   8. (sing′ krə nīz) _____

4. (simp′ təm) _____   9. (sing′ kə pāt) _____

5. (kō ô′ thər) _____   10. (kō äp′ ər ə tiv) _____

List Words

1. coauthor
2. collateral
3. copilot
4. symptom
5. synagogue
6. coexist
7. coordinate
8. syllable
9. symmetry
10. synchronize
11. coherent
12. cooperative
13. symphonic
14. synthesis
15. syncopate
16. coincide
17. symbolize
18. symposium
19. syntax
20. syllabus

Practice

Word Analysis

Write the List Word that has the same root as the word given.

1. syncopation _____

2. synthetic _____

3. authorize _____

4. autopilot _____

5. cooperation _____

6. coincidence _____

7. nonexisting _____

8. symmetrical _____

9. coordination _____

10. symbolic _____

Write the List Words that contain double letters.

1. _____

2. _____

3. _____

4. _____

5. _____

6. _____

Proofreading

Use the proofreading marks to correct the mistakes in the sentences. Then write the misspelled words correctly on the lines.

```
              Proofreading Marks
◯ spelling mistake          /  small letter
# add space               ⌄ ⌄  add quotes
⊙ ? !  add period, question mark, or exclamation mark
```

1. David asked his coauthor, "Could you cordinate our meetings? _____

2. A symposium on symphonec music will be held Tomorrow night. _____

3. The copilot and I had to syncronize ourwatches before the flight. _____

4. What do the stripes on our flag simbolize " asked a student. _____

5. We heard a cohearent speech on the importance of Computers. _____

6. What beautiful symmetry of design on that sinagog _____

7. Our visit during the Summer will coinside with yours. _____

8. Mr. Warren said, Learn to spell each sylabble inthis word." _____

9. "Our next project will be a cooprative one," said the Teacher. _____

10. The sentence sintax can give you clues toa word's meaning. _____

List Words

coauthor	coexist	coherent	coincide
collateral	coordinate	cooperative	symbolize
copilot	syllable	symphonic	symposium
symptom	symmetry	synthesis	syntax
synagogue	synchronize	syncopate	syllabus

Puzzle

Use the List Words to complete the crossword puzzle.

ACROSS

1. having to do with the sounds a symphony makes

5. a writer who works with another writer

6. a meeting to discuss some particular subject

8. the assistant pilot of an airplane

9. a word or part of a word

12. the putting together of parts or elements to make a whole

16. speaking or thinking in a way that makes sense

17. the way words are put together in sentences; sentence structure

18. to be the symbol of something; represent

DOWN

2. to bring together in a proper relation

3. a sign that something else exists, especially in sickness

4. helpful, willing to cooperate

5. to happen at the same time

7. an outline or summary

9. a temple where Jewish people gather for worship

10. property given as a pledge to repay a loan

11. to make agree in time or rate of speed

13. to shift the musical accent of a beat

14. balance or harmony

15. living together in peace

Test Yourself

In each pair of List Words, underline the misspelled List Word and write it correctly on the line.

1. sincopate, symptom   _____

2. synagog, symposium   _____

3. simphonic, syntax   _____

4. sylabus, synthesis   _____

5. copilot, coperative   _____

6. cordinate, collateral   _____

7. coincide, cohearant   _____

8. coauther, coexist   _____

Challenges

Express Yourself

A **review** is a critical examination of a movie, TV show, book, or play. It also expresses the personal opinion of the reviewer. Write a review of a movie, television show, or play that you have seen or a book you have read recently. Give a short summary of its story and then tell why you liked or disliked it. Proofread and revise your review. Then compile your work with that of your classmates in a book. Create one book for movie reviews, one for television show reviews, and so on. Add reviews to the books periodically.

Bonus Words: Theater

amphitheater	critique	prologue	melodrama	coliseum
pageant	soliloquy	vaudeville	scenario	cinema

Write Bonus Words to answer the questions.

Which word relates to film or movies?

1. _____

Which word might discuss a play or film?

2. _____

Which words name buildings or structures?

3. _____

4. _____

Which words describe or name kinds of performances?

5. _____   6. _____   7. _____

Which words name parts of particular plays?

8. _____   9. _____   10. _____

Prefixes Meaning <u>Not</u>

Game Plan

Many different prefixes mean <u>not</u>. Some of these prefixes change their spellings before certain letters. The prefix **a**, for example, becomes **an** before a vowel. The prefix **in** becomes **im** before **m**, **b**, and **p**. Look at how these words are spelled:

<u>an</u>archy   <u>in</u>cognito   <u>im</u>mobilize   <u>im</u>promptu

Other prefixes meaning <u>not</u> include **non** and **neg**, as in <u>non</u>existent and <u>neg</u>ative.

Warm Up

1. *anarchy*	
2. *imprudent*	
3. *impersonate*	
4. *incognito*	
5. *negligent*	
6. *anesthesia*	
7. *immobilize*	
8. *impatiently*	
9. *indecisive*	
10. *negative*	
11. *anemia*	
12. *immaculate*	
13. *inaccurate*	
14. *invalid*	
15. *nonchalant*	
16. *anonymous*	
17. *impromptu*	
18. *inactive*	
19. *neglect*	
20. *nonexistent*	

Vocabulary Development

Write the List Word that matches each synonym or definition.

1. unfavorable   _____

2. idle   _____

3. in disguise   _____

4. without advance planning _____

5. unnamed   _____

6. null and void   _____

7. cool and composed   _____

8. prevent movement   _____

9. clean   _____

10. mimic or copy   _____

11. incorrect   _____

12. hesitant   _____

Dictionary Skills

Rewrite each of the following List Words to show how they are divided into syllables.

1. neglect _____
2. anemia _____
3. anarchy _____
4. invalid _____
5. negligent _____

6. impatiently _____
7. anesthesia _____
8. immobilize _____
9. nonexistent _____
10. imprudent _____

Practice

Word Analysis

Write the List Word formed by adding a prefix that means <u>not</u> to each base given.

1. valid _____

2. decisive _____

3. mobilize _____

4. accurate _____

5. prudent _____

6. personal _____

7. active _____

8. patiently _____

Word Application

Replace the underlined word or words in each sentence with a List Word. Write the List Word on the line.

1. Make sure you do not <u>abandon</u> your duty. _____

2. These troops are <u>not on active duty</u>. _____

3. Ellen is so <u>composed</u>, and I am so nervous. _____

4. First, the doctor will have to <u>prevent motion in</u> that broken leg. _____

5. The police received a call from a <u>nameless</u> person. _____

6. We decided to have a <u>spur-of-the-moment</u> party. _____

7. To avoid photographers, the star travelled <u>in disguise</u>. _____

8. This surgery will require only local <u>painkiller</u>. _____

9. Make sure you do not make <u>wrong</u> claims about your product. _____

10. The Washington family keeps their home <u>very clean</u>. _____

11. The nurse will test you for <u>a blood disorder</u>. _____

12. In the fog, my ocean view was <u>not there</u>. _____

13. People often try to <u>pretend they are</u> famous people. _____

14. Spending all your money would be <u>unwise</u>. _____

15. A leader is not allowed to be <u>wavering</u>. _____

16. After the revolution, <u>an absence of government</u> ruled. _____

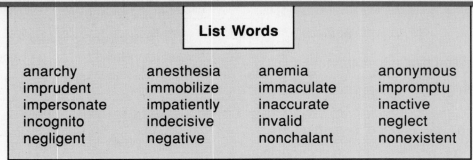

List Words

anarchy   anesthesia   anemia   anonymous
imprudent   immobilize   immaculate   impromptu
impersonate   impatiently   inaccurate   inactive
incognito   indecisive   invalid   neglect
negligent   negative   nonchalant   nonexistent

Puzzle

This is a crossword puzzle without clues. Use the length and the
spelling of each List Word to complete the puzzle.

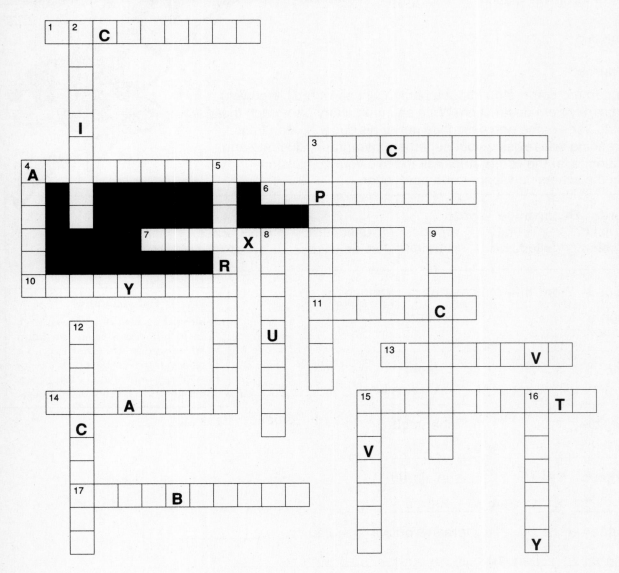

Proofreading

Use the proofreading marks to correct the mistakes in the poem below. Then write the misspelled List Words on the lines.

If you want to be be a good superhero
you must must be prepared to go incogneto.
You must act nonshalant in in every way
until you can show that "crime does not pay."
And then with a whoosh, you fly through the skies
and quickly imobilize a bunch of bad guys

1. _____

2. _____

3. _____

Challenges

Express Yourself

Create a superhero comic strip about a person whose incredible powers save an entire city from destruction. Write an introductory paragraph that tells the character's name and describes her or his super human traits. After proofreading and revising your superhero paragraph, illustrate and write the dialogue for the comic strip. Ask to have your comic strip published in the school newspaper or a newsletter.

Bonus Words: Descriptive Words

altruistic	articulate	arduous	unscathed	boisterous
laudable	winsome	staunch	vindictive	dynamic

Write the Bonus Word that matches each synonym.

vengeful

1. _____

difficult

2. _____

intelligible

3. _____

energetic

4. _____

cute

5. _____

loud

6. _____

loyal

7. _____

charitable

8. _____

uninjured

9. _____

praiseworthy

10. _____

Did you know?

Nonchalant is a word borrowed from French and comes from two Latin words meaning "to be not warm." A person who is *nonchalant* does not get warm or passionate about things, but seems always to be cool or lukewarm.

Game Plan

You have already studied several words and prefixes that have Latin roots. Knowing the meanings of Latin roots that appear frequently in English words will help you to analyze unfamiliar words for correct meaning and spelling.

Latin Root	Meaning	English Words	Meaning
documentum	lesson, example	**document**	paper relied on for proof
		documentary	film that teaches
optio	wish, desire	**option**	the power to choose
		optional	not mandatory; elective
opticus	eye	**optician**	one who makes eyeglasses

1. *auditor*
2. *exorbitant*
3. *molecular*
4. *ordinance*
5. *Republican*
6. *documentary*
7. *insecticide*
8. *optician*
9. *publicity*
10. *suburban*
11. *dominion*
12. *juvenile*
13. *option*
14. *quarantine*
15. *vermin*
16. *exhilarated*
17. *maximum*
18. *opulent*
19. *regime*
20. *verdict*

Warm Up

Vocabulary Development

Write the List Word that matches each definition clue.

1. law _____
2. excessive _____
3. young _____
4. choice _____
5. wealthy _____
6. bug poison _____
7. promotion _____
8. political party _____
9. eye specialist _____
10. jury's decision _____
11. nonfiction film _____
12. animal pests _____

Dictionary Skills

Write the List Word that matches each etymology.

1. Latin **sub-** ("under, near") + **urbs** ("town") _____
2. Latin **vermus** ("worm") _____
3. Latin **vere-** ("truly") + **dictum** ("said") _____
4. Latin **dominus** ("master") _____
5. Latin **regere** ("to rule") _____
6. Latin **ex-** ("intensive") + **hilaris** ("glad") _____
7. Italian **quaranta** ("forty") from Latin **quattuor** ("four") _____
8. Latin **audire** ("to hear") _____
9. Latin **maximus** ("greatest") _____
10. Latin **moles** ("mass") _____

Practice

Word Analysis

Write the List Word with the same Latin root as the word given.

1. order _____

2. maxim _____

3. dominate _____

4. quarter _____

5. orbit _____

6. urban _____

7. hilarious _____

8. regiment _____

9. adopt _____

10. audition _____

Classification

Write a List Word to complete each series.

1. atomic, cellular, _____

2. Democrat, Socialist, _____

3. wealthy, luxuriant, _____

4. testimony, evidence, _____

5. _____ , adolescent, adult

6. parasites, predators, _____

7. dentist, dietitian, _____

8. newscast, biography, _____

9. hospitalization, bed rest, _____

10. minimum, average, _____

11. announcement, promotion, _____

12. bookkeeper, treasurer, _____

Word Application

Select a List Word from the choices in parentheses to complete each sentence. Write your answer on the line.

1. The _____ formula of water is H_2O. (documentary, molecular, quarantine)

2. Commuters from _____ towns take trains to the city. (dominion, ordinance, suburban)

3. Ralph used_____ to rid his garden of aphids and beetles. (vermin, publicity, insecticide)

4. I was shaken but_____ by the roller coaster rider. (exhilarated, exorbitant, opulent)

5. Your posters provided great _____ for my campaign. (publicity, dominion, documentary)

6. The movie was set in the _____ palace of Catherine the Great. (maximum, opulent, exhilarated)

7. The _____ of Queen Victoria lasted from 1837 to 1901. (opulent, regime, verdict)

List Words			
auditor	documentary	dominion	exhilarated
exorbitant	insecticide	juvenile	maximum
molecular	optician	option	opulent
ordinance	publicity	quarantine	regime
Republican	suburban	vermin	verdict

Puzzle

Use the List Words to complete the crossword puzzle.

ACROSS

4. related to the particles in an element or compound

5. related to young people

7. a law, especially one made by a city government

11. excessive in number or size

13. rule or power to rule

15. period of time in which a certain person is in power

16. person who makes eye care products

17. nonfiction film

18. insects or small animals, such as termites and rats

19. material geared to announce events or provide information to the public

DOWN

1. jury's decision

2. period in which a diseased person or animal is isolated

3. bug poison

6. feeling cheerful and lively

8. person who checks financial accounts and records

9. the greatest possible amount

10. a political party in the United States

12. related to areas situated near a city

14. power to choose; one particular choice

16. rich or luxurious

Proofreading

Use the proofreading marks to correct the mistakes in the article below. Then write the misspelled List Words on the lines.

Proofreading Marks	
⬯ spelling mistake	ⱽ add apostrophe
ⱽⱽ add quotation marks	/ small letter

Francisco Vásquez de Coronado was one of Spain's explorers who set out to search for gold and exorbetant wealth in the 1500s. Coronado, however, didnt discover any opyulent towns in his Exploration of what is now Americas southwest. He claimed Territory for the Spanish kings domminion. Coronado remarked exhilerated, I have found country that has fresh Rivers and grass like that of Castile in Spain.

1. _____

2. _____

3. _____

4. _____

Challenges

Express Yourself

Vasco Núñez de Balboa was the first to view the Pacific Ocean from the North American coast. Francisco Vásquez de Coronado was the first European to see the Grand Canyon. Pick one of these explorers to research. Based on your study, write a report in which you, as the explorer, announce your discovery to the King of Spain. After proofreading and revising your report, read it aloud to the class or a group. Discuss whether your description helped them picture what you saw.

Bonus Words: Earth

igneous	avalanche	erosion	mesa	atoll
sedimentary	topography	geyser	crevasse	alluvial

Write the Bonus Word that matches each definition clue.

1. deep crack in land or ice _____

2. wearing away of soil _____

3. ring-shaped island _____

4. high, steep-sided plateau _____

5. study of land surfaces _____

6. boiling spring _____

7. containing matter deposited by water or wind, as sand or soil _____

8. made up of sand or clay washed down by flowing water _____

9. matter produced by the action of volcanoes or other intense heat _____

10. sudden, swift slide of a mass of loosened snow, earth, or rocks _____

Game Plan

Many English words have Greek origins. Knowing the meanings of Greek roots and prefixes will help you spell and define unfamiliar words.

Greek Prefix/Root	Meaning	English Word	Meaning
meter + polis	mother city	**metropolis**	major city
theo + logos	the gods' words	**theology**	religious studies
archi + tekton	chief carpenter	**architect**	building designer

Warm Up

Vocabulary Development

Write the List Word that matches each synonym or definition.

1. school _____
2. ancient _____
3. rubbery _____
4. urgent _____
5. find fault _____
6. universe _____
7. government rules _____
8. document library _____
9. careful study _____
10. word puzzle _____
11. worldwide _____

Dictionary Skills

Write a List Word to match each Greek etymology.

1. **aēr** ("air") + **naus** ("ship") _____
2. **theo** ("god") + **logos** ("word") _____
3. **dēmos** ("the people") + **kratos** ("strength") _____
4. **Magnētis** ("stone from Magnesia") _____
5. **politikos** ("of a citizen") _____
6. **meter** ("mother") + **polis** ("city") _____
7. **Akadēmos** ("figure in Greek myths") _____
8. **ana** ("back") + **gramma** ("letter") _____
9. **oikos** ("house") + **nomos** ("law") _____
10. **archi** ("chief") + **tekton** ("carpenter") _____
11. **ana** ("up") + **lysis** ("loosening") _____
12. **ek** ("out") + **leipein** ("to leave") _____

1. *academy*
2. *archive*
3. *cosmopolitan*
4. *economical*
5. *metropolis*
6. *aeronautics*
7. *archaic*
8. *criticize*
9. *elastic*
10. *democracy*
11. *analysis*
12. *architect*
13. *crisis*
14. *cosmos*
15. *politics*
16. *anagram*
17. *bureaucracy*
18. *eclipse*
19. *magnetic*
20. *theology*

Practice

Word Analysis

Write the List Word that has the same root as the word given.

1. polite _____

2. magnesium _____

3. economy _____

4. Minneapolis _____

5. analyze _____

6. airplane _____

7. academic _____

8. telegram _____

> **Did you know?**
>
> **Academy** comes from the Greek word for a grove of trees near Athens. Plato, an ancient Greek philosopher and teacher, taught his students in that grove. The Greeks thought that it had once belonged to a hero in Greek legend named Akademos.

Analogies

Write a List Word to complete each analogy.

1. Difficult is to easy as _____ is to modern.

2. Communism is to the Soviet Union as _____ to the United States.

3. Portrait is to artist as building is to _____ .

4. Brittle is to break as _____ is to stretch.

5. Archaeology is to early civilizations as _____ is to religious doctrines.

6. Applaud is to "yes" as _____ is to "no."

7. Library is to book as _____ is to document.

8. Island is to ocean as galaxy is to _____ .

Word Application

Select a List Word from the choices in parentheses to complete each sentence. Write your answer on the line.

1. Red tape is a slang term for the complexities of

_____ . (aeronautics, bureaucracy, crisis)

2. A _____ person travels all over the world with ease. (politics, cosmopolitan, democracy)

3. Scientists who design rockets are experts in _____ . (aeronautics, metropolis, crisis)

4. The moon may totally cover the sun in a solar

_____ . (bureaucracy, cosmos, eclipse)

5. The tornado created a _____ in the city. (metropolis, crisis, cosmos)

List Words			
academy	aeronautics	analysis	anagram
archive	archaic	architect	bureaucracy
cosmopolitan	criticize	crisis	eclipse
economical	elastic	cosmos	magnetic
metropolis	democracy	politics	theology

Syllables

Write each List Word under the correct category.

Words with Two Syllables

1. _____

2. _____

3. _____

4. _____

Words with Three Syllables

5. _____

6. _____

7. _____

8. _____

9. _____

10. _____

11. _____

Words with Four Syllables

12. _____

13. _____

14. _____

15. _____

16. _____

17. _____

18. _____

Words with Five Syllables

19. _____

20. _____

Definitions

Write a List Word to solve each definition clue.

1. storage vault   _____

2. thorough examination _____

3. emergency   _____

4. to pass judgment   _____

5. a word puzzle   _____

6. force that attracts   _____

7. educational institution _____

8. leading city   _____

Proofreading

Use the proofreading marks to correct the mistakes in the how-to article. Then write the misspelled List Words on the lines.

Proofreading Marks

⬭ spelling mistake   ? add question mark
⊙ add period   ¶ new paragraph

Did you know that making your own greeting cards can be quite econnomical Just use paper, glue, photos, markers, and your imagination Your cards can be works of art and can be preserved in a family arkive.

    Where can you find ideas for cards Try illustrating a character or scene from a movie or a work of art from a museum. Include a quote or poem Cards can be traditional or cosmopoliten. Even archayc designs may be reused. However you decide to design your cards, enjoy!

1. _____
2. _____
3. _____
4. _____

Challenges

Express Yourself

Compose a greeting card to cheer up a friend or relative who is ill. First, write an opening line or lines for the front of the card. Then write several lines—in prose or poetry—for the inside. Proofread and revise your card. Send your card to someone.

Bonus Words: Medical Terms

therapeutic	convalescent	surgery	gurney	intravenous
rehabilitate	pediatrics	dispensary	syringe	radiology

Write a Bonus Word to complete each sentence.

1. A _____ is a stretcher or cot on wheels.

2. To _____ injured muscles, doctors often prescribe physical therapy.

3. Doctors sometimes perform _____ to repair damaged organs.

4. Vaccines are often given by _____ injection.

5. A _____ is a vial of medicine with a needle designed to penetrate a vein.

6. Drinking liquids and getting plenty of rest is _____ for the common cold.

7. A patient's _____ period after surgery is sometimes spent in the hospital.

8. The hospital stores medicines in the _____ .

9. _____ is a medical specialty involving X-rays.

10. _____ is a medical specialty involving the health care of young persons.

Game Plan

The List Words contain Greek roots that appear frequently in English words. Many English words are a combination of two Greek roots.

Greek Root	Meaning	English Word	Meaning
chronos	time	**chronic**	lasting a long time
thermos	hot	**thermostat**	device for regulating heat system
metron	measure	**thermometer**	device for measuring heat level
		chronometer	an extremely accurate clock

1. aristocrat
2. biography
3. thermostat
4. octagon
5. parasite
6. barometer
7. chronic
8. geographical
9. parallel
10. pharmacy
11. biological
12. dialogue
13. geological
14. parable
15. televise
16. hydrant
17. enthusiasm
18. neon
19. paralysis
20. thermos

Warm Up

Vocabulary Development

Write the List Word that matches each synonym or definition.

1. drugstore _____
2. eagerness _____
3. conversation _____
4. life story _____
5. short story _____
6. helpless inactivity _____
7. insulated bottle _____
8. eight-sided figure _____
9. recurring often _____
10. colorless gas _____

Dictionary Skills

Write the List Word that comes between each pair of dictionary guide words.

1. parade/parallelogram _____
2. biohazard/biometry _____
3. geoid/geometry _____
4. thermoscope/thesaurus _____
5. humor/hydrogen _____
6. telephone/thermodynamic _____
7. geodesic/geologic _____
8. banner/beacon _____
9. aqua/aster _____
10. parameter/parboil _____
11. pepper/phase _____

Practice

Word Analysis

Write the List Word derived from the Greek roots given.

1. **para** ("beside") + **allēlos** ("one another") _____

2. **bios** ("life") + **logos** ("word, thought") _____

3. **aristos** ("best") + **kratos** ("power") _____

4. **geo** ("earth") + **logos** ("word, thought") _____

5. **bios** ("life") + **graphē** ("writing") _____

6. **para** ("beside") + **sitos** ("food") _____

7. **geo** ("earth") + **graphē** ("writing") _____

8. **para** ("beside") + **lysis** ("destruction") _____

9. **thermos** ("heat") + **statos** ("standing") _____

10. **baros** ("weight") + **metron** ("measure") _____

11. **dia** ("across") + **logos** ("word, thought") _____

12. **oktō** ("eight") + **gōnia** ("angle") _____

> **Did you know?**
> **Enthusiasm** comes from a Greek word meaning "inspired by a god." Poets and prophets long ago were thought to be inspired by a god. The earliest meaning of *enthusiasm* was "the inspiration of a poet or prophet."

Classification

Write a List Word to complete each series.

1. fable, myth, _____

2. photograph, transmit, _____

3. soup bowl, mug, _____

4. hydrogen, helium, _____

5. duke, noble, _____

6. supermarket, shoe store, _____

7. perpendicular, diagonal, _____

8. pep, vigor, _____

9. hose, sprinkler, _____

10. triangle, square, _____

11. journal, memoir, _____

12. monologue, discourse, _____

Word Application

Select a List Word from the choices in parentheses to complete each sentence. Write your answer on the line.

1. _____ studies concern rocks and minerals. (geographical, geological)

2. A _____ is an animal that gains food by living on a host animal. (parable, parasite)

3. A _____ is a device that measures atmospheric pressure. (barometer, thermostat)

4. A firefighter often uses a _____ for water to extinguish flames. (thermos, hydrant)

List Words

aristocrat	barometer	biological	hydrant
biography	chronic	dialogue	enthusiasm
thermostat	geographical	geological	neon
octagon	parallel	parable	paralysis
parasite	pharmacy	televise	thermos

Syllables

Write each List Word under the correct category.

Words with Two Syllables

1. _____

2. _____

3. _____

4. _____

Words with Four Syllables

5. _____

6. _____

7. _____

8. _____

Words with Five Syllables

9. _____

10. _____

11. _____

12. _____

Puzzle

Each clue is an example, or illustration, of a List Word. Write the List Words in the answer spaces. Then transfer the numbered letters to the spaces below to answer the question.

1. She jumped for joy.   _ _ _ _ _ _ _ _ _
                                    2 15

2. *The Life of Helen Keller* _ _ _ _ _ _ _ _ _
                            1   6   12

3. a stop sign   _ _ _ _ _ _ _
                 5   16

4. a long illness   _ _ _ _ _ _ _ _ _
                    11   8

5. "Who's there?"
   "It's John."   _ _ _ _ _ _ _ _
                  13   3

6. _____   _ _ _ _ _ _
                 10   4

7. Davidson's Drugstore   _ _ _ _ _ _ _ _
                          9 14

8. work at Channel 6   _ _ _ _ _ _ _ _
                       17   7

QUESTION: What two List Words could describe this elephant?

ANSWER: _ _ _ _ _ _ _ _ _ _   _ _ _ _ _ _ _
           1 2 3 4 5 6 7 8 9 10   11 12 13 14 15 16 17

Proofreading

Use the proofreading marks to correct the mistakes in the article below. Then write the misspelled List Words on the lines.

Proofreading Marks	
⬭ spelling mistake	ⱽ add apostrophe
⌣⌣ ⌣⌣ add quotation marks	⌃ add comma

   A biograffy of Pecos Bill might include tall tales about how he roped a cyclone with enthusiazm and turned it into a breeze. When it hadn't rained for months in Texas, people said Go see Bill. He'll know what to do. Cowboys said that he created the Southwests geografical features such as the valleys formed by scraping his boot heels. Pecos Bills fans would enjoy other tall tales about geologjical events such as the rivers he dug when he was thirsty.

1. _____   3. _____

2. _____   4. _____

Challenges

Express Yourself

Have you ever felt "as hungry as a bear"? Such exaggerated expressions are called **hyperboles.** They are used in speech and literature to overstate reality, often for comic effect. Write about a funny experience. Use hyperboles to "stretch" the facts for added humor. After proofreading and revising your hyperboles, tell your "tall tales" to your group.

Bonus Words: Language				
mimicry	synonymous	rhetoric	euphemism	epigram
sarcasm	epithet	paradox	memoir	anachronism

Write a Bonus Word to complete each sentence.

1. Words that are _____ have similar meanings.

2. *He passed away* is a _____ for *he died.*

3. *The child is father of the man* is an example of _____ .

4. Early Romans driving fancy sports cars is an example of _____ .

5. The title *Richard the Lion-Hearted* is an example of _____ .

6. In a personal _____ , someone might recall important events in his or her life.

7. Edison's saying "Genius is 1% inspiration and 99% perspiration" is a famous _____ .

8. To say "Thanks a lot" to a person who has not been helpful is to use _____ .

9. To use "ten-dollar words" that sound eloquent but do not communicate clearly is

   to use _____ .

10. Onomatopoetic words, such as *honk, sputter, clatter,* and *buzz* are examples of _____ .

Game Plan

The prefixes **co** and **syn** mean together. Examples include coauthor and synonym. When it is added to a root beginning with **l**, **syn** changes to **syl**, as in syllable. It changes to **sym** when it is added to roots beginning with **b**, **m**, or **p**. Examples include symbol, symmetry, and sympathy.

The prefixes **non**, **neg**, **in**, **im**, and **a** mean not. Examples include nonchalant, negligent, indecisive, impossible, and apolitical. The prefix **a** becomes **an** when it is added to a root beginning with a vowel. Examples include anarchy and anemia.

Many English words have Greek or Latin origins. Knowing the meanings of Greek and Lain prefixes and roots will help you to define and spell many unfamiliar words.

Prefix/Root	Source	Meaning	English Word	Meaning
ex + orbita	Latin	out of track	**exorbitant**	excessive
optio	Latin	wish, desire	**option**	power to choose
sub + urbs	Latin	near town	**suburban**	just outside a city
ex + hilaris	Latin	very glad	**exhilarated**	cheerful, lively
aér + naus	Greek	air ship	**aeronautics**	science of aircraft
bios + logos	Greek	life words	**biology**	study of living things
okto + gonia	Greek	eight angles	**octagon**	eight-sided figure

Practice

Select a List Word from the choices in parentheses to complete each sentence. Write the answer on the line.

Lesson **19**

coherent symmetry
coordinate symptom
synchronize syntax
symphonic coincide
synagogue symbolize

_____

_____

1. A rash of small red dots is a _____ of measles. (syntax, symptom)

2. Let's _____ our watches. (synchronize, coincide)

3. In my poem, the sun will _____ power. (synagogue, symbolize)

4. Hal has been chosen to _____ the project. (coincide, coordinate)

5. He worships at a _____ . (synagogue, symmetry)

6. This year, school vacation will _____ with my father's business trip to Argentina. (coincide, symbolize)

7. Mozart wrote many beautiful _____ works. (symphonic, coordinate)

8. We study grammar and _____ . (syntax, coherent)

9. Maria got an A on her oral report because it was interesting and _____ . (symphonic, coherent)

10. Pieces of art that are balanced have _____ . (symmetry, synchronize)

Each of these sentences contains the wrong List Word. Cross out the word and write the correct List Word on the line.

1. No one knew who sent the anesthesia note. _____

2. I'm afraid I was nonexistent, and forgot to feed the cat last night. _____

3. Don't let shyness immaculate you when new friends invite you to join them in a game. _____

4. To protect her privacy, the movie star decided to travel negligent. _____

5. The comedian will inaccurate a gorilla. _____

6. The doctor will administer anemia to the patient prior to surgery. _____

7. The city's plans to enlarge the library will be postponed because the funds are anonymous. _____

8. Ask honest people to avoid incognito facts. _____

9. Eat foods that are rich in iron to protect yourself from impersonate. _____

10. The players' immobilize white uniforms became wet and grimy because the field was covered with mud. _____

Lesson **20**

anonymous	immobilize
impersonate	anemia
inaccurate	immaculate
negligent	incognito
nonexistent	anesthesia

_____

_____

Write a List Word to answer each definition clue.

1. related to a particle in an element or compound _____

2. rich or luxuriant _____

3. excessive in number or size _____

4. person who makes eye care products _____

5. nonfiction film _____

6. period during which an ill person or animal is isolated _____

7. related to young people _____

8. cheerful and lively _____

9. person who manages financial accounts _____

10. a law _____

Lesson **21**

auditor	quarantine
exorbitant	documentary
exhilarated	opulent
juvenile	optician
ordinance	molecular

_____

_____

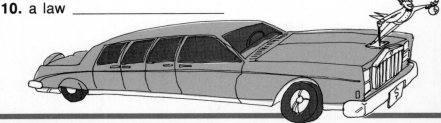

Write a List Word to complete each sentence.

1. _____ is the study of religion.

2. A building is designed by an _____.

3. The form of government of ancient Greece was a

   _____ .

4. _____ is the science, study, or design of aircraft.

5. To _____ a film is to describe its strengths and weaknesses.

6. A law firm might file source documents in its

   _____ .

7. Something that is _____ to buy is considered a bargain.

8. Chemists might conduct an _____ of a compound to discover what elements it contains.

9. One of the _____ laws that once existed in Arizona made hunting for camels illegal.

10. New York City is the largest _____ in the United States.

Lesson **22**

archaic	analysis
metropolis	archive
architect	aeronautics
economical	criticize
democracy	theology

_____

_____

Use the List Words to complete the crossword puzzle.

Lesson **23**

paralysis	pharmacy
enthusiasm	chronic
biological	parable
dialogue	parallel
parallel	geographical
	thermostat

_____

_____

ACROSS
3. story that teaches a lesson
5. related to the study of living things
6. device to regulate heat level
7. related to the study of the earth's surface
9. drugstore
10. inability to move

DOWN
1. at the same distance apart, at every point
2. intense or eager interest
4. conversation
8. enduring; continuous

synchronize	symbolize	coherent
inaccurate	nonexistent	anesthesia
optician	auditor	exorbitant
architect	criticize	economical
geographical	chronic	pharmacy

Mixed Practice

Write each List Word under the correct category.

Nouns Naming People

1. _____
2. _____
3. _____

Adjectives

4. _____
5. _____
6. _____
7. _____
8. _____
9. _____
10. _____

Verbs

11. _____
12. _____
13. _____

Nouns Naming Things

14. _____
15. _____

Words with Suffix **al**

16. _____
17. _____

Words with Suffix **ent**

18. _____
19. _____

Words with Prefixes meaning <u>not</u>

20. _____
21. _____
22. _____

Words with Greek root <u>chronos</u>

23. _____
24. _____

Test Yourself

In each of the following groups of words, one word is misspelled. Fill in the circle that appears before that word.

1. o auditer
   o thermostat
   o symbolize
   o architect

2. o symmetry
   o exhorbitant
   o archive
   o inaccurate

3. o impersonate
   o parable
   o theology
   o exilarated

4. o pharmacy
   o coordinate
   o archaic
   o nonexistant

5. o coincide
   o molecular
   o aeronotics
   o parallel

6. o quarentine
   o economical
   o negligent
   o syntax

7. o biological
   o anemia
   o documentry
   o analysis

8. o democracy
   o paralysis
   o anesthesia
   o synagoge

9. o ordinance
   o geographical
   o critisize
   o incognito

10. o dialogue
    o optitian
    o metropolis
    o immaculate

11. o opulant
    o immobilize
    o coherent
    o chronic

12. o enthusiasm
    o syncronize
    o anonymous
    o symphonic

Words Ending in **ize, ise, ent, ant**

Game Plan

Some word endings are easy to confuse. Listen for the ending sounds of <u>enterprise</u> and <u>apologize</u>. They sound alike, but they are spelled differently. Study words with these endings carefully. Other sounds are also easy to confuse. The ending sounds of <u>prudent</u> and <u>relevant</u> sound alike, but have different spellings. You must memorize which words end in **ent** and which in **ant**.

Warm Up

Vocabulary Development

Write the List Word that matches each definition.

1. eternal _____
2. a business _____
3. joyful _____
4. showing good judgment _____
5. express regrets _____
6. save money _____
7. relying on another _____
8. agreeable or pleasing _____
9. able _____
10. watchful _____
11. direction hands of clock move _____
12. meaningful _____
13. list _____

Dictionary Skills

Write the List Word that matches each sound-spelling.

1. (käm´ prə mīz) _____
2. (pʉr´ mə nənt) _____
3. (leṅgkth´ wīz) _____
4. (əb zʉr´ vənt) _____
5. (rash´ ən ə līz) _____
6. (plez´´ nt) _____
7. (här´ mə nīz) _____
8. (rel´ ə vənt) _____
9. (prev´ ə lənt) _____
10. (fran´ chīz) _____

1. pleasant
2. competent
3. rationalize
4. jubilant
5. prevalent
6. enterprise
7. compromise
8. franchise
9. lengthwise
10. prudent
11. apologize
12. dependent
13. harmonize
14. observant
15. relevant
16. clockwise
17. economize
18. itemize
19. permanent
20. significant

Practice

Word Analysis

Write each List Word under its ending.

ise

1. _____
2. _____
3. _____
4. _____
5. _____

ize

11. _____
12. _____
13. _____
14. _____
15. _____

ant

6. _____
7. _____
8. _____
9. _____
10. _____

ent

16. _____
17. _____
18. _____
19. _____
20. _____

Write the List Word that has the same root as each word given.

1. economy _____
2. please _____
3. rational _____
4. observe _____

5. items _____
6. dependable _____
7. prevail _____
8. unobserved _____

Word Application

Replace the underlined word or words in each sentence with a List Word. Write the List Word on the line.

1. On the round edges, paint <u>in the direction the clock hands turn</u>, but on the floor, paint <u>with the length</u>.

_____　_____

2. Mrs. Flores is supervising the entire <u>job</u>, and she seems <u>delighted</u> with the results.

_____　_____

3. It would be <u>wise</u> to try to <u>save money</u> on non-essential features.

_____　_____

4. When their voices all <u>sing in agreement</u>, they make a <u>pleasing</u> sound.

_____　_____

List Words

pleasant	enterprise	apologize	clockwise
competent	compromise	dependent	economize
rationalize	franchise	harmonize	itemize
jubilant	lengthwise	observant	permanent
prevalent	prudent	relevant	significant

Puzzle

Use the List Words to complete the crossword puzzle.

ACROSS

3. in the direction of the length
5. a right given to sell something
7. to make conform to reason
8. to sing in harmony
10. lasting forever
12. meaningful to a certain situation or thing
15. careful; cautious
16. having the ability to do what is needed
18. full of meaning
19. to list each item

DOWN

1. a settling of an argument by both sides giving in
2. in the direction of the clock
4. be thrifty
6. relying on another
9. a business or undertaking
10. happening over a wide area
11. to say that one is sorry
13. joyful and proud
14. paying careful attention
17. nice; agreeable

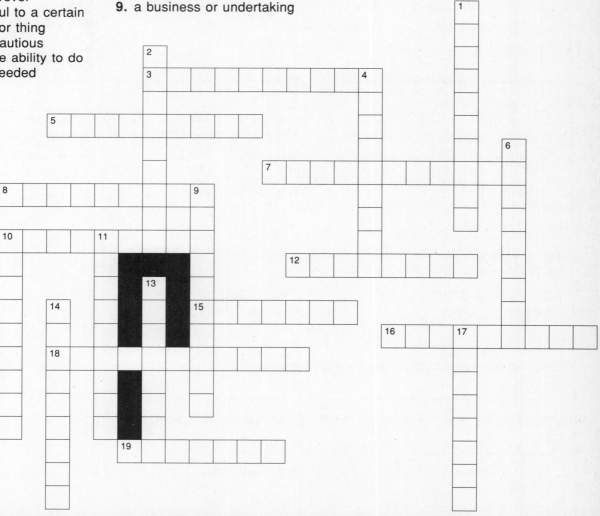

Proofreading

Use the proofreading marks to correct the mistakes in the advertisement. Then write the misspelled List Words on the lines.

> **Proofreading Marks**
> ⬭ spelling mistake   ✗ delete word
> ! add exclamation mark   / small letter

You will be be jubilent with our Software You'll be able to ecconomize and and itimize your Whole budget with just a few Keystrokes. You may even see signifikant returns on Taxes! Don't wait to buy buy this new computer program

1. _____

2. _____

3. _____

4. _____

Challenges

Express Yourself

A **simile** compares two things using the words "like" or "as." For example, "These fans will sell like hot cakes!" is a simile. Think like a business person and write an advertisement for a product. These examples may give you ideas:

. . . as fast as the wind. . .   . . . like home. . .

Proofread and revise your ads, then read them aloud.

Bonus Words: Business

| inflation | corporation | proprietary | proxy | mercantile |
| securities | conglomerate | diversify | negotiation | liquidate |

Write the Bonus Word that matches each clue given.

discussion to reach agreement

1. _____

authority to act for another

2. _____

more dollars buy less

3. _____

stocks and bonds, for example

4. _____

commercial

5. _____

give variety to

6. _____

a legal entity

7. _____

convert assets into cash

8. _____

many companies in one big one

9. _____

held under patent or trademark

10. _____

Game Plan

The suffix **ity** can form a noun from an adjective. For example, legal becomes legality. When the suffix is added to words ending in **ble**, the ending of the base word changes, as in visible/visibility. A few other words, such as generous and hospitable, change in different ways to become generosity and hospitality.

Warm Up

Vocabulary Development

Write the List Word that matches each definition.

1. ability to be on time _____

2. ability to move _____

3. ability to be taken or purchased _____

4. singularity _____

5. following prescribed customs _____

6. abilities not yet developed _____

7. ability to be seen _____

8. state of being lesser _____

9. ability to bend _____

10. temperament _____

11. unselfish act _____

12. a possible event _____

Dictionary Skills

Rewrite each of the following List Words to show how they are divided into syllables.

1. legality _____   6. superiority _____

2. similarity _____   7. hospitality _____

3. eligibility _____   8. practicality _____

4. liability _____   9. technicality _____

5. formality _____   10. capability _____

List Words

1. punctuality
2. personality
3. liability
4. practicality
5. formality
6. individuality
7. technicality
8. availability
9. inferiority
10. mobility
11. visibility
12. hospitality
13. eligibility
14. capability
15. generosity
16. eventuality
17. superiority
18. legality
19. flexibility
20. similarity

Practice

Word Analysis

Form List Words by adding the suffix **ity** to these adjectives to make nouns.

1. mobile _____
2. inferior _____
3. practical _____
4. formal _____
5. liable _____
6. personal _____
7. punctual _____
8. available _____
9. individual _____
10. technical _____

11. visible _____
12. similar _____
13. hospitable _____
14. eventual _____
15. superior _____
16. generous _____
17. capable _____
18. legal _____
19. flexible _____
20. eligible _____

Word Application

Write the correct form of each underlined word on the line.

1. Dean was well known for his <u>punctual</u>. _____
2. This engine has the <u>capable</u> to pull both boxcars. _____
3. Bowing before the Prince is merely a <u>formal</u>. _____
4. Tara called to let us know of her <u>available</u> for the job. _____
5. Emily's clothing reflected her sense of <u>individual</u>. _____
6. We always knew that glass door breaking was an <u>eventual</u>. _____
7. Our insurance company has <u>liable</u> for the accident. _____
8. Rick, who is known for his <u>practical</u>, chose the smallest dog. _____
9. Not all aerobic exercises increase the body's <u>flexible</u>. _____
10. The crossing guards wear orange ponchos for high <u>visible</u>. _____
11. Your voice and your father's have a great <u>similar</u>. _____
12. Ellen's wheelchair has greatly increased her <u>mobile</u>. _____
13. This city has an orchestra thanks to one company's <u>generous</u>. _____
14. Two lawyers had to research the <u>legal</u> of the situation. _____

List Words			
punctuality	individuality	visibility	eventuality
personality	technicality	hospitality	superiority
liability	availability	eligibility	legality
practicality	inferiority	capability	flexibility
formality	mobility	generosity	similarity

Puzzle

On the spaces at the right, unscramble each List Word. Then transfer the numbered letters to the spaces below to solve the riddle. Not every List Word is used.

1. lenittchcaiy — — — — __ — — — — — — __ —
                          2   6

2. tivabyaiilla — — — — — — __ — — — — — —
                              11

3. cuttiypunal — — __ — — — — — — — —
                     14

4. pioyurerits — — — __ — — — — — — —
                     3

5. ernoitifiry — — — __ — — __ — — — —
                     16   18

6. tyinegrose — — __ — — __ — — — —
                    4   13

7. mitboily — — — __ — — —
                  5

8. tiallibiy — — — — — __ — — —
                          9

9. undidailyivit — — — __ — — — — __ — — — — __ —
                          10   8   19

10. spoalyernit — __ — — — — — — — —
                       15

11. sitopithaly — __ — — — __ — — — —
                       17   1

12. yuittneeval — — __ — — — — — — —
                        12

13. mayrlfito — __ — — — — — —
                     7

RIDDLE: Why isn't your nose twelve inches long?

ANSWER: __ __ __ __ __ __ W __ __ __ __ __ __ __ __ __ __ __ __ __
             1 2 3 4 5 6   7 8 9 10 11 12 13 14 15 16 17 18 19

Proofreading

Use the proofreading marks to correct the mistakes in the following article. Then write the misspelled List Words on the lines.

Proofreading Marks		
⬭ spelling mistake	⊙ add period	
≡ capital letter	🐿 add space	

   mathematics is an old traveler thathas moved with great mobilite for thousands of years It is also a character thatshows great flexebility and prakticality in its different forms Some early mathematicians with great capeability, such as Anaxagoras of Clazomenae and Hippocrates of chios, came from greece.

1. _____
2. _____
3. _____
4. _____

Challenges

Express Yourself

A **metaphor** compares two things without using the words "like" or "as." For example, "Mathematics is a beautiful puzzle," and "Numbers are the alphabet of arithmetic," are metaphors. Write a description of mathematics using metaphors. Be as silly or as serious as you like. Proofread and revise your description. Compare your descriptions with those of your classmates.

Bonus Words: Mathematics

trigonometry	calculus	logarithm	correlation	statistical
geometric	finite	analytical	numerical	abacus

Write the Bonus Word that matches each clue.

1. not infinite _____

2. having lines, circles, or other forms _____

3. early kind of calculator _____

4. kind of exponent _____

5. a mutual relationship _____

6. able to analyze _____

7. based on numerical facts or data _____

8. math that deals with triangles _____

9. expressed by numbers _____

10. math dealing with changes _____

Words Ending in **ary, ory**

Game Plan

The word endings **ary** and **ory** sometimes sound alike. Listen for the ending sounds in <u>compulsory</u> and <u>infirmary</u>. They sound similar but are spelled differently. Study and memorize words with these endings carefully.

Warm Up

Vocabulary Development

Write the List Word that matches each synonym or definition.

1. flattering _____
2. mythical _____
3. words of a language _____
4. modern _____
5. bringing radical change _____
6. meeting a need or wish _____
7. a safe place _____
8. a viewing place _____
9. first _____
10. health clinic _____
11. financial _____
12. tasty _____
13. remarkable _____
14. needed _____

Dictionary Skills

Write the List Word that matches each sound-spelling.

1. (prī´ mer´ ē) _____
2. (səb sid´ ē er´ ē) _____
3. (nes´ ə ser´ ē) _____
4. (sā´ vər ē) _____
5. (kəm pul´ ser ē) _____
6. (man´ də tôr´ ē) _____
7. (sat´ is fak´ tə rē) _____
8. (in´ trə duk´ tər ē) _____
9. (əd vī´ zər ē) _____
10. (vō kab´ yə ler´ ē) _____

1. advisory
2. extraordinary
3. mandatory
4. preliminary
5. satisfactory
6. compulsory
7. infirmary
8. monetary
9. primary
10. savory
11. complimentary
12. introductory
13. necessary
14. revolutionary
15. subsidiary
16. contemporary
17. legendary
18. observatory
19. sanctuary
20. vocabulary

Practice

Word Analysis

Write the List Word that contains the same root as the word given.

1. legend _____

2. infirm _____

3. compliment _____

4. observe _____

5. satisfy _____

6. prime _____

7. savor _____

8. advise _____

9. introduce _____

10. revolution _____

11. mandate _____

12. compel _____

Write the List Words that have the ending **ory**.

13. _____

14. _____

15. _____

16. _____

17. _____

18. _____

19. _____

Did you know?

In colonial days, a child's first reading book was called a primer, and today, the first grades of school are called the primary grades. **Primary** is taken from the Latin word, *prime*, which means "the first in order." Today we use this same word, to describe the first or the best of something, like the prime rib of beef.

Word Application

Replace the underlined word or words in each phrase with a List Word. Write the List Word on the line.

1. a <u>division</u> of Worldwide Manufacturers _____

2. the <u>opening</u> round of competition _____

3. an artist who is <u>living and working today</u> _____

4. a free <u>preliminary</u> offer _____

5. a storm and hurricane <u>warning bulletin</u> _____

6. an <u>out of the ordinary</u> piece of music _____

7. a <u>famous</u> cartoon character

_____

8. a national wildlife <u>protected place</u> for birds _____

9. many <u>money</u> considerations

_____

10. the solar <u>viewing place</u>

_____

List Words			
advisory	compulsory	complimentary	contemporary
extraordinary	infirmary	introductory	legendary
mandatory	monetary	necessary	observatory
preliminary	primary	revolutionary	sanctuary
satisfactory	savory	subsidiary	vocabulary

Puzzle

This is a crossword puzzle without clues. Use the length and the spelling of each List Word to complete the puzzle.

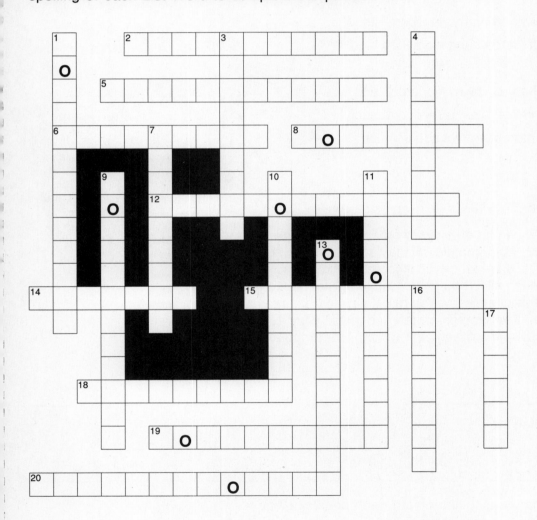

Proofreading

Use the proofreading marks to correct the mistakes in the article below. Then write the misspelled List Words on the lines.

Proofreading Marks

⬭ spelling mistake   ⌃ add comma
? add question mark   ¶ new paragraph

Where did money come from? Records from ancient Mesopotamia more than 4,500 years ago reveal that money was nesesary, but instead of coins and banknotes, they used weighted amounts of silver. Other primeary sources of money were stones, feathers, shells, and beads. Contemporory money consists of bank notes, coins, credit cards, and checking and savings accounts.

Today, each country has its own monatory unit. If your write down the name of the currency in each country, you'll have an interesting vocabulery list.

1. _____

2. _____

3. _____

4. _____

5. _____

Challenges

Express Yourself

Alliteration is a literary device that employs two or more words with the same beginning sounds. For example, "Sandy sang a simple song of sunny Sundays sailing," is an example of alliteration. Write two sentences containing as much alliteration as possible. Write them on the topic of foreign or domestic currency. You might say, for instance, "In France the franc is fine." After you proofread and revise your alliterative sentences, combine them with others from your group and create a poem about currency.

Bonus Words: Currencies

franc	mark	rupee	yen	ruble
peso	pound	lira	guilder	shekel

Write the Bonus Word that is associated with each country given.

1. Netherlands _____   5. Israel _____   9. Germany _____

2. Mexico _____   6. England _____   10. Japan _____

3. India _____   7. U.S.S.R. _____

4. Italy _____   8. France _____

Game Plan

Several English words have French roots. For example, the English word <u>porcelain</u> comes from the French word <u>porcelaine</u>. The English word <u>surgeon</u> comes from the French word <u>surgien</u>.

Many other English words have been borrowed directly, in original form, from the French language. Examples include <u>fiancée</u>, <u>bouillon</u>, <u>souvenir</u>, and <u>sauté</u>. The spelling of such words can be tricky. Some, like <u>sauté</u>, contain accent marks. Others contain sounds spelled by letter combinations that are common to French words but rare to English words. For example, the letters **et** at the end of <u>croquet</u> and the **ée** at the end of <u>fiancée</u> stand for long **a**.

1. *bouillon*	
2. *fiancée*	
3. *opaque*	
4. *racquet*	
5. *scallop*	
6. *croquet*	
7. *finesse*	
8. *corsage*	
9. *resumé*	
10. *soufflé*	
11. *endive*	
12. *marionette*	
13. *porcelain*	
14. *sauté*	
15. *souvenir*	
16. *etiquette*	
17. *menu*	
18. *protégé*	
19. *scavenger*	
20. *surgeon*	

Warm Up

Vocabulary Development

Write the List Word that matches each definition clue.

1. manners _____
2. puppet _____
3. keepsake _____
4. shellfish _____
5. egg dish _____
6. broth _____
7. tennis equipment _____
8. to fry quickly _____
9. medical specialist _____
10. dinner choices _____
11. small bouquet _____
12. lawn game _____

Dictionary Skills

Write the List Word that matches each sound-spelling.

1. (krō kā´) _____
2. (fē´ än sā´) _____
3. (en´ dīv) _____
4. (skav´ in jər) _____
5. (pôr´ s'l in) _____
6. (fi nes´) _____
7. (prōt´e zhā) _____
8. (soo flā´) _____
9. (rez´ oo mā´) _____
10. (ō pāk´) _____

> **Did you know?**
> **Etiquette** is a French word that actually means "ticket," "label," or "list." It was first used on the lists of rules that were posted in a court or army camp. We might also say that **etiquette** can be a *ticket* that allows a person to enter polite society.

Practice

Word Analysis

Write List Words to answer the following questions.

In which words does **et**, **e**, or **ee** spell the long **a** sound, as in day?

1. _____   3. _____   5. _____

2. _____   4. _____   6. _____

Which words contain the letter combination **que**?

7. _____ 8. _____ 9. _____ 10. _____

Which words contain these double consonants?

ss 11. _____   tt 13. _____   ll 15. _____

tt 12. _____   ff 14. _____   ll 16. _____

Analogies

Write a List Word to complete each analogy.

1. Bat is to baseball as _____ is to tennis.

2. Judge is to courtroom as _____ is to operating room.

3. Gems are to bracelet as flowers are to _____ .

4. Fork is to silver as cup is to _____ .

5. Flour is to bread as eggs are to _____ .

6. Lion is to predator as buzzard is to _____ .

7. Back is to forth as transparent is to _____ .

8. Apple is to lemon as cabbage is to _____ .

Word Application

Write a List Word to complete each sentence.

1. Ellen kept the ticket stub as a _____ of her wonderful trip.

2. The waiter told us about the dinner specials that were not listed on the _____ .

3. The magician fooled us with cleverness and _____ .

4. It is considered to be poor _____ to talk with your mouth full of food.

5. Two weeks before the wedding, we had a party for Jeff and his _____ , Joanie.

6. Sally listed all her summer jobs on her _____ .

7. While learning to play the piano, I was lucky to become the _____ of a gifted pianist.

List Words

bouillon	croquet	endive	etiquette
fiancée	finesse	marionette	menu
opaque	corsage	porcelain	protégé
racquet	resumé	sauté	scavenger
scallop	soufflé	souvenir	surgeon

Classification

Write a List Word to complete each series.

1. chowder, soup, _____

2. china, earthenware, _____

3. ball, _____ , net

4. apprentice, student, _____

5. bake, boil, _____

6. style, cleverness, _____

Puzzle

Use the List Words to complete the crossword puzzle.

ACROSS
- **1.** egg dish
- **3.** not transparent
- **6.** doctor who operates
- **9.** animal that feeds on decaying organic matter
- **10.** list of jobs and related experiences
- **13.** to fry briefly
- **15.** list of dinner selections
- **16.** sporting equipment
- **17.** leafy green plant
- **18.** game with mallets, balls, and wickets
- **19.** engaged female

DOWN
- **2.** skill; artfulness; craft
- **4.** code of acceptable manners
- **5.** ceramic material used for dishes
- **7.** bouquet that is worn
- **8.** stringed puppet
- **11.** scrapbook item
- **12.** clear soup or broth
- **13.** shellfish
- **14.** person who receives help or guidance from another

Proofreading

Use the proofreading marks to correct the mistakes in the article below. Then write the misspelled List Words on the lines.

Proofreading Marks	
⬯ spelling mistake	ⱽ add apostrophe
≡ capital letter	⌀ delete word

diamonds are one of of the most precious gemstones. When diamonds are dug out of mines, they may appear opake. It's the diamond cutters job to make them sparkle. A diamond cutter must have finese and hands as steady as those of of a surgin to cut such valuable stones. Although other gemstones are popular, a woman may still wish for a diamond engagement ring from her feancé.

1. _____

2. _____

3. _____

4. _____

Challenges

Express Yourself

Research two of these gemstones: sapphire, turquoise, onyx, garnet, diamond, pearl, ruby, emerald. Report the etymology of their names and compare their colors and other physical properties, their sources in nature, and their relative values. Proofread and revise your report. Then include it in a class reference book on gemstones.

Bonus Words: Gemstones

impurity	facets	crystalize	turquoise	obsidian
refraction	dispersion	amethyst	sapphire	diamond

Write a Bonus Word to complete each sentence.

1. The _____ is a hard, black stone that is formed by the intense heat of volcanoes.

2. A tiny crack or _____ , even if invisible to the eye, can make a gem's value plunge.

3. The polished surfaces of a cut gem are called _____ .

4. The _____ of light reflecting off a cut gem can create a rainbow effect.

5. Due to _____ of light, you'll see a distorted image by looking through a cut gem.

6. The _____ is a colorless stone that is the hardest natural substance known.

7. The _____ , which is named after the planet Saturn, is usually deep blue.

8. Most gems are formed when minerals _____ .

9. The _____ is a greenish-blue stone containing the elements aluminum and copper.

10. The _____ , which is purple or violet, is a variety of quartz or corundum.

Game Plan

Many English words do not follow ordinary spelling rules. The best way to become familiar with these **hurdle words** is to study, memorize, and practice using them.

Hurdle Word	"Trick"	Hurdle Word	"Trick"
schedules **jeopardy**	d = j eo = /e/	**emphatically** **accessory**	ph = /f/ cc, ss double consonants

Warm Up

1. *accessory*
2. *emphatically*
3. *attendant*
4. *schedules*
5. *vulnerable*
6. *allotted*
7. *fascinate*
8. *notarize*
9. *tranquil*
10. *wharf*
11. *dilapidated*
12. *fulfilled*
13. *precinct*
14. *tyranny*
15. *yeast*
16. *disastrous*
17. *jeopardy*
18. *scarcity*
19. *umbrella*
20. *zinnia*

Vocabulary Development

Write the List Word that matches each synonym.

1. servant _____
2. pier _____
3. shabby _____
4. allowed _____
5. peaceful _____
6. dictatorship _____
7. timetables _____
8. completed _____
9. intrigue _____
10. sensitive _____

Dictionary Skills

Write the List Word that comes between each pair of dictionary guide words.

1. scan/scene _____
2. wheat/zinc _____
3. instant/key _____
4. display/far _____
5. tyrant/vulgar _____
6. yellow/zoom _____
7. mystery/odd _____
8. over/python _____
9. dimple/embrace _____
10. able/alive _____

Practice

Word Analysis

Fill in the missing letters to form List Words. Then write the
completed List Words on the lines.

1. vuln __ __ __ ble   _____

2. not __ r __ __ e   _____

3. pre __ i __ __ t   _____

4. di __ as __ __ __ us   _____

5. a __ __ e __ __ __ ry   _____

6. __ m __ __ atic __ __ ly _____

7. s __ __ ed __ les _____

8. s __ ar __ __ ty _____

9. fa __ __ inate   _____

10. t __ r __ __ ny   _____

11. w __ __ __ f   _____

12. tra __ __ __ il   _____

Classification

Write a List Word to complete each series.

1. waiter, valet, _____

2. charm, enchant, _____

3. calm, restful, _____

4. raincoat, boots, _____

5. trouble, danger, _____

6. scarf, pin, _____

7. witness, sign, _____

8. freighter, harbor, _____

9. marigold, petunia, _____

10. dough, bread, _____

Word Application

Replace each underlined word or words in the sentences with a
List Word. Write the List Word on the line.

1. He <u>strongly</u> denied that he was responsible for the <u>ruinous</u> accident.

_____   _____

2. The landlord <u>satisfied</u> his promise to repair the <u>run down</u> apartment building.

_____   _____

3. Because of the <u>shortage</u> of seats, each graduate was <u>given</u> only four tickets for the immediate
family.

_____   _____

4. The sergeant posted <u>lists of times</u> for patrol officers assigned to his <u>division</u>.

_____   _____

List Words

accessory	allotted	dilapidated	disastrous
emphatically	fascinate	fulfilled	jeopardy
attendant	notarize	precinct	scarcity
schedules	tranquil	tyranny	umbrella
vulnerable	wharf	yeast	zinnia

Puzzle

Use the List Words to complete the crossword puzzle.

ACROSS

3. great danger or peril
6. something extra
7. free from disturbance
9. to witness a legal signing
11. a wooden structure in a harbor where ships load and unload goods
12. substance used in baking to make dough rise
13. a person who helps or serves someone
15. to make happen; completed
17. having great destruction or misfortune
18. lists of arriving and departing trains and buses
19. very cruel and unjust use of power

DOWN

1. a portable covering to protect from rain
2. a showy garden flower
4. the district or area patrolled by police
5. open to harm or danger
8. distributed little by little
10. run down; in ruin
14. with force of expression
15. to delight or charm
16. a lacking or shortage of something

Proofreading

Use the proofreading marks to correct the mistakes in the poem below. Then write the misspelled List Words on the lines.

Proofreading Marks	
⬭ spelling mistake	⌃ add comma
⊙ add period	/ small letter

The howl of a wolf Breaks the tranqul night
awakening Those who are vulnerible to fright.
Yet the wolf is emfaticly a peaceful Beast
who only when Hungry would look for a feast.
Yet the lone wolf continues to fasinate us
though the old Tales are now seen as ludicrous

1. _____

2. _____

3. _____

4. _____

Challenges

Express Yourself

Onomatopoeia is a word in which the sound gives the word its meaning.

Plink, plink went the raindrops as they fell on the puddle.

Write five examples of onomatopoeia in complete sentences. The sounds these objects make may give you ideas: a chain saw, a speed boat, a skidding car, a wolf, a bulldozer. Proofread and revise your onomatopoetic sentences. Then compare them with those of your classmates and discuss which ones best define the words.

Bonus Words: Sound

vociferous	enunciate	timbre	amplification	taciturn
reverberate	inaudible	intonation	strident	reticent

Write the Bonus Word that matches each clue given.

1. cause a sound to echo _____

2. cannot be heard _____

3. loud; noisy; vehement _____

4. say clearly and distinctly _____

5. making sound louder _____

6. harsh-sounding; shrill _____

Write the words that are synonyms or near-synonyms for the words given.

distinguishing quality of a voice   almost always silent

7. _____   **9.** _____

8. _____   **10.** _____

Did you know?

In England, during the 16th century, when a chess player was forced to make a move with which he could lose the game, his position was called *iuparti*. During the 17th century, the letter *j* came into general use in the English language, and the beginning *i* in *iuparti* was changed to *j*. The word eventually became **jeopardy**, and came to describe any situation in which winning or losing hung in a delicate balance.

Game Plan

Understanding word endings can help you spell many words correctly. Some endings are easy to confuse, such as **ise** and **ize**, **ent** and **ant**, and **ary** and **ory**. Pay close attention to the spelling of words with similar endings. Here are several examples:

prevalent, relevant
franchise, harmonize
advisory, preliminary

The ending **ity** forms a noun from an adjective, as when formal becomes formality. When this suffix is added to words ending in **ble**, an **i** is inserted before the **l**, so that words like liable become liability. In some words, the base word changes in different ways. For example, hospitable becomes hospitality.

Many English words come from French and may contain letter combinations that are common in French words but unusual in English words, such as the ending of finesse. Other words from the French may contain accent marks like the one in sauté.

Our language also has words that do not follow the usual spelling rules. These may contain unusual spellings for certain sounds or unexpected double consonants. In the word jeopardy, for example, the vowel sound for short **e** is spelled **eo**. The word allotted has two pairs of double consonants.

The best way to learn words with unusual spellings is to study them and use them.

Practice

Replace the underlined word or words in each sentence with a List Word. Write the List Word on the line.

Lesson 25

pleasant competent
apologize economize
compromise jubilant
dependent enterprise
observant itemize

_____

_____

1. The Captain of the hockey team was <u>very happy</u> when she was named Player of the Year. _____
2. Make sure you go to a <u>skilled</u> mechanic. _____
3. Thanks to a quick call from an <u>aware</u> neighbor, firefighters extinguished the fire before it spread. _____
4. The breeze makes this room quite <u>nice</u>. _____
5. If you can <u>reach an agreement through negotiation</u>, you can both get what you want. _____
6. This <u>business</u> will not be sold! _____
7. Everyone in the family can <u>save money</u> by buying generic brands whenever possible. _____
8. When we go camping, we are no longer <u>relying</u> on city facilities for entertainment. _____
9. I want to <u>say I'm sorry</u> for arriving late. _____
10. <u>Make a list of</u> the ingredients you need. _____

Write the List Word with the same root as the word given.

dissimilar

1. _____

individualized

2. _____

inhospitable

3. _____

nonflexible

4. _____

incapable

5. _____

invisibly

6. _____

generously

7. _____

unavailable

8. _____

ineligible

9. _____

impersonate

10. _____

Lesson 26

hospitality   flexibility
availability   generosity
individuality   personality
eligibility   capability
similarity   visibility

_____

_____

Write a List Word to complete each sentence.

1. If people or animals are safe in a place, the place may be a _____ .

2. Financial plans affect a nation's _____ system.

3. If something is essential, it is _____ .

4. If someone says that Seth looked wonderful, that person is making a _____ statement.

5. The _____ pitcher was inducted into the Baseball Hall of Fame.

6. If you feel sick, go to the _____ .

7. Health is the _____ reason for exercising.

8. If you and your family are generally pleased, the carpenter did a _____ job.

9. If a dancer's performance is truly outstanding, you might also call it an _____ performance.

10. If seatbelts are required, they are _____

Lesson 27

infirmary   monetary
legendary   primary
mandatory   sanctuary
necessary   extraordinary
satisfactory   complimentary

_____

_____

Write List Words to answer the questions.

Which words contain the vowel combination **ue**?

1. _____ 3. _____

2. _____ 4. _____

Which word contains the vowel combination **eo**?

5. _____

Which words contain the vowel combination **ou**?

6. _____ 8. _____

7. _____

Which word completes each series?

9. earthenware, plastic, _____

10. doll, puppet, _____

11. soup, chowder, _____

12. pediatrician, neurologist, _____

Lesson 28

bouillon   surgeon
etiquette   opaque
porcelain   croquet
racquet   marionette
souvenir   soufflé

_____

_____

Use the List Words to complete the crossword puzzle.

ACROSS
4. charm or bewitch
6. able to be hurt
7. causing great damage
9. lack or shortage
10. carried out

DOWN
1. pier or dock
2. timetables
3. bread ingredient
5. tie, scarf, or glove, for instance
8. serene

Lesson 29

accessory   fulfilled
fascinate   scarcity
schedules   tranquil
vulnerable   wharf
disastrous   yeast

_____

_____

compromise	capability	etiquette
eligibility	bouillon	competent
croquet	enterprise	dependent
disastrous	complimentary	fascinate
flexibility	fulfilled	extraordinary

Mixed Practice

Write the List Words that come between each pair of dictionary guide words. Write the words in alphabetical order.

bluster/diverge

1. _____
2. _____
3. _____
4. _____
5. _____
6. _____
7. _____
8. _____

elegant/gabardine

9. _____
10. _____
11. _____
12. _____
13. _____
14. _____
15. _____

Test Yourself

In each of the following groups of words, one word is misspelled. Fill in the circle that appears before that word.

1. o accessory
o fulfilled
o compromise
o jubilent

2. o individuality
o personality
o neccesary
o extraordinary

3. o etiquette
o opaqeu
o hospitality
o yeast

4. o fascinate
o scarcity
o dependant
o enterprise

5. o complimentery
o monetary
o satisfactory
o infirmary

6. o porcelain
o croquet
o observent
o itemize

7. o pleasant
o compitent
o similarity
o flexibility

8. o legendary
o primery
o eligibility
o capability

9. o racquet
o marionette
o scheduels
o tranquil

10. o apologize
o economize
o avaliability
o generosity

11. o manditory
o sanctuary
o bouillon
o surgeon

12. o souvenir
o visability
o vulnerable
o disastrous

Game Plan

The study of science involves the recognition and comprehension of many unfamiliar words. Words such as <u>indigestion</u>, <u>microorganism</u>, and <u>respiration</u> may seem complicated and difficult to spell. With practice, you can master these challenging words.

All the List Words are from science. Memorize and practice spelling these words.

Warm Up

1. allergy
2. indigestion
3. physics
4. neutron
5. vaccinate
6. fungus
7. larynx
8. psychology
9. transmitter
10. voltage
11. diagnose
12. microorganism
13. satellite
14. transfusion
15. friction
16. iodine
17. perennial
18. respiration
19. turbine
20. zoology

Classification

Write a List Word to complete each series.

1. current, wattage, _____

2. air, lungs, _____

3. space, orbit, _____

4. esophagus, trachea, _____

5. inoculate, serum, _____

6. electron, proton, _____

7. mold, parasite, _____

8. annual, biennial, _____

9. mammals, birds, _____

10. microscope, bacteria, _____

Dictionary Skills

Write the List Word that matches each sound-spelling.

1. (tʉr´ bin) _____

2. (ī´ ə dīn) _____

3. (fiz´ iks) _____

4. (frik´ shən) _____

5. (al´ ər jē) _____

6. (trans mit´ ər) _____

7. (in´ di jes´ chən) _____

8. (trans fyo͞o´ zhən) _____

9. (sī kä l´ə jē) _____

10. (dī´ əg nōs´) _____

Practice

Word Analysis

Write each List Word under the correct category.

Words with Two Syllables

1. _____
2. _____
3. _____
4. _____
5. _____
6. _____
7. _____

Words with Three Syllables

8. _____
9. _____
10. _____
11. _____
12. _____
13. _____
14. _____

Words with Four Syllables

15. _____
16. _____
17. _____
18. _____
19. _____

Word with Six Syllables

20. _____

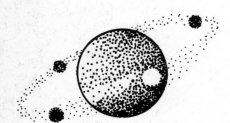

Proofreading

Use the proofreading marks to correct the mistakes in the letter. Then write misspelled List Words correctly on the lines.

	Proofreading Marks
⬭	spelling mistake
⚲	delete word
/	small letter
⌃	add comma
¶	new paragraph

Dear Mrs. Jacobs

After weeks of tests, I can finally diegnose your Daughter Jean's medical condition. One reason for the the problem affecting her resparation seems to be that she is allergic to microrganisms in feathers. Whenever she comes in contact with birds, particles from their plumes irritate her larinks. She can correct this problem by sleeping on pillows made of foam rubber or or other synthetic materials.
Jean also said that her symptoms worsen in spring and fall when we have the perrenial problem of high pollen counts in the air. I suggest that we treat Jean with Antihistamines. If that that doesn't help, we may wish to vacinnate her against the irritants. Call my office soon.

Sincerely

Dr. Maria Juarez

1. _____
2. _____
3. _____
4. _____
5. _____
6. _____

List Words

allergy	fungus	diagnose	iodine
indigestion	larynx	microorganism	perennial
physics	psychology	satellite	respiration
neutron	transmitter	transfusion	turbine
vaccinate	voltage	friction	zoology

Puzzle

Use the List Words to complete the crossword puzzle.

ACROSS

1. mold, mildew, mushroom
4. something that sends signals
6. the study of human behavior
9. discomfort caused by inability to digest foods properly
11. a sensitivity to a substance such as food or plants
13. science dealing with energy, matter, and movement
14. detect an illness
17. inject a serum to protect against a disease
18. upper part of the throat
19. returning or becoming active again and again

DOWN

2. uncharged particle of an atom
3. an object in orbit around the earth
5. bacteria not visible to the human eye
7. the act of moving blood from one person to another
8. the study of animals and their behavior
10. purplish-colored disinfectant
12. breathing
15. the resistance to motion of two objects that touch
16. a steam engine
17. measurement of electrical current

Test Yourself

In each pair of List Words, underline the misspelled word and write it correctly on the line.

1. perenial, transmitter _____

2. resperation, psychology _____

3. microrganism, fungus _____

4. transfusion, voltige _____

5. indegestion, satellite _____

6. physics, nutron _____

7. turbine, vacinate _____

8. alergy, zoology _____

9. diagnose, iodyne _____

10. larinx, friction _____

> **Did you know?**
>
> A **turbine** is an engine that generates electricity. It got its name from the Latin word *turbare* meaning "to twist about." This is quite reasonable since a *turbine* must be turning in order to work. *Turbare* also gives us the word *trouble*. And indeed, if you were twisted about in a *turbine*, you would certainly be in a great deal of trouble.

Challenges

Express Yourself

Which field of science interests you—zoology, biology, microbiology, or physics? Write a persuasive speech that tells why the field you're interested in should receive more grants for research than any other field. After proofreading and revising your speech, get together with others that wrote about the same field. Hold a class debate to decide which field of science merits more funding.

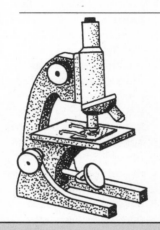

Bonus Words: Organizations				
cartel	confederation	fraternity	sorority	guild
syndicate	affiliation	clique	troupe	faction

Write the Bonus Word that matches each definition clue.

1. a small exclusive circle of people _____

2. a small group within an organization working against goals of the main body _____

3. a group of women or girls with similar interests _____

4. an alliance; a political union of states _____

5. an association that fixes prices and monopolizes an industry _____

6. connected with a particular group _____

7. a group of actors, singers, performers _____

8. a group of men or boys with similar interests _____

9. an association formed to transact a planned financial project _____

10. a trade union _____

Words from Occupations

Game Plan

Words that name occupations are usually another form or a word related to that occupation. The endings **or**, **er**, **an**, **ist**, or **ive** are added to make the word mean <u>one who does something</u>. For example, a <u>librarian</u> is <u>one who works in a library</u>. Here are some other examples.

manicure—manicurist announce—announcer
arbitrate—arbitrator represent—representative

The List Words name occupations. Notice the special spelling patterns of each word. Memorize and practice spelling them.

List Words

1. administrator
2. librarian
3. therapist
4. proprietor
5. electrician
6. arbitrator
7. vendor
8. paramedic
9. veterinarian
10. chemist
11. comedian
12. technician
13. representative
14. announcer
15. pharmacist
16. hygienist
17. analyst
18. manicurist
19. carpenter
20. researcher

Warm Up

Classification

Write a List Word to complete each series.

1. hammer, nails, _____
2. jokes, laughter, _____
3. prescription, drugstore, _____
4. books, catalogue cards, _____
5. animals, medicine, _____
6. microphone, radio, _____
7. dentist, teeth, _____
8. nail file, polish, _____
9. wiring, outlets, _____
10. laboratory, chemicals, _____

Dictionary Skills

Rewrite each of the following List Words to show how they are divided into syllables.

1. proprietor _____
2. researcher _____
3. arbitrator _____
4. therapist _____
5. representative _____
6. administrator _____
7. analyst _____
8. vendor _____
9. paramedic _____
10. technician _____

Practice

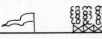

Word Analysis

Fill in the missing letters to form List Words. Then write the completed List Words on the lines.

1. ph __ rm__ c __ st _____

2. res __ __ rch __ r _____

3. lib __ __ __ __ an _____

4. p __ r __ med __ __ __ _____

5. rep __ __ sen __ __ __ ive _____

6. ven __ __ r _____

7. pr __ p __ __ __ t __ r _____

8. arb __ t __ __ t __ r _____

9. a __ __ ounc __ __ r _____

10. man __ c __ __ r __ st _____

Vocabulary Development

Write the List Word that matches each derivative given.

1. chemistry _____

2. electricity _____

3. therapy _____

4. technical _____

5. carpentry _____

6. analyze _____

7. comedy _____

8. administrate _____

9. hygiene _____

10. veterinary _____

Word Application

Write a List Word to complete each sentence.

1. The _____ filled Grandpa's medicine prescription.

2. The _____ of the store listened to the customer's complaint.

3. Mr. Ortega is an _____ who settles disputes between labor and management.

4. Cathy is a _____ trying to find new ways to recycle trash.

5. The _____ treated the injured people at the scene of the accident.

6. Tabby, our pet cat, was examined by Dr. Swartz, the _____ .

7. The _____ built new bookcases for the library.

8. The dental _____ discussed proper brushing techniques with me.

List Words

administrator	arbitrator	comedian	hygienist
librarian	vendor	technician	analyst
therapist	paramedic	representative	manicurist
proprietor	veterinarian	announcer	carpenter
electrician	chemist	pharmacist	researcher

Puzzle

Use the List Words to complete the crossword puzzle.

ACROSS

1. one who fixes fingernails
3. a specialist in physical or mental disorders
7. a doctor for animals
9. a person who installs electrical wiring
10. an expert in chemistry
12. a person who examines the details of something
13. one who assists a trained medical professional
14. a person who tells jokes and amusing stories
17. one who sells; a peddler
19. one who investigates in order to establish facts
20. one who manages or directs

DOWN

2. one who builds and repairs wooden things
4. one who dispenses medicines
5. a person skilled in the technicalities of a subject
6. one who speaks or acts for someone or something
8. one who introduces radio or television programs
11. a person who assists a dentist
15. one who settles disputes
16. one who owns and operates a business
18. a person who manages a library

Proofreading

Use the proofreading marks to correct the mistakes in the article. Then write the misspelled List Words on the lines.

Proofreading Marks
- ⬭ spelling mistake ⱽ ⱽ add quotation marks
- ! add exclamation mark ¶ new paragraph

A repersentativ of the Ormand Company has just announced a most amazing discovery A company resercher has found a new species of plant in the Amazon rain forest that might hold the key to a cancer cure. An administrater for the project reports, The plant was part of a general collection made over several months. A tecknician actually first noticed it because of its unusual color.

The company's kemist says, Preliminary reports have shown this plant to be very promising. A local pharmasist says, This will be great if it is true

1. _____
2. _____
3. _____
4. _____
5. _____
6. _____

Challenges

Express Yourself

Imagine you are a researcher in the field of medicine or health care. You have just been awarded a grant to conduct research in the area of your choice. Write two or three paragraphs explaining what disease or health care issue you will research. Proofread and revise your paragraphs. Then share them with the class. Discuss why your research is important and how it might possibly be achieved.

Bonus Words: Health

| enzyme | plaque | arthritis | stimulant | addiction |
| hypertension | cholesterol | nicotine | depressant | tolerance |

Write the Bonus Word that matches each definition clue.

1. a slavish dependence on a substance _____
2. poisonous substance found in tobacco leaves _____
3. organic compound that aids in digestion _____
4. high blood pressure _____
5. a waxy substance found in animal fats _____
6. the ability to resist the effects of stimuli _____
7. lowers the rate of nervous or muscular activity _____
8. increases the rate of brain cell activity _____
9. inflammation of the joints _____
10. sticky film on teeth _____

Words from Literature

Game Plan

Like science and math, the field of literature and composition has a specific vocabulary of technical terms. Words such as <u>fiction</u>, <u>sonnet</u>, and <u>prose</u> describe types of literature. Other words, including <u>simile</u>, <u>metaphor</u>, and <u>personification</u>, describe types of figurative language.

All of the List Words are related to literature and composition. Knowing how to define and spell them will be of great benefit to you throughout your studies.

1. *alliteration*
2. *caricature*
3. *literature*
4. *parody*
5. *proverb*
6. *allegory*
7. *couplet*
8. *narrative*
9. *personification*
10. *pseudonym*
11. *analogy*
12. *exposition*
13. *fiction*
14. *poetic*
15. *simile*
16. *bibliography*
17. *idiom*
18. *prose*
19. *stanza*
20. *sonnet*

Warm Up

Vocabulary Development

Write the List Word that matches each definition.

1. list of source materials for a nonfiction work _____

2. art or writing that exaggerates someone's features _____

3. false "pen" name used by a writer _____

4. poem of fourteen lines with one central theme _____

5. old, familiar saying that states a simple truth _____

6. repetition of the same beginning sound _____

7. symbolic story that teaches or explains _____

8. all literature that is not poetry _____

9. literature that explains true facts or events _____

10. two lines of poetry _____

Dictionary Skills

Write the List Words in alphabetical order.

1. _____   8. _____   15. _____

2. _____   9. _____   16. _____

3. _____   10. _____   17. _____

4. _____   11. _____   18. _____

5. _____   12. _____   19. _____

6. _____   13. _____   20. _____

7. _____   14. _____

Practice

Word Analysis

Write the List Word that has the same root as the word given.

1. verb _____

2. personally _____

3. sonic _____

4. narrate _____

5. ode _____

6. stand _____

7. name _____

8. couple _____

9. similar _____

10. expose _____

Word Application

Select a List Word from the choices in parentheses to complete each sentence. Write your answer on the line.

1. _____ lines contain rhythm, meter, and often rhyme. (poetic, simile)

2. _____ , a general class of literature, includes novels and plays. (exposition, fiction)

3. Through _____ , the relationships between words are analyzed. (allegory, analogy)

4. The shifting sands of summer is an example of _____ . (simile, alliteration)

5. A section of a poem, usually four or more lines in length, is a _____ .(stanza, couplet)

6. An example of _____ is My dog voted to sample my lunch. (personification, allegory)

7. Stories, nonfiction articles, and plays are _____ . (exposition, literature)

8. Mark Twain was the _____ used by Samuel Langhorne Clemens. (bibliography, pseudonym)

9. The _____ I heard it on the grapevine means I heard it through gossip. (idiom, proverb)

10. The cartoonist drew a _____ of the president. (narrative, caricature)

11. Entries are alphabetized, by author's last name, in the _____ . (exposition, bibliography)

12. All literature that is not poetry is called _____ . (narrative, prose)

13. A story about a character overcoming a dragon named "Greed" is an _____ . (allegory, analogy)

List Words			
alliteration	allegory	analogy	bibliography
caricature	couplet	exposition	idiom
literature	narrative	fiction	prose
parody	personification	poetic	stanza
proverb	pseudonym	simile	sonnet

Puzzle

Each of these clues is an example of a literary term defined by a List Word. Write your answers in the spaces. Then transfer the numbered letters to the spaces below to answer the question.

1. "A stitch in time saves nine."
   —Ben Franklin

— — — — — —
1 15   11

2. "I shall be as secret as the grave."
   —Miguel de Cervantes

— — — — —
10   9   12

3. "A little Madness in the Spring is wholesome even for the King."
   —Emily Dickinson

— — — — — — —
        4   18

4. "The Yankee is one who, if he once gets his teeth on a thing, all creation can't make him let go."
   —Ralph Waldo Emerson

— — — — —
5

5. "Hail, Columbia! happy land! Hail, ye heroes! heaven-born band!"
   —Joseph Hopkinson

— — — — — — — — — —
        19   16   7

6. Thy head is as full of quarrels as an egg is full of meat."
   —William Shakespeare

— — — — — — —
20   8

7. "The bluebird carries the sky on his back."
   —Henry David Thoreau

— — — — — — — — — —
2   14   17

8. "A young man named Ernest Hemingway lives in Paris, writes for the *Transatlantic Review* and has a brilliant future."
   —F. Scott Fitzgerald

— — — — — — — —
3   6   13

QUESTION: Who was Mrs. Silence Dogwood?

ANSWER: one of many — — — — — — — — — — used by
                        1 2 3 4 5 6 7 8 9 10

— — — — — — — K — — —
11 12 13   14 15 16 17   18 19 20

Proofreading

Use the proofreading marks to correct the mistakes in the article. Then write the misspelled List Words on the lines.

Proofreading Marks

◯ spelling mistake   ⚲ delete word
= capital letter   🏠 add space

much of science ficshon is is now considered literatoore rather thanthe misunderstood proze it once was. some authors in this this field mayhave once written under a psudonym because of the lack of respect toward the genre, but many are now now famousand respected. Three of the biggest have been Isaac asimov, Arthur c. Clarke, and robert A. heinlein.

1. _____

2. _____

3. _____

4. _____

_____

Challenges

Express Yourself

Most science fiction is set in the future. It builds on today's established facts, stretching them to imagine new technology or areas of exploration. Write a science fiction story. Include at least one new invention, alien creature, or bold exploration. Proofread and revise your story. Then place it in a science fiction corner for others to read.

Bonus Words: Space

| nebula | module | relativity | inertia | planetarium |
| luminosity | centrifugal force | celestial | momentum | encapsulate |

Write a Bonus Word to complete each sentence.

1. You can view stars and constellations at a _____ .

2. The planet Saturn is a _____ body surrounded by rings.

3. A _____ is a cloud of interstellar gas or dust.

4. According to Einstein's theory of _____ , no energy can travel faster than light.

5. The tendency for a being at rest to stay at rest is called _____ .

6. When something orbits around a central core, _____ pulls it outward.

7. To calculate the _____ of a moving object, physicists multiply mass times speed.

8. The moon's _____ is created by reflected light from the sun.

9. Astronauts _____ themselves in suits equipped with oxygen supplies.

10. In 1969, the first lunar _____ to be piloted by humans landed on the moon.

Game Plan

You are probably familiar with many words that refer to English usage and language arts. Many of these common words, such as <u>grammar</u>, <u>preposition</u>, <u>capitalization</u>, and <u>homonym</u> are often misspelled.

All the List Words name words from language arts. Study the spelling patterns of each word. Memorize and practice spelling them.

Warm Up

Vocabulary Development

Write the List Word that matches each definition.

1. shows surprise _____

2. an incomplete sentence _____

3. the mark used in a contraction _____

4. a word's meaning _____

5. a joining word _____

6. the use of upper case letters _____

7. changing the meaning of _____

8. word formed with letters of a word _____

9. verb used as a noun, ending in **ing** _____

10. verb that takes a direct object _____

Dictionary Skills

Write the List Words that come between each pair of dictionary guide words. Write the words in alphabetical order.

List Words

1. acronym
2. conjunction
3. gerund
4. modifying
5. parenthesis
6. apostrophe
7. exclamation
8. grammar
9. glossary
10. preposition
11. predicate
12. definition
13. homonym
14. paraphrase
15. transitive
16. capitalization
17. fragment
18. infinitive
19. participle
20. interrogative

gesture/interrupt	parade/press
1. _____	6. _____
2. _____	7. _____
3. _____	8. _____
4. _____	9. _____
5. _____	10. _____

Practice

Word Analysis

Write List Words to answer the following questions.

Which words contain the letter combination **nym**?

1. _____   2. _____

Which words contain the following double consonants?

3. rr _____   4. ss _____   5. mm _____

Word Application

Write a List Word to complete each sentence.

1. Use _____ whenever you begin a sentence or write a proper name.

2. A word's first _____ listed in the dictionary is its most common meaning.

3. Adjectives are usually found _____ a noun or another adjective.

4. <u>Soar</u> is a _____ for the word <u>sore</u>.

5. A sentence _____ is a part of a sentence missing either a subject or predicate.

6. A sentence that asks a question is called an _____ sentence.

7. An _____ mark at the end of a sentence shows strong feelings or surprise.

8. The complete _____ includes the verb and all its modifiers in a sentence.

9. Look up the word in the _____ at the end of your reading textbook.

10. When you repeat something in different words, you _____ it.

11. <u>Radar</u> is an _____ for <u>radio detecting and ranging</u>.

12. In the phrase <u>to the store</u>, <u>store</u> is the object of the _____ .

13. _____ is the study of English usage.

14. The present _____ of <u>have</u> is <u>having</u>.

15. A _____ verb shows action and takes a direct object.

Write the List Word that matches each clue.

1. ( )   _____   5. ?   _____

2. !   _____   6. <u>Washington</u>   _____

3. Mary's _____   7. in, for, at   _____

4. to go   _____   8. The boy to the store   _____

List Words

acronym	apostrophe	predicate	capitalization
conjunction	exclamation	definition	fragment
gerund	grammar	homonym	infinitive
modifying	glossary	paraphrase	participle
parenthesis	preposition	transitive	interrogative

Puzzle

Unscramble the List Words to complete the crossword puzzle.

ACROSS

2. CMINELAOTAX
4. PPRAEAHASR
5. REPPIOISNTO
8. OAYLSGSR
9. NERIOITEARGTV
12. MOMOYHN
14. EUDRGN
15. TAEFGRMN
16. PAIACIANTILZTO
17. FNEINIIITV

DOWN

1. FNDIINIETO
3. IAIERNSTTV
4. EIEPADRCT
5. RPETEASNHSI
6. DIYMOGFIN
7. RCNOMAY
8. RMRMAGA
10. POTESPAROH
11. ONCCJINUNTO
13. ACIERPTIPL

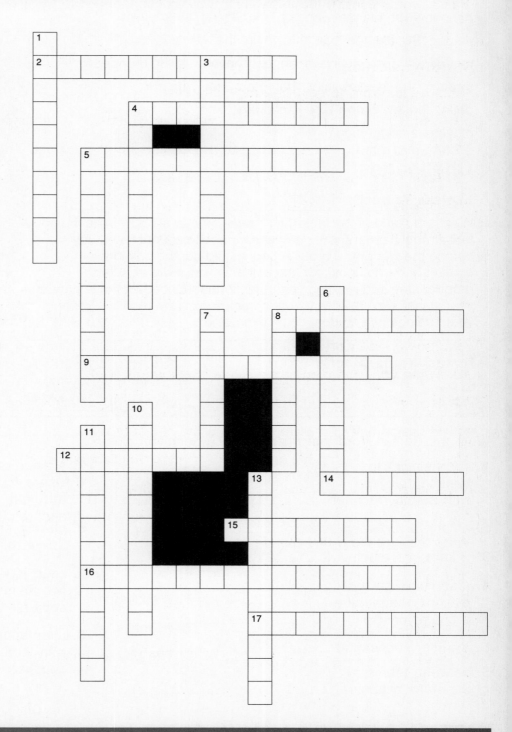

Proofreading

Use the proofreading marks to correct the mistakes in the news report. Then write the misspelled List Words on the lines.

Proofreading Marks
⬭ spelling mistake   ? add question mark
⊙ add period   ⱱ add apostrophe

To parafrase last nights events, our school's girls basketball team is going to the finals How did this happen The team's work on modefying their plays helped So did the ball thrown in the game's last minute. The crowd gave an exclmaytion as it dropped through the basket. Isnt that great Look up the definetion of *happy* in a dictionary, and youll see our players smiling faces.

1. _____

2. _____

3. _____

4. _____

Challenges

Express Yourself

What are some of the important issues at your school? What do you feel strongly about? Write a questionnaire to conduct a survey among the students at your school to find out the opinions of the student body. It should contain at least six questions. After proofreading and revising your questionnaire, conduct the survey in your classroom. Tally and write a summary of the results. Present your findings at a student council meeting.

Bonus Words: Sports

intramural	participation	tournament	skiing	volleyball
facility	interscholastic	racquetball	lacrosse	Rugby

Write the Bonus Word that matches each definition clue.

1. sport similar to handball played with a small racquet _____

2. among or between schools _____

3. a form of football _____

4. a series of games played to determine a championship _____

5. a winter snow sport _____

6. between teams of the same school _____

7. a place or building where sports events are held _____

8. playing an active role _____

9. sport in which two teams are separated by net _____

10. team sport played with long-handled pouched sticks _____

Game Plan

Some words are especially difficult to spell because they contain silent letters, such as the **h** in <u>scheme</u> and the **i** in <u>marriage</u>. Other "hurdle words" contain the schwa sound /ə/ in unstressed syllables. Although it sounds like short **e**, it may be spelled with any of the vowels. Examples include the first **o** in <u>oppose</u>, the **a** and final **e** in <u>equivalent</u>, and the **o** and **io** in <u>solution</u>.

Warm Up

Vocabulary Development

Write the List Word that matches each synonym or definition.

1. device
2. laboratory
3. obstacle
4. primitive
5. situation
6. dilemma
7. marriage
8. opportunities
9. procedure
10. solution
11. equivalent
12. metropolitan
13. oppose
14. scheme
15. peculiar
16. exhibit
17. miniature
18. optimistic
19. several
20. zinc

1. many _____
2. hopeful _____
3. problem _____
4. wedding _____
5. equal _____
6. answer _____
7. tiny _____
8. show _____

9. contraption _____
10. strange or odd _____
11. disagree with _____
12. urban _____
13. chances _____
14. circumstances _____
15. testing room _____
16. simple; rough _____

Dictionary Skills

Write the List Word that comes between each pair of dictionary guide words.

1. oat/open _____
2. pebble/pray _____
3. zebra/zoo _____
4. say/scratch _____
5. private/prune _____
6. mauve/mince _____
7. prime/probe _____
8. mace/meter _____
9. eon/ether _____
10. opposite/option _____

Practice

Word Analysis

Write the List Word containing the same root as the word given.

1. primates _____

2. dissolve _____

3. unequal _____

4. unopposed _____

5. obstruction _____

6. inopportune _____

7. pessimistic _____

8. politician _____

Antonyms

Write the List Word that matches each antonym.

1. problem _____

2. divorce _____

3. accept _____

4. ordinary _____

5. few _____

6. advanced _____

7. rural _____

8. discouraged _____

Analogies

Write a List Word to complete each analogy.

1. Kitchen is to cook as _____ is to scientist.

2. Gate is to go as _____ is to stop.

3. Performance is to drama as _____ is to photograph.

4. Tall is to giraffe as _____ is to mouse.

5. Wood is to oak as metal is to _____ .

6. Memories are to past as _____ are to future.

7. "Yes" is to agree as "no" is to _____ .

8. Three is to few as eight is to _____ .

Word Application

Select a List Word from the choices in parentheses to complete each sentence. Write your answer on the line.

1. John was hopeful that his _____ would work. (optimistic, scheme)

2. The _____ became confused while the cafeteria was painted. (solution, situation)

3. The paint roller is a clever, time-saving _____ . (device, dilemma)

List Words

device	dilemma	equivalent	exhibit
laboratory	marriage	metropolitan	miniature
obstacle	opportunities	oppose	optimistic
primitive	procedure	scheme	several
situation	solution	peculiar	zinc

Classification

Write a List Word to complete each series.

1. copper, aluminum, _____

2. chances, occasions, _____

3. _____ , average, enormous

4. ancient, simple, _____

5. hurdle, sand trap, _____

6. gallery, museum, _____

7. few, some, _____

8. plot, plan, _____

9. invention, machine, _____

10. sum, remainder, _____

Puzzle

Use the List Words to complete the crossword puzzle.

ACROSS
  2. a place for experiments
  7. chances
  8. a metallic element
  9. something that gets in the way
  11. pertaining to a large city
  13. position or circumstances
  15. ancient; simple; rough
  17. the answer to a problem
  18. many; more than a few
  19. a difficult problem

DOWN
  1. union; wedding
  3. to disagree or work against
  4. a tool or machine
  5. a method of doing something
  6. strange; unusual; rare
  10. tiny
  12. equal
  14. hopeful
  16. a public show
  18. a plan or system

Proofreading

Use the proofreading marks to correct the mistakes in the article. Then write the misspelled List Words on the lines.

Proofreading Marks
⬭ spelling mistake   ⌄⌄ ⌄⌄ add quotation marks
≡ capital letter   ⌃ add comma

The first primetive computer, a calculating divice called the Difference Engine, was created in 1822 by charles Babbage an english mathematician. the programming procidure was developed by Ada byron Lovelace. Because opotunities for women were few in the early nineteenth century Lovelace was not well recognized for her contribution.

1. _____

2. _____

3. _____

4. _____

5. _____

Challenges

Express Yourself

Thomas Edison changed the world when he invented the electric light bulb. Now it's your turn. Invent a machine. Draw a diagram of it, labeling its parts. Write a description of what it does, how it does it, and why it will "change the world." Proofread and revise your work. Then display it in the classroom. Discuss which inventions might really work.

Bonus Words: Machines

hydraulic	implement	electromagnetic	combustion	conduit
lathe	fabricate	ventilator	incinerator	mechanical

Write a Bonus Word to complete each sentence.

1. Rubbish can be burned in the _____ .

2. A _____ allows for the passage and circulation of fresh air.

3. _____ is synonymous with <u>tool</u>.

4. A stapler is a _____ device for attaching together sheets of paper.

5. _____ brakes are operated by the movement and force of brake fluid.

6. A _____ is a carpentry device that can turn square timbers into cylindrical poles.

7. In a _____ engine, fuel mixes with oxygen and is then ignited to create energy.

8. Workers on that assembly line manufacture, or _____ , cardboard boxes.

9. Current passes through wire, creating _____ energy to run the motor.

10. The electric wires are encased in a protective _____ to avoid fires and shocks.

Game Plan

Knowing how to define and spell words from various fields of study is an advantage to any student. In this unit, you learned many words related to specific subjects. Practice using and spelling these words.

Here are examples of words from science.

physics   psychology   zoology

Pay special attention to the endings of words that name occupations.

librarian   paramedic   chemist

The field of literature has its technical terms.

caricature   parody   exposition

Words from language arts are familiar but often difficult to spell.

exclamation   transitive   capitalization

Hurdle Words have unexpected spellings, with irregular spelling patterns. These words are especially difficult to spell because they do not follow normal spelling rules. Memorize and practice spelling these challenging words.

device   dilemma   metropolitan   several

Practice

Write the List Word that matches each definition.

Lesson 31

allergy   diagnose
neutron   microorganism
vaccinate   satellite
larynx   iodine
voltage   respiration

_____

_____

1. to inject a serum in an attempt to ward off a disease

_____

2. inhaling and exhaling air _____

3. a hypersensitivity to a specific substance _____

4. muscle and cartilage in the throat _____

5. to decide the nature of a disease after careful examination

_____

6. the measure of electrical force _____

7. a man-made object rocketed into orbit around the earth

_____

8. an uncharged elementary particle of an atom with the same mass as a proton _____

9. a chemical element used as an antiseptic _____

10. any microscopic animal or vegetable organism

Write a List Word to complete each sentence.

1. If people talk to you about personal problems, you are an _____ .

2. If you purchase a store, you are the _____ .

3. If you clean people's teeth, you are a dental _____ .

4. If you practice medicine dealing with diseases in animals, you are a _____ .

5. If you stand on a corner selling trinkets, you are a street _____ .

6. To speak for the voters, be a state _____ .

7. If you can make people laugh, be a _____ .

8. To share medical expertise about prescriptions, be a _____ .

9. To manage a business be an _____ .

10. If you are fascinated by radios and televisions, be an electronics _____ .

Lesson 32

hygienist   technician
proprietor   representative
vendor   pharmacist
analyst   administrator
comedian   veterinarian

_____

_____

Write List Words to answer the questions.

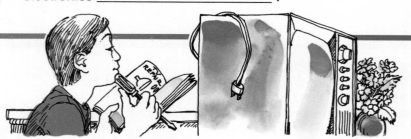

Which words contain the vowel combination **io**?

1. _____   3. _____

2. _____   4. _____

Which words contain the following vowel combinations

5. **oe** _____   7. **eu** _____

6. **ou** _____

Which word contains the double consonant **rr**?

8. _____

Which word begins with the Latin root **sim** meaning <u>alike</u>?

9. _____

Which word contains letters in the same order as these four words: <u>all</u>, <u>leg</u>, <u>ego</u>, <u>gory</u>?

10. _____

Lesson 33

alliteration   pseudonym
allegory   poetic
couplet   simile
narrative   personification
bibliography   idiom

_____

_____

Write the List Words that come between each pair of dictionary guide words. Write the words in alphabetical order.

Lesson **34**

paraphrase   definition
conjunction   homonym
parenthesis   acronym
apostrophe   fragment
interrogative grammar

_____

_____

abhor/gradual

1. _____

2. _____

3. _____

4. _____

5. _____

friction/partial

6. _____

7. _____

8. _____

9. _____

10. _____

Unscramble the List Words to complete the crossword puzzle.

ACROSS
2. MESHEC
3. BOATLECS
4. LEANVIQUET
5. PEOSPO
7. IRATEMUNI
8. PUREILCA

DOWN
1. BOATROARYL
2. LOUSONIT
5. MITTPICSOI
6. BIXHITE

Lesson **35**

laboratory   scheme
obstacle   peculiar
solution   exhibit
equivalent   miniature
oppose   optimistic

_____

_____

147

respiration	pharmacist	paraphrase
vaccinate	narrative	interrogative
voltage	pseudonym	peculiar
proprietor	poetic	scheme
vendor	definition	exhibit

Mixed Practice

Write the List Word that matches each synonym.

1. peddler _____

2. lyrical _____

3. reword _____

4. wattage _____

5. druggist _____

6. plan _____

7. asking _____

8. owner _____

9. breathing _____

10. story _____

11. odd _____

12. display _____

13. inoculate _____

14. pen name _____

15. meaning _____

Test Yourself

In each of the following groups of words, one word is misspelled. Fill in the circle that appears before the word.

1. o equivalent
   o exhibit
   o microorganism
   o nutron

2. o analist
   o pharmacist
   o pseudonym
   o simile

3. o technician
   o representative
   o definition
   o grammer

4. o minature
   o fragment
   o larynx
   o obstacle

5. o alliteration
   o sattelite
   o couplet
   o allergy

6. o hygienist
   o comedean
   o conjunction
   o paraphrase

7. o optamistic
   o vaccinate
   o narrative
   o bibliography

8. o peculiar
   o parenthisis
   o oppose
   o laboratory

9. o idium
   o poetic
   o solution
   o homonym

10. o interrogative
   o scheme
   o proprietor
   o personafication

11. o apostrophy
   o veterinarian
   o vendor
   o iodine

12. o diagnose
   o allagory
   o administrator
   o scheme

Writing and Proofreading Guide

1. Select a topic to write about.

2. Write your first draft without worring about mistakes.

3. Now organize your writing so that it makes sense.

4. Use the proofreading marks to revise your work.

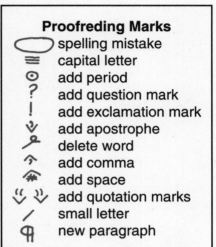

Proofreding Marks
- ⟨◯⟩ spelling mistake
- ≡ capital letter
- ⊙ add period
- ? add question mark
- ! add exclamation mark
- ⌄ add apostrophe
- ⌀ delete word
- ⌃ add comma
- ⌂ add space
- ⟨"⟩ ⟨"⟩ add quotation marks
- / small letter
- ¶ new paragraph

seemed hours

I had been wandering for what ⟨seemd⟩ like ⟨ours,⟩ trying to find ~~my~~ way out of the jungle⊙ Why was i walking in circles ? All of a sudden I heard a voice saying, "Why dont you use your compass?" In my quandary I had forgotten all about my backpack containing food ⌃ a flashlight, and my compass.

5. Write your final copy.

I had been wandering for what seemed like hours, trying to find my way out of the jungle. Why was I walking in circles? All of a sudden I heard a voice saying, "Why don't you use your compass?" In my quandary I had forgotten all about my backpack containing food a flashlight, and my compass.

Using Your Dictionary

The Spelling Workout Dictionary shows you many things about your spelling words.

The **entry word** listed in alphabetical order is the word you are looking up.

The **respelling** tells how to pronounce the word.

The **part of speech** is given as an abbreviation.

The **definition** tells what the word means.

Other **forms** of the word are given.

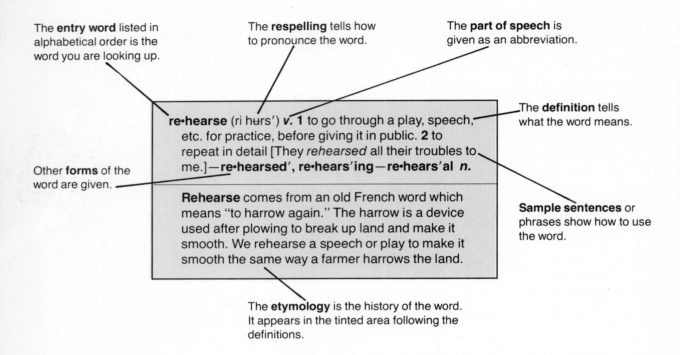

re·hearse (ri hurs′) **v. 1** to go through a play, speech, etc. for practice, before giving it in public. **2** to repeat in detail [They *rehearsed* all their troubles to me.]—**re·hearsed′, re·hears′ing**—**re·hears′al** *n.*

Rehearse comes from an old French word which means "to harrow again." The harrow is a device used after plowing to break up land and make it smooth. We rehearse a speech or play to make it smooth the same way a farmer harrows the land.

Sample **sentences** or phrases show how to use the word.

The **etymology** is the history of the word. It appears in the tinted area following the definitions.

Pronunciation Key

SYMBOL	KEY WORDS	SYMBOL	KEY WORDS	SYMBOL	KEY WORDS	SYMBOL	KEY WORDS
a	ask, fat	oo	look, pull	b	bed, dub	w	will, always
ā	ape, date	ōō	ooze, tool	d	did, had	y	yet, yard
ä	car, lot			f	fall, off	z	zebra, haze
		yoo	unite, cure	g	get, dog		
e	elf, ten	yōō	cute, few	h	he, ahead	ch	chin, arch
er	berry, care	ou	out, crowd	j	joy, jump	ng	ring, singer
ē	even, meet	u	up, cut	k	kill, bake	sh	she, dash
		ʉr	fur, fern	l	let, ball	th	thin, truth
i	is, hit			m	met, trim	*th*	then, father
ir	mirror, here	ə	a in ago	n	not, ton	zh	s in pleasure
ī	ice, fire		e in agent	p	put, tap		
			e in father	r	red, dear	′	as in (ā′b′l)
ō	open, go		i in unity	s	sell, pass		
ô	law, horn		o in collect	t	top, hat		
oi	oil, point		u in focus	v	vat, have		

An Americanism is a word or usage of a word that was born in this country. An open star before an entry word or definition means that the word or definition is an Americanism.

These dictionary entries are taken, by permission, in abridged or modified form from *Webster's New World Dictionary for Young Readers.* Copyright © 1989 by Simon & Schuster, Inc.

Aa

ab·a·cus (ab′ə kəs) **n.** a frame with groups of beads sliding back and forth on wires. The abacus is used for doing arithmetic quickly without writing. —*pl.* **ab′a·cus·es**

a·ban·don (ə ban′dən) **v. 1** to give up completely [Don't *abandon* hope of being saved.] **2** to leave; desert [The crew *abandoned* the burning ship.] ◆*n.* freedom of actions or feelings, with no control [to dance with wild *abandon*]. —**a·ban′don·ment n.**

ab·hor (əb hôr′) **v.** to feel great fear, disgust, or hatred for; hate very much [Frank *abhors* fighting.] —**ab·horred′, ab·hor′ring**

a·bol·ish (ə bäl′ish) **v.** to do away with completely; get rid of [Congress may *abolish* a law.]

a·brupt (ə brupt′) **adj. 1** coming or happening suddenly, without warning [to make an *abrupt* stop]. **2** very blunt or gruff [He answered with an *abrupt* "No!"] —**a·brupt′ly adv.** —**a·brupt′ness n.**

ab·solve (əb zälv′) **v. 1** to say that a person is free of guilt or blame or will not be punished for sin [I was *absolved* of the crime. The priest *absolved* the sinner.] **2** to make someone free from a duty or promise. —**ab·solved′, ab·solv′ing**

ab·stain (əb stān′) **v.** to do without willingly; hold oneself back [to *abstain* from meat during Lent.]

ab·stract (ab strakt′ *or* ab′strakt) **adj. 1** thought of apart from a particular act or thing [A just trial is a fair one, but justice itself is an *abstract* idea.] **2** hard to understand [That explanation is too *abstract*.] **3** formed with designs taken from real things, but not actually like any real object or being [an *abstract* painting].

ab·surd (əb surd′ *or* ab zurd′) **adj.** so clearly untrue or unreasonable as to be something to laugh at or make fun of [It is *absurd* to eat peas with a knife.] —**ab·surd′ly adv.**

a·cad·e·my (ə kad′ə mē) **n. 1** a private high school. **2** any school for special training, as in music, art, or military science. **3** a society of scholars, writers, artists, etc. working in the interests of the arts or sciences. —*pl.* **a·cad′e·mies**

Academy comes from the Greek name for a grove of trees near Athens. Plato, an ancient Greek philosopher and teacher, taught his students in that grove. The Greeks thought that it had once belonged to a hero in Greek legend named *Akademos*.

a·cap·pel·la (ä′ kə pel′ə) without instrumental accompaniment.

ac·cept·ance (ək sep′təns) **n. 1** an accepting or being accepted [the *acceptance* of an award]. **2** approval or belief [That theory now has the *acceptance* of most scientists.]

ac·ces·so·ry (ək ses′ər ē) **n. 1** something extra; thing added, as for convenience, comfort, or decoration [A radio and air conditioner are *accessories* on a car. A purse and gloves are *accessories* to an outfit.] **2** a person who helps another to break the law, although absent at the time of the crime [The doorkeeper became an *accessory* by helping the murderer escape.] —*pl.* **ac·ces′so·ries** ◆*adj.* being something extra or added to help the more important thing [The vacuum cleaner has *accessory* attachments.]

ac·ci·den·tal (ak′sə den′t'l) **adj.** happening by chance [Goodyear's discovery of how to vulcanize rubber was *accidental*.] —**ac′ci·den′tal·ly adv.**

ac·quit (ə kwit′) **v.** to rule that a person accused of something is not guilty [The judge *acquitted* the suspect.] —**ac·quit′ted, ac·quit′ting**

☆**ac·ro·nym** (ak′rə nim) **n.** a word that is formed from the first letters, or first syllables, of two or more words ["Comsat" is an *acronym* formed from "communication satellite."]

ad·dict (ad′ikt) **n.** a person who has a habit so strong that he cannot easily give it up [a drug *addict*]. ◆*v.* (ə dikt′) to give oneself up to some strong habit [Some people are *addicted* to watching television.] —**ad·dic′tion n.**

ad·jec·tive (aj′ik tiv) **n.** a word used with a noun or pronoun to tell which, what kind of, how many, or whose [In the sentence "Every egg was fresh," the words "every" and "fresh" are *adjectives*.] —**ad·jec·ti·val** (aj′ik tī′v'l) **adj.**

ad-lib (ad′lib′) **v.** to make up and put in words, gestures, etc. not in the script as one is performing: *used only in everyday talk* [Good actors learn to *ad-lib* when they forget their lines.] —**ad′-libbed′, ad′-lib′bing**

Ad-lib is a shortened form of a Latin phrase *ad libitum*, meaning "as one pleases," that is used in music to mark a part that performers can change or leave out as they please.

ad·min·is·tra·tor (əd min′ə strāt′ər) **n.** a person who administers or directs something; executive; manager.

ad·mit (əd mit′) **v. 1** to permit or give the right to enter [One ticket *admits* two persons.] **2** to have room for [The hall *admits* 500 people.] **3** to take or accept as being true; confess [Lucy will not *admit* her mistake.] —**ad·mit′ted, ad·mit′ting**

abacus

ad·verb (ad′vʉrb) **n.** a word used with a verb, adjective, or another adverb to tell when, where, how, what kind, or how much. *Quickly* tells how in "run *quickly*"; *always* tells when in "*always* sad"; *bright* tells what kind in "*bright* red dress"; *very* tells how much in "run *very* quickly." —**ad·ver·bi·al** (ad vʉr′bē əl) **adj.**

ad·vi·so·ry (əd vī′zər ē) **adj.** advising or able to advise [*advisory* experts]. ◆**n.** a warning that bad weather is on the way. —*pl.* **ad·vi·so·ries**

ad·vo·cate (ad′və kāt) **v.** to speak or write in support of; be in favor of [The senator *advocated* a new housing bill.] —**ad′vo·cat·ed, ad′vo·cat·ing** ◆**n.** (ad′və kit *or* ad′və kāt) **1** a person who speaks or writes in favor of something. **2** a person who argues another's case; especially, a lawyer.

aer·o·nau·tics (er′ə nô′tiks) **n.pl.** the science of making and flying aircraft: *used with a singular verb.* —**aer′o·nau′ti·cal** *or* **aer′o·nau′tic adj.**

af·fa·ble (af′ə b'l) **adj.** pleasant and easy to talk to; friendly. —**af′fa·bil′i·ty n.** —**af′fa·bly adv.**

af·fi·da·vit (af′ə dā′vit) **n.** a statement written by a person who swears that it is the truth [He signed an *affidavit* saying that he had paid the debt.]

af·fil·i·ate (ə fil′ē āt) **v.** to take in or be taken in as a member or another part; join [Our store has become *affiliated* with a large supermarket chain.] —**af·fil′i·at·ed, af·fil′i·at·ing** ◆**n.** (ə fil′ē it) an affiliated person or organization [a local *affiliate* of a national group]. —**af·fil·i·a′tion n.**

af·firm·a·tive (ə fʉr′mə tiv) **adj.** saying that something is true; answering "yes" [an *affirmative* reply]. ◆**n.** **1** a word, phrase, or action showing that one approves or agrees [She nodded her head in the *affirmative*.] **2** the side that favors or agrees with the point being debated [There were more votes in the negative than in the *affirmative*.]

af·flu·ent (af′lo̅o̅ wənt *or now also* af lo̅o̅ ′ənt) **adj.** having much money or property; prosperous; rich.

ag·gra·vate (ag′rə vāt) **v.** **1** to make worse; make more troublesome [You will *aggravate* your sprained ankle by walking.] **2** to make impatient; annoy; bother: *used only in everyday talk* [The talking in the audience began to *aggravate* us.] —**ag′gra·vat·ed, ag′gra·vat·ing** —**ag′gra·va′tion n.**

ag·gres·sive (ə gres′iv) **adj.** **1** ready to start fights or quarrels [an *aggressive* bully]. **2** bold and active; full of energy and ideas [an *aggressive* leader]. —**ag·gres′sive·ly adv.** —**ag·gres′sive·ness n.**

al·le·go·ry (al′ə gôr′ē) **n.** a story used to teach or explain an idea or moral rule. In allegories people, animals, and things have hidden meanings beside the ones that are easily seen [Aesop's fables are short *allegories*.] —*pl.* **al′le·go′ries** —**al′le·gor′i·cal adj.**

☆**al·ler·gy** (al′ər jē) **n.** a condition in which one becomes sick, gets a rash, etc. by breathing in, touching, eating, or drinking something that is not harmful to most people [Hay fever is usually caused by an *allergy* to certain pollens.] —*pl.* **al′ler·gies**

al·li·ga·tor (al′ə gāt′ər) **n.** **1** a large lizard like the crocodile, found in warm rivers and marshes of the U.S. and China. **2** a scaly leather made from its hide.

al·lit·er·a·tion (ə lit′ə rā′shən) **n.** a repeating of the same sound at the beginning of two or more words, as in a line of poetry [There is an *alliteration* of *s* in "Sing a song of sixpence."]

al·lot (ə lät′) **v.** **1** to divide or give out in shares or by lot [The land was *allotted* equally to the settlers.] **2** to give to a person as a share [Each speaker is *allotted* five minutes.] —**al·lot′ted, al·lot′ting**

al·lu·vi·al (ə lo̅o̅′vē əl) **adj.** made up of the sand or clay washed down by flowing water [*alluvial* deposits at the mouth of the river].

al·tru·is·tic (al′tro̅o̅ is′tik) **adj.** putting the good of others ahead of one's own interests; unselfish. —**al′tru·is′ti·cal·ly adv.**

am·bas·sa·dor (am bas′ə dər) **n.** **1** an official of highest rank sent by a country to represent it in another country. **2** any person sent as a representative or messenger [the U.S. *ambassador* to the UN].

am·e·thyst (am′ə thist) **n.** **1** a purple stone, especially a kind of quartz, that is used as a jewel. **2** purple or violet.

am·phib·i·ous (am fib′ē əs) **adj.** **1** that can live both on land and in water [an *amphibious* plant]. **2** that can operate or travel on both land and water [an *amphibious* truck].

am·phi·the·a·ter *or* **am·phi·the·a·tre** (am′fə thē′ə tər) **n.** a round or oval building having rising rows of seats around an open space in which sports events, plays, etc. are held.

am·pli·fi·ca·tion (am′plə fi kā′shən) **n.** **1** an amplifying, or making larger or stronger; increase. **2** more details [Your report needs *amplification*.]

amphitheater

am·pli·fi·er (am′plə fī′ər) **n. 1** a person or thing that amplifies. **2** a device, especially one with vacuum tubes or semiconductors, used to make electric or radio waves stronger before they are changed into sounds, as in a phonograph or radio.

a·nach·ro·nism (ə nak′rə niz′m) **n. 1** the connecting of a person, thing, or happening with another that came later in history [Shakespeare was guilty of an *anachronism* when he had a clock striking in a play about ancient Rome.] **2** anything that is or seems to be out of its proper time in history [A horse on a city street is an *anachronism* today.]

an·a·gram (an′ə gram) **n. 1** a word or phrase made from another word or phrase by changing the order of the letters ["Dare" is an *anagram* of "read."] **2 anagrams**, *pl.* a game played by forming words from letters picked from a pile.

a·nal·o·gy (ə nal′ə jē) **n.** likeness in some ways between things that are otherwise unlike; resemblance in part [How a jet airplane flies can be explained by showing an *analogy* with air escaping fast from a toy balloon.] —*pl.* **a·nal′o·gies**

a·nal·y·sis (ə nal′ə sis) **n.** a separating or breaking up of something into its parts so as to examine them and see how they fit together [A chemical *analysis* of a substance will tell what elements are in it. The *analysis* of a problem will help tell what caused it.] —*pl.* **a·nal·y·ses** (ə nal′ə sēz)

an·a·lyst (an′ə list) **n. 1** a person who analyzes. **2** *a shorter form of* **psychoanalyst**.

an·a·lyt·i·cal (an′ə lit′i k′l) or **an·a·lyt·ic** (an′ə lit′ik) **adj. 1** having to do with analysis [an *analytical* prosess]. **2** good at analyzing [an *analytical* person]. —**an′a·lyt′i·cal·ly** *adv.*

an·arch·y (an′ər kē) **n. 1** the complete absence of government and law. **2** a condition of disorder or confusion. —**an·ar·chic** (an är′kik) *adj.*

an·ces·tor (an′ses tər) **n. 1** a person who comes before one in a family line, especially someone earlier than a grandparent; forefather [Their *ancestors* came from Poland.] **2** an early kind of animal from which later kinds have developed [The *ancestor* of the elephant was the mammoth.]

an·chor (aŋ′kər) **n. 1** a heavy object let down into the water by a chain to keep a ship from drifting. It is usually a metal piece with hooks that grip the ground at the bottom of the water. **2** anything that keeps something else steady or firm [In time of trouble, faith was the old folks' *anchor*.] ◆*v.* **1** to keep from drifting or coming loose by using an anchor. **2** to attach or fix firmly [The shelves are *anchored* to the wall.]

a·ne·mi·a (ə nē′mē ə) **n.** a condition in which a person's blood does not have enough red corpuscles or hemoglobin so that it does not carry a normal amount of oxygen. The person becomes pale and tired.

an·es·the·sia (an′əs thē′zhə) **n.** a condition in which one has no feeling of pain, heat, touch, etc. in all or part of the body.

an·gu·lar (aŋ′gyə lər) **adj. 1** having angles or sharp corners [an *angular* building]. **2** measured by an angle [the *angular* motion of a pendulum]. **3** with bones that jut out; gaunt [an *angular* face].

an·nex (ə neks′) **v.** to add on or attach a smaller thing to a larger one [Texas was *annexed* to the Union in 1845.] ◆*n.* (an′eks) something added on; especially, an extra part built on or near a building to give more space. —**an′nex·a′tion** *n.*

an·ni·hi·late (ə nī′ə lāt) **v.** to destroy completely; wipe out [An atomic bomb can *annihilate* a city.] —**an·ni′hi·lat·ed, an·ni′hi·lat·ing** —**an·ni′hi·la′tion** *n.*

an·no·tate (an′ə tāt) **v.** to add notes that explain something or give one's opinions [Scholars *annotate* the plays of Shakespeare.] —**an′no·tat·ed, an′no·tat·ing**

an·nounce·ment (ə nouns′mənt) **n. 1** an announcing of something that has happened or will happen. **2** something announced, often in the form of a written or printed notice [The wedding *announcements* are here.]

an·nounc·er (ə nouns′ər) **n.** a person who announces; especially, one who introduces radio or television programs, reads commercials, etc.

an·nul (ə nul′) **v.** to do away with; put an end to; make no longer binding under the law; cancel [The marriage was *annulled* after a week.] —**an·nulled′, an·nul′ling** —**an·nul′ment** *n.*

a·non·y·mous (ə nän′ə məs) **adj. 1** whose name is not known [an *anonymous* writer]. **2** written, given, etc. by a person whose name is kept secret [an *anonymous* gift]. —**a·non′y·mous·ly** *adv.*

an·te·ced·ent (an′tə sēd′ənt) **adj.** coming or happening before; previous [The pilot told of the storm *antecedent* to the crash.] ◆*n.* **1** a thing or happening coming before something else. **2** one's ancestry, past life, etc. **3** the word or group of words to which a pronoun refers [In "the guide who led us," "guide" is the *antecedent* of "who."]

an·te·ri·or (an tir′ē ər) **adj. 1** at or toward the front; forward. **2** coming before; earlier.

an·te·room (an′ti rōōm) **n.** a room leading to a larger or more important room; waiting room.

anchor

☆**an·ti·bi·ot·ic** (an′ti bī ät′ik) *n.* a chemical substance produced by bacteria, fungi, etc., that can kill, or stop the growth of, germs. Antibiotics, such as penicillin, are used in treating diseases.

an·ti·his·ta·mine (an′ti his′tə mēn) *n.* a medicine used to relieve asthma, hay fever, and, sometimes, the common cold.

an·ti·so·cial (an′ti sō′shəl) *adj.* **1** not liking to be with other people [Are you so *antisocial* that you never have visitors?] **2** harmful to society in general [All crimes are *antisocial* acts.]

anx·i·e·ty (aŋ zī′ə tē) *n.* **1** the condition of feeling uneasy or worried about what may happen; concern [She waited with *anxiety* to hear what the doctor would say.] **2** an eager but often uneasy desire [He fumbled the ball in his *anxiety* to do well.] —*pl.* **anx·i′e·ties**

a·pol·o·gize (ə päl′ə jīz) *v.* to make an apology; say that one is sorry for doing something wrong or being at fault [They *apologized* for being late.] —**a·pol′o·gized, a·pol′o·giz·ing**

a·pos·tro·phe (ə päs′trə fē) *n.* the mark (′) used: **1** in a shortened word or phrase to show that a letter or letters have been left out [*ne′er* for *never*; *I′ll* for *I will*]. **2** to show the possessive case [the *soldier′s* uniform; the *teachers′* lounge]. **3** to form certain plurals [five *6′s*; to dot the *i′s*].

arcade

ap·pe·tite (ap′ə tīt) *n.* **1** a desire or wish for food [Exercise gave her a strong *appetite*.] **2** any strong desire [He has an *appetite* for good books.]

ap·pli·ca·ble (ap′li kə b′l) *adj.* that can be applied or used; suitable [Your suggestion is not *applicable* to the problem.] —**ap′pli·ca·bil′i·ty** *n.*

aq·ua·ma·rine (ak′wə mə rēn′) *n.* **1** a clear, pale blue-green mineral, used in jewelry. **2** a pale blue-green color.

a·quar·i·um (ə kwer′ē əm) *n.* **1** a glass tank or bowl in which living fishes, water animals, and water plants are kept. **2** a building where collections of such animals and plants are shown to the public. —*pl.* **a·quar′i·ums** or **a·quar·i·a** (ə kwer′ē ə)

a·quat·ic (ə kwät′ik or ə kwat′ik) *adj.* **1** growing or living in or upon water [*aquatic* plants]. **2** done in or upon the water [*aquatic* sports].

ar·bi·tra·tor (är′bə trāt′ər) *n.* a person chosen to judge a dispute.

ar·cade (är kād′) *n.* **1** a covered passageway, as through a building, often with an arched roof; especially, such a passage with small shops on both sides. **2** a row of arches supported by columns.

ar·cha·ic (är kā′ik) *adj.* **1** belonging to an earlier time; ancient or old-fashioned [a yard with an *archaic* iron fence]. **2** that is now seldom used except in poetry, the Bible, etc. ["Thou art" is an *archaic* form of "you are."]

ar·chi·tect (är′kə tekt) *n.* a person who works out the plans for buildings, bridges, etc. and sees that these plans are carried out by the builders.

ar·chive (är′kīv) *n. usually* **archives**, *pl.* **1** a place where old public records or papers of historical interest are kept. **2** such records or papers.

ar·du·ous (är′joo wəs) *adj.* **1** hard to do; difficult [*arduous* work]. **2** using much energy; strenuous [*arduous* efforts]. —**ar′du·ous·ly** *adv.*

a·ris·to·crat (ə ris′tə krat) *n.* **1** a member of the aristocracy, or upper class. **2** a person who acts, thinks, or believes like people of the upper class.

ar·thri·tis (är thrīt′is) *n.* a disease in which the joints of the body swell up and become sore and stiff. —**ar·thrit·ic** (är thrit′ik) *adj.*

ar·tic·u·late (är tik′yə lit) *adj.* **1** spoken in such a way that all the sounds and words are clear and distinct [an *articulate* reply]. **2** able to speak in this way; also, able to tell one′s thoughts clearly so they are understood [an *articulate* speaker]. ◆*v.* (är tik′yə lāt) to say in a clear, distinct way. —**ar·tic′u·lat·ed, ar·tic′u·lat·ing**

ar·ti·fi·cial (är′tə fish′əl) *adj.* **1** made by a human being, not by nature; not natural [*artificial* flowers made of plastic]. **2** put on just for an effect; not sincere; false [an *artificial* smile]. —**ar·ti·fi·ci·al·i·ty** (är′tə fish′ē al′ə tē) *n.* —**ar′ti·fi′cial·ly** *adv.*

as·cer·tain (as′ər tān) *v.* to find out in such a way as to be sure [We *ascertained* the facts about the case by reading through old newspapers.] —**as′cer·tain′a·ble** *adj.* —**as′cer·tain′ment** *n.*

as·sist·ance (ə sis′təns) *n.* help; aid.

at·oll (a′tôl or ā′täl) *n.* a coral island that is shaped like a ring around a lagoon.

at·tend·ant (ə ten′dənt) *adj.* **1** attending or taking care [an *attendant* nurse]. **2** that goes along; joined with; accompanying [Every job has its *attendant* problems.] ◆*n.* a person who attends, or serves; servant, keeper, etc. [an *attendant* at the zoo; the queen and her *attendants*].

attorney general the chief law officer of a country or State [The U.S. *Attorney General* is the head of the Justice Department.] —*pl.* **attorneys general** or **attorney generals**

au·di·tion (ô dish′ən) *n.* a hearing in which an actor or musician who is being tested for a job gives a short performance. ◆☆*v.* **1** to give an audition to. **2** to perform in an audition.

au·di·tor (ô′də tər) *n.* **1** a listener or hearer. **2** a person whose work is auditing accounts.

☆**au·to·mo·bile** (ôt′ə mə bēl′ or ôt′ə mə bēl′) *n.* a car moved by an engine that is part of it, used for traveling on streets or roads; motorcar.

auxiliary verb a verb that is used to form tenses, moods, or voices of other verbs.

Have, be, may, can, must, do, shall, will are used as auxiliary verbs. In the sentence "He will be late, but she may not be," *will* and *may* are auxiliary verbs.

a·vail·a·ble (ə vā′lə b'l) *adj.* that can be got, used, or reached [This style is *available* in three colors.] —**a·vail′a·bil′i·ty** *n.*

av·a·lanche (av′ə lanch) *n.* **1** a large mass of snow, ice, rocks, etc. sliding swiftly down a mountain. **2** anything that comes suddenly and in large numbers [an *avalanche* of mail; an *avalanche* of blows].

Bb

bank·rupt (baŋk′rupt) *adj.* **1** not able to pay one's debts and freed by law from the need for doing so [Any property a *bankrupt* person may still have is usually divided among those to whom the person owes money.] **2** that has failed completely [The school's policy on this matter seems *bankrupt*.] ◆*n.* a person who is bankrupt. ◆*v.* to make bankrupt.

Bankrupt comes from two Italian words meaning "broken bench." Moneylenders used to carry on their business at a bench or table. They would be put out of business if the bench were broken, just as nowadays people are put out of business if they cannot pay their debts.

bar·be·cue (bär′bə kyōō) *n.* **1** a hog, ox, etc. roasted whole on a spit over an open fire. **2** any meat roasted over an open fire. ☆**3** a picnic or party at which such meat is served. **4** a stove or pit for cooking outdoors. ◆*v.* **1** to roast on a spit over an open fire. **2** to broil or roast meat or fish in a highly seasoned sauce (called **barbecue sauce**). —**bar′be·cued, bar′be·cu·ing**

ba·rom·e·ter (bə räm′ə tər) *n.* **1** an instrument that measures the pressure of the air around us. It is used in forecasting changes in the weather and finding the height above sea level. **2** anything that shows changes in conditions [The stock market is a *barometer* of business.] —**bar·o·met·ric** (bar′ə met′rik) *adj.*

ben·e·fac·tor (ben′ə fak′tər) *n.* a person who has given money or other help to someone in need.

ben·e·fit (ben′ə fit) *n.* **1** help or advantage; also, anything that helps [Speak louder for the *benefit* of those in the rear.] **2** *often* **benefits**, *pl.* money paid by an insurance company, the government, etc. as during old age or sickness, or for death. **3** any public event put on to raise money for a certain person, group, or cause [The show is a

benefit for crippled children.] ◆*v.* **1** to do good for; aid; help [The new tax law *benefits* big businesses.] **2** to be helped; profit [You'll *benefit* from exercise.]

be·nign (bi nīn′) *adj.* **1** good-natured; kindly [a *benign* smile]. **2** doing little or no harm; not likely to cause death [a *benign* tumor]. —**be·nign′ly** *adv.*

bib·li·og·ra·phy (bib′lē äg′rə fē) *n.* a list of writings about a certain subject or by a certain author. —*pl.* **bib′li·og′ra·phies** —**bib·li·o·graph·i·cal** (bib′lē ə graf′i k'l) *adj.*

bi·og·ra·phy (bī äg′rə fē) *n.* the story of a person's life written by another person. —*pl.* **bi·og′ra·phies** —**bi·o·graph·i·cal** (bī′ə graf′i k'l) *adj.*

bi·o·log·i·cal (bī′ə läj′i k'l) *adj.* having to do with biology. —**bi·o·log′i·cal·ly** *adv.*

biv·ou·ac (biv′wak *or* biv′ōō wak′) *n.* a camp of soldiers outdoors with little or no shelter, set up for a short time. ◆*v.* to camp outdoors. —**biv′ou·acked, biv′ou·ack·ing**

bois·ter·ous (bois′tər əs) *adj.* **1** rough and stormy. **2** noisy and lively [a *boisterous* party].

bor·ough (bur′ō) *n.* **1** a town or village that has a charter to govern itself. **2** one of the five main divisions of New York City.

bouil·lon (bool′yän) *n.* a clear soup.

boy·cott (boi′kät) *v.* to join together in refusing to buy, sell, or use something or to have any dealings with someone [We all *boycotted* the ice cream store because it was dirty.] ◆☆*n.* the act of boycotting a business, etc.

The word **boycott** comes from the name of Captain Charles C. Boycott, who collected rent for a landlord in Ireland. After he raised the rents of his neighbors in 1880, they had no more to do with him. They wouldn't even sell him groceries.

broad·cast (brôd′kast) *v.* **1** to send over the air by means of radio or television [to *broadcast* a program]. —**broad′cast** or **broad′cast·ed, broad′cast·ing 2** to scatter or spread widely. —**broad′cast, broad′cast·ing** ◆*n.* **1** the act of broadcasting. **2** a radio or television program [the six o'clock news *broadcast*].

bu·reauc·ra·cy (byoo rä′krə sē) *n.* **1** government by appointed officials who follow all rules without question and without exceptions. **2** such officials, as a group, or the way they govern. —*pl.* **bu·reauc′ra·cies**

but·tress (but′ris) *n.* **1** a support built against a wall to make it strong. **2** any support or prop. ◆*v.* to prop up or support [to *buttress* a wall; to *buttress* an argument].

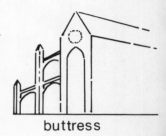

buttress

a	ask, fat
ā	ape, date
ä	car, lot
e	elf, ten
er	berry, care
ē	even, meet
i	is, hit
ir	mirror, here
ī	ice, fire
ō	open, go
ô	law, horn
oi	oil, point
oo	look, pull
ōō	ooze, tool
yoo	unite, cure
yōō	cute, few
ou	out, crowd
u	up, cut
ur	fur, fern
ə	a in ago
	e in agent
	e in father
	i in unity
	o in collect
	u in focus
ch	chin, arch
ng	ring, singer
sh	she, dash
th	thin, truth
th	then, father
zh	s in pleasure
′	as in (ā′b'l)

canopy

ca·dence (kād'′ns) *n.* **1** flow or rhythm with a regular beat [to march in fast *cadence*; the *cadence* of waves breaking on the shore]. **2** the rise or fall of the voice or the tone of the voice in speaking. **3** the final chords or other ending of a section of music.

cal·cu·lus (kal'kyə ləs) *n.* a kind of mathematics used to solve hard problems in science and statistics.

> **Calculus** is a Latin word meaning "pebble." The early Romans used little stones for counting or "calculating" in doing arithmetic.

can·cel·la·tion (kan's'l ā'shən) *n.* **1** the act of canceling. **2** something canceled. **3** a mark that cancels, as on a postage stamp.

can·o·py (kan'ə pē) *n.* **1** a cloth or other covering fastened as a roof above a throne, bed, etc., or held on poles over a person or sacred thing. **2** anything that seems to cover like a canopy [We walked through the woods beneath a *canopy* of leaves.] —*pl.* **can'o·pies** ◆*v.* to put or form a canopy over. —**can'o·pied, can'o·py·ing**

ca·pa·bil·i·ty (kā'pə bil'ə tē) *n.* the power to do something; ability [She has the *capability* to become a lawyer.] —*pl.* **ca'pa·bil'i·ties**

cap·i·tal·i·za·tion (kap'ə t'l ə zā'shən) *n.* **1** the act of capitalizing. **2** the stocks and bonds that stand for the total capital of a business.

car·i·ca·ture (kar'ə kə chər) *n.* **1** a picture or imitation of a person or thing in which certain features or parts are exaggerated in a joking or mocking way. **2** the skill or work of making such pictures, etc. ◆*v.* to make or be a caricature of [Cartoonists often *caricature* the President.] —**car'i·ca·tured, car'i·ca·tur·ing** —**car'i·ca·tur·ist** *n.*

car·pen·ter (kär'pən tər) *n.* a worker who builds and repairs wooden things, especially the wooden parts of buildings, ships, etc.

car·tel (kär tel') *n.* a group of companies joined together to have complete control over the production and prices of certain products; trust or monopoly [an international *cartel* of oil producers].

ce·les·tial (sə les'chəl) *adj.* **1** of the heavens or sky [The stars are *celestial* bodies.] **2** of the finest or highest kind; perfect [*celestial* bliss].

Cel·si·us (sel'sē əs) *adj.* of or describing a thermometer on which the freezing point of pure water is 0° and the boiling point is 100°: *also called* **centigrade**.

caricature

cen·sor (sen'sər) *n.* an official who has the power to examine books, news stories, mail, movies, etc. and to remove or change anything the government does not wish people to see or hear. ◆*v.* to examine books, letters, movies, etc. and to remove or hold back anything thought not right for people to see or hear. —**cen'sor·ship** *n.*

cen·ti·grade (sen'tə grād) *adj., n.* same as **Celsius**.

cen·ti·me·ter (sen'tə mēt'ər) *n.* a unit of measure, equal to 1/100 meter.

cen·tral·ize (sen'trə līz) *v.* to bring or come to a center; especially, to bring under one control [All government powers were *centralized* under a dictator.] —**cen'tral·ized, cen'tral·iz·ing** —**cen'tral·i·za'tion** *n.*

cen·trif·u·gal force (sen trif'yə gəl) the force that pulls a thing outward when it is spinning rapidly around a center.

cer·e·bral (ser'ə brəl *or* sə rē'brəl) *adj.* having to do with the brain or with the cerebrum.

chan·de·lier (shan də lir') *n.* a lighting fixture hanging from the ceiling with branches for several lights.

chem·ist (kem'ist) *n.* an expert in chemistry.

Chil·e (chil'ē) a country on the southwestern coast of South America. —**Chil'e·an** *adj., n.*

☆**chi·ro·prac·tor** (kī'rə prak'tər) *n.* a person who practices a system of treating diseases by pressing and moving the spine and the joints of the body with the hands.

cho·les·ter·ol (kə les'tə rōl) *n.* a waxy substance found in the body and in certain foods. When there is much of it in the blood, it is thought to cause hardening of the arteries.

chron·ic (krän'ik) *adj.* **1** going on for a long time or coming back again and again [a *chronic* disease]. **2** having been one for a long time; constant or habitual [a *chronic* complainer; a *chronic* invalid]. —**chron'i·cal·ly** *adv.*

cin·e·ma (sin'ə mə) *n.* **1** a movie; motion picture. **2** a movie theater. **3** the art or business of making movies.

clas·si·cal (klas'i k'l) *adj.* describing a kind of music that is not simple in form and that requires much study and training to write and perform [Symphonies, concertos, sonatas, etc. are called *classical* music.] —**clas'si·cal·ly** *adv.*

clause (klôz) *n.* **1** a group of words that includes a subject and verb, but that forms only part of a sentence. In the sentence "She will visit us if she can," *She will visit us* is a clause that could be a complete sentence, and *if she can* is a clause that depends on the first clause. **2** any of the separate points or articles in a law, contract, treaty, etc.

cli·ché (klē shā′) **n.** an expression or idea that has become stale from too much use ["As old as the hills" is a *cliché*.]

clique (klēk *or* klik) **n.** a small group of people who are friendly only with one another and have little to do with outsiders.

clock·wise (kläk′wīz) **adv., adj.** in the direction in which the hands of a clock move [When you turn the knob *clockwise*, the radio goes on.]

closed circuit a system of sending television signals by cable to just a certain number of receiving sets for some special purpose.

co·au·thor (kō ô′thər) **n.** an author who works with another author in writing something, as a book.

co·ex·ist (kō′ig zist′) **v. 1** to go on living or existing together at the same time. **2** to live together in a peaceful way even though there are political or other differences. —**co′ex·ist′ence n.**

co·her·ent (kō hir′ənt) **adj. 1** sticking together [a *coherent* blob of jelly]. **2** having all parts connected in a proper way; clear [She told a rambling story that was not very *coherent*.] **3** speaking or thinking in a way that makes sense [He was terrified and no longer *coherent*.] —**co·her′ence n.** —**co·her′ent·ly adv.**

co·in·cide (kō′in sīd′) **v. 1** to be exactly alike in shape and size [If one circle fits exactly over another, they *coincide*.] **2** to happen at the same time [Our birthdays *coincide*.] **3** to agree; be the same [Our interests do not *coincide*.] —**co′in·cid′ed, co′in·cid′ing**

col·i·se·um (käl′ə sē′əm) **n.** a large building or stadium for sports events, shows, etc.

col·lab·o·rate (kə lab′ə rāt) **v. 1** to work together in preparing something [Charles and Mary Lamb *collaborated* in writing "Tales from Shakespeare."] **2** to help or work with an enemy that has invaded one's country. —**col·lab′o·rat·ed, col·lab′o·rat·ing** —**col·lab′o·ra′tion n.** —**col·lab′o·ra′tor n.**

col·lat·er·al (kə lat′ər əl) **adj.** that goes along with the main thing, but in a less important way; additional or secondary [*collateral* evidence]. ◆**n.** ☆stocks, bonds, or other property that is given to a lender of money to hold as a pledge that the loan will be repaid.

col·league (käl′ēg) **n.** a person who works in the same office, the same profession, etc.; fellow worker.

col·lec·tion (kə lek′shən) **n. 1** the act of gathering [Rubbish *collection* is on Friday.] **2** things collected [a *collection* of coins]. **3** something gathered into a mass or pile [a *collection* of dust]. **4** money collected [a *collection* for a church].

col·li·sion (kə lizh′ən) **n. 1** the act of coming together with force; crash [an automobile *collision*]. **2** a clash of ideas, interests, etc.

col·lo·qui·al (kə lō′kwē əl) **adj.** being or containing the words and phrases that are used only in everyday talk, or in writing that is like everyday talk ["My buddy flunked the exam" is a *colloquial* way of saying "My close friend failed the examination."] —**col·lo′qui·al·ly adv.**

col·on·nade (käl ə nād′) **n.** a row of columns as along the side of a building.

col·o·ny (käl′ə nē) **n. 1** a group of people who settle in a distant land but are still under the rule of the country from which they came. **2** the place where they settle [the Pilgrim *colony* at Plymouth]. **3** a land that is ruled by a country some distance away [Java was once a Dutch *colony*.] —*pl.* **col′o·nies**

co·los·sal (kə läs′'l) **adj.** very large or very great; enormous or immense.

com·bus·tion (kəm bus′chən) **n.** the act or process of burning [An internal-*combustion* engine is one in which the fuel is burned within the engine itself.]

co·me·di·an (kə mē′dē ən) **n.** an actor who plays comic parts, or one who tells jokes and does funny things to make people laugh.

com·mem·o·rate (kə mem′ə rāt) **v.** to honor or keep alive the memory of [The Washington Monument *commemorates* our first President.] —**com·mem′o·rat·ed, com·mem′o·rat·ing**

com·mence·ment (kə mens′mənt) **n. 1** a beginning or start. **2** the graduation ceremony of a school or college, when graduates receive their degrees or diplomas.

com·ment (käm′ent) **n.** a remark or note that explains or gives an opinion [The teacher's *comments* on the poem helped us to understand it.] ◆**v.** to make comments or remarks [Doctors should not *comment* on their patients to others.]

com·men·tar·y (käm′ən ter′ē) **n. 1** a series of comments or notes on a book, play, etc. [You need to read *commentaries* in order to understand Shakespeare's plays.] **2** something serving like a comment or illustration [This political scandal is a *commentary* on our corrupt society.] —*pl.* **com′men·tar′ies**

com·merce (käm′ərs) **n.** the buying and selling of goods, especially when done on a large scale between cities, states, or countries; trade.

com·mis·sion·er (kə mish′ə nər) **n. 1** a member of a commission. **2** the head of a government commission or department [a water *commissioner*].

com·mit·ment (kə mit′mənt) **n. 1** a committing or being committed. **2** a promise; pledge.

colonnade

a	ask, fat
ā	ape, date
ä	car, lot
e	elf, ten
er	berry, care
ē	even, meet
i	is, hit
ir	mirror, here
ī	ice, fire
ō	open, go
ô	law, horn
oi	oil, point
൦൦	look, pull
ōō	ooze, tool
yൄ	unite, cure
yōō	cute, few
ou	out, crowd
u	up, cut
ʉr	fur, fern
ə	a in ago
	e in agent
	e in father
	i in unity
	o in collect
	u in focus
ch	chin, arch
ŋ	ring, singer
sh	she, dash
th	thin, truth
th	then, father
zh	s in pleasure
′	as in (ā′b'l)

com·mod·i·ty (kə mäd′ə tē) **n.** anything that is bought and sold; article of trade or commerce. —pl. **com·mod′i·ties**

com·mon·wealth (käm′ən welth) **n.** 1 the people of a nation or state. 2 a nation or state in which the people hold the ruling power; democracy or republic. ☆3 sometimes, any State of the United States.

com·mu·nal (käm′yoon ′l or kə myoon′′l) **adj.** 1 of or belonging to the community; public [This park is *communal* property.] 2 of a commune. —**com·mu′nal·ly adv.**

com·mune (käm′yoon) **n.** 1 the smallest district that has a local government in France, Belgium, and some other countries in Europe. ☆2 a small group of people living together and sharing their earnings, the work to be done, etc.

com·mute (kə myoot′) **v.** ☆1 to travel as a commuter. 2 to change a punishment, duty, etc. to one that is less harsh [to *commute* a prisoner's sentence from five to three years]. —**com·mut′ed, com·mut′ing** —**com·mu·ta·tion** (käm′yə tā′shən) **n.**

com·pe·tent (käm′pə tənt) **adj.** having enough ability to do what is needed; capable [a *competent* typist]. —**com′pe·tent·ly adv.**

com·plex (kəm pleks′ or käm′pleks) **adj.** made up of different parts connected in a way that is hard to understand; not simple; intricate [A computer is a *complex* machine. Unemployment is a *complex* problem.] ◆**n.** (käm′pleks) 1 a group of connected ideas, things, etc. that form a single whole [the *complex* of roads in a State]. 2 a mixed-up feeling about something that makes one show fear, dislike, etc. [an inferiority *complex*; a *complex* about traveling in airplanes].

com·pli·ca·tion (käm′plə kā′shən) **n.** 1 a complicated or mixed-up condition; confusion or intricacy. 2 a happening that makes something more complicated or involved [the *complications* of a plot; a disease with *complications*].

com·pli·men·ta·ry (käm′plə men′tər ē) **adj.** 1 paying a compliment; giving praise or admiring [*complimentary* remarks]. 2 given free [a *complimentary* ticket to a play].

com·pro·mise (käm′prə mīz) **n.** a settling of an argument or dispute in which each side gives up part of what it wants. ◆**v.** 1 to settle by a compromise [They *compromised* by taking turns on the bicycle.] 2 to put in danger of being criticized or disgraced [Do not *compromise* your reputation by cheating.] —**com′pro·mised, com′pro·mis·ing**

com·pul·so·ry (kəm pul′sər ē) **adj.** that must be done; required [*compulsory* training].

con·cen·tric (kən sen′trik) **adj.** having the same center [*concentric* circles].

concentric

con·duit (kän′dit or kän′doo wit) **n.** 1 a pipe or passage for carrying fluids, as a gas pipe, gutter, or sewer. 2 a tube for protecting electric wires or cables.

con·fed·er·a·tion (kən fed′ə rā′shən) **n.** 1 a uniting or being united in a league or alliance. 2 nations or states joined in a league, as for defense; alliance.

con·fer (kən fur′) **v.** 1 to give or grant [They *conferred* a medal upon the hero.] 2 to meet for a discussion; have a talk [The mayor will *confer* with the city council.] —**con·ferred′, con·fer′ring**

con·fron·ta·tion (kän′frən tā′shən) **n.** a face-to-face meeting, as of two persons who hold opposite views on some matter.

con·glom·er·ate (kən gläm′ə rāt) **v.** to form or collect into a rounded mass. —**con·glom′er·at·ed, con·glom′er·at·ing** ◆**adj.** (kən gläm′ər it) made up of separate parts or materials formed into one mass [A *conglomerate* rock is made up of pebbles and stones cemented together in hard clay and sand.] ◆**n.** (kən gläm′ər it) ☆2 a large corporation made up of a number of companies dealing in different products or services. —**con·glom′er·a′tion n.**

con·junc·tion (kən jungk′shən) **n.** 1 a joining together; combination [High winds, in *conjunction* with rain, made travel difficult.] 2 a word used to join other words, phrases, or clauses [*And, but, or, if,* etc. are *conjunctions.*]

con·quer (käng′kər) **v.** 1 to get or gain by using force, as by winning a war [The Spaniards *conquered* Mexico.] 2 to overcome by trying hard; get the better of; defeat [She *conquered* her bad habits.] —**con′quer·or n.**

con·ser·va·to·ry (kən sur′və tôr′ē) **n.** a school of music, art, etc. —pl. **con·ser·va·to′ries**

con·sol·i·date (kən säl′ə dāt) **v.** 1 to join together into one; unite; merge [The corporation was formed by *consolidating* many companies.] 2 to make or become strong or firm [The troops *consolidated* their position by bringing up heavy guns.] —**con·sol′i·dat·ed, con·sol′i·dat·ing** —**con·sol′i·da′tion n.**

con·spir·a·cy (kən spir′ə sē) **n.** 1 a secret plan by two or more people to do something bad or unlawful; plot [a *conspiracy* to kill the king]. 2 a working or joining together [A *conspiracy* of events kept me from the party.] —pl. **con·spir′a·cies**

con·tem·po·rar·y (kən tem′pə rer′ē) **adj.** existing or happening in the same period of time. ◆**n.** a person living in the same period as another [The painters Mary Cassatt and Edgar Degas were *contemporaries.*] —pl. **con·tem′po·rar′ies**

con·tra·band (kän′trə band) **n.** things that it is against the law to bring into or take out of a country; smuggled goods.

con·tra·dict (kän trə dikt′) **v. 1** to say the opposite of; deny the things said by someone [The witness *contradicted* the story told by the suspect.   Stop *contradicting* me.] **2** to be opposite to or different from; go against [The facts *contradict* your theory.]

Contradict comes from a Latin word that means "to speak against."   In English to contradict someone means "to deny what someone else has said," which is one way of speaking against that person.

con·trar·y (kän′trer ē) **adj. 1** opposite; completely different [to hold *contrary* opinions]. **2** opposed; being or acting against [*contrary* to the rules]. **3** (*often* kən trer′ē) opposing in a stubborn way; perverse [such a *contrary* child, always saying "No!"]. ◆**n.** the opposite [Just the *contrary* of what you say is true.]

con·trast (kən trast′) **v. 1** to compare in a way that shows the differences [to *contrast* France and England]. **2** to show differences when compared [Golf *contrasts* sharply with tennis as a sport.] ◆**n.** (kän′trast) **1** a difference between things being compared [the *contrast* between air and rail travel]. **2** something showing differences when compared with something else [Reading a novel is quite a *contrast* to seeing a movie based on the novel.]

con·trol·ler (kən trōl′ər) **n. 1** a person in charge of spending, as for a company or government. **2** a person or thing that controls.

con·tro·ver·sial (kän′trə vur′shəl) **adj.** that is or can be much argued about; debatable [a *controversial* book]. —**con′tro·ver′sial·ly adv.**

con·va·les·cent (kän′və les′′nt) **adj.** getting back health and strength after illness. ◆**n.** a convalescent person.

co·op·er·a·tive (kō äp′ər ə tiv *or* kō äp′rə tiv) **adj. 1** willing to cooperate; helpful. **2** that is or belongs to a group whose members produce goods together or sell them and share the profits [Local farmers have started a *cooperative* store.] ◆**n.** a cooperative group, store, etc.

co·or·di·nate (kō ôr′də nāt) **v.** to bring together in the proper relation; make work well together [She was able to *coordinate* the efforts of dozens of volunteers.] —**co·or′di·nat·ed, co·or′di·nat·ing**

co·pi·lot (kō′pī lət) **n.** the assistant pilot of an airplane.

cor·dial (kôr′jəl) **adj.** deeply felt; hearty; sincere [a *cordial* welcome]. ◆**n.** a sweet and rather thick alcoholic drink. —**cor′dial·ly adv.**

Co·rin·thi·an (kə rin′thē ən) **adj. 1** of Corinth. **2** describing a highly decorated style of ancient Greek architecture in which the columns have fancy carvings of leaves at the top.

cor·o·ner (kôr′ə nər) **n.** an official whose duty is to find out the cause of any death that does not seem to be due to natural causes.

cor·po·ra·tion (kôr′pə rā′shən) **n.** a group of people who get a charter that gives the group some of the legal powers and rights that one person has [Cities and colleges, as well as businesses, can be organized as *corporations*.]

cor·re·la·tion (kôr′ə lā′shən) **n.** the relation or connection between things [the high *correlation* between ignorance and prejudice].

cor·rupt (kə rupt′) **adj.** changed from good to bad; having become evil, rotten, dishonest, incorrect, etc. [*corrupt* officials; *corrupt* business practices; a *corrupt* version of a book]. ◆**v.** to make or become corrupt. —**cor·rupt′ly adv.**

cor·sage (kôr säzh′ *or* kôr säj′) **n.** ☆a small bunch of flowers for a woman to wear, as at the waist or shoulder.

cos·mo·pol·i·tan (käz′mə päl′ə t'n) **adj. 1** having to do with the world as a whole. **2** interested in and liking the people and cultures of all countries; feeling at home anywhere. ◆**n.** a cosmopolitan person.

cos·mos (käz′məs) **n. 1** the universe as a system with order. **2** any whole system with order.

cou·plet (kup′lit) **n.** two lines of poetry that go together and are usually rhymed. Example
He that fights and runs away
May live to fight another day.

cou·ri·er (koor′ē ər *or* kur′ē ər) **n.** a messenger sent in a hurry with an important message.

cour·te·sy (kur′tə sē) **n. 1** courteous or polite behavior; good manners [Thank you for your *courtesy* in writing to me.] **2** a polite act or remark. —*pl.* **cour′te·sies**

cre·scen·do (krə shen′dō) **adj., adv.** gradually becoming louder or stronger: *a direction in music shown by the sign* <. ◆**n.** a gradual increase in loudness. —*pl.* **cre·scen′dos**

cre·vasse (kri vas′) **n.** a deep crack or crevice, especially in a glacier.

crim·i·nal (krim′ə n'l) **adj. 1** being a crime; that is a crime [a *criminal* act]. **2** having to do with crime [*criminal* law]. ◆**n.** a person guilty of a crime. —**crim′i·nal·ly adv.**

cri·sis (krī′sis) **n. 1** any turning point, as in history. **2** a time of great danger or trouble. —*pl.* **cri·ses** (krī′sēz)

crit·i·cize (krit′ə sīz) **v. 1** to judge as a critic. **2** to find fault with; disapprove of [The boss *criticizes* everything I do.] —**crit′i·cized, crit′i·ciz·ing**

cri·tique (kri tēk′) **n.** a piece of writing that gives a careful judgment of a book, play, etc.

cro·quet (krō kā′) **n.** an outdoor game in which the players use mallets to drive a wooden ball through hoops in the ground.

corsage

a	ask, fat
ā	ape, date
ä	car, lot
e	elf, ten
er	berry, care
ē	even, meet
i	is, hit
ir	mirror, here
ī	ice, fire
ō	open, go
ô	law, horn
oi	oil, point
oo	look, pull
ōō	ooze, tool
yoo	unite, cure
yōō	cute, few
ou	out, crowd
u	up, cut
ur	fur, fern
ə	a in ago
	e in agent
	e in father
	i in unity
	o in collect
	u in focus
ch	chin, arch
ng	ring, singer
sh	she, dash
th	thin, truth
th	then, father
zh	s in pleasure
′	as in (ā′b'l)

davenport

cru·el (krōō′əl) *adj.* **1** liking to make others suffer; having no mercy or pity [The *cruel* Pharaoh made slaves of the Israelites.] **2** causing pain and suffering [*cruel* insults; a *cruel* winter]. —**cru′el·ly** *adv.*

crys·tal·lize (kris′tə līz) *v.* **1** to form crystals [Boil the maple syrup until it *crystallizes*.] **2** to take on or give a definite form [Their customs were *crystallized* into law.] —**crys′tal·lized, crys′tal·liz·ing** —**crys′tal·li·za′tion** *n.*

cu·ri·os·i·ty (kyoor′ē äs′ə tē) *n.* **1** a strong feeling of wanting to know or learn [*Curiosity* is a child's best teacher.] **2** a strange or unusual thing [A fire engine pulled by horses is now a *curiosity*.] —*pl.* **cu′ri·os′i·ties**

cus·tom·ar·y (kus′tə mer′ē) *adj.* in keeping with custom; usual [It is *customary* to tip a waiter or waitress.] —**cus′tom·ar′i·ly** *adv.*

cus·tom·er (kus′tə mər) *n.* a person who buys, especially one who buys regularly [I have been a *customer* of that shop for many years.]

Dd

daunt·less (dônt′lis) *adj.* that cannot be frightened or discouraged; fearless [The *dauntless* rebels fought on.] —**daunt′less·ly** *adv.*

dav·en·port (dav′ən pôrt) *n.* ☆a large sofa.

dec·ade (dek′ād) *n.* a period of ten years.

de·cant·er (di kan′tər) *n.* a decorative glass bottle.

de·ceased (di sēst′) *adj.* dead.

de·cep·tion (di sep′shən) *n.* **1** a deceiving or fooling. **2** something that fools, as a fraud.

dec·i·li·ter (des′ə lēt′ər) *n.* a unit of volume, equal to 1/10 liter.

dec·i·mal (des′ə m'l) *adj.* of or based upon the number ten; counted by tens [The metric system of measure is a *decimal* system.] ◆*n.* a fraction with a denominator of 10, or of 100 or 1,000, etc. It is shown by a point (**decimal point**) before the numerator, as .5 (5/10) or .63 (63/100).

dec·i·me·ter (des′ə mēt′ər) *n.* a measure of length, equal to 1/10 meter.

de·ci·sion (di sizh′ən) *n.* the act of deciding or settling something, or the opinion or choice decided on [The *decision* of the judges will be final.]

decanter

de·cline (di klīn′) *v.* **1** to bend or slope downward [The lawn *declines* to the sidewalk.] **2** to become less, as in health, power, or value; decay [A person's strength usually *declines* in old age.] **3** to refuse something, especially in a polite way [I am sorry I must *decline* your invitation.] —**de·clined′, de·clin′ing** ◆*n.* a becoming less, smaller, or weaker; decay [a *decline* in prices].

de·com·pose (dē kəm pōz′) *v.* **1** to rot or decay. **2** to break up into its separate basic parts [Water can be *decomposed* into hydrogen and oxygen.] —**de·com·posed′, de·com·pos′ing** —**de·com·po·si·tion** (dē′käm pə zish′ən) *n.*

de·cre·scen·do (dē′krə shen′dō) *adj., adv.* gradually becoming softer: *a direction in music usually shown by the sign* τ. ◆*n.* a decrease in loudness. —*pl.* **de′cre·scen′dos**

de·fense·less (di fens′lis) *adj.* having no defense; not able to protect oneself.

de·fer (di fur′) *v.* to put off until a later time; postpone [The judge *deferred* the trial until the following week.] —**de·ferred′, de·fer′ring** —**de·fer′ment** *n.*

def·i·ni·tion (def′ə nish′ən) *n.* **1** a defining or being defined. **2** a statement that tells what a thing is or what a word means. **3** the clearness or sharpness of an outline.

de·moc·ra·cy (di mäk′rə sē) *n.* **1** government in which the people hold the ruling power, usually giving it over to representatives whom they elect to make the laws and run the government. **2** a country, state, etc. with such government. **3** equal rights, opportunity, and treatment for all [The student council wants more *democracy* in our school.] —*pl.* **de·moc′ra·cies**

☆**dental hygienist** a dentist's assistant, who cleans teeth, takes X-rays of the teeth, etc.

de·pend·ent (di pen′dənt) *adj.* **1** controlled or decided by something else [The size of my allowance was *dependent* on our family income.] **2** relying on another for help or support [A baby is completely *dependent* on its parents.] ◆*n.* a person who depends on someone else for support.

de·plete (di plēt′) *v.* to empty or use up; exhaust [Lack of rain will soon *deplete* our water supply. My energy was *depleted*.] —**de·plet′ed, de·plet′ing** —**de·ple′tion** *n.*

de·pres·sant (di pres′ənt) *adj.* lowering the rate of nervous or muscular activity ◆*n.* a depressant drug; sedative.

de·pres·sion (di presh′ən) *n.* **1** sadness; gloominess [to suffer from a fit of *depression*]. **2** a hollow or low place [Water collected in the *depressions* in the ground.] ☆**3** a period during which there is less business and many people lose their jobs.

de·scend·ant (di sen′dənt) *n.* a person who is descended from a certain ancestor.

des·per·a·tion (des′pə rā′shən) *n.* **1** the condition of being desperate. **2** recklessness that comes from despair [In *desperation* the hunted deer leaped across the chasm.]

de·struc·tion (di struk′shən) *n.* the act of destroying or the condition of being destroyed; ruin [The forest fire caused much *destruction*.]

de·ter (di tʉr′) *v.* to keep a person from doing something through fear, doubt, etc.; discourage [Does the death penalty *deter* crime?] —**de·terred′, de·ter′ring**

de·ter·mine (di tʉr′mən) *v.* **1** to settle or decide on [I haven't *determined* whether to go to college.] **2** to set one's mind on something; resolve [She is *determined* to be a lawyer.] **3** to find out exactly [First *determine* the area of the floor.] **4** to be the thing that decides; have an important effect on [One's hobbies often *determine* what one chooses to do for a living.] —**de·ter′mined, de·ter′min·ing**

de·tour (dē′tŏŏr) *n.* **1** a turning aside from the direct or regular route. **2** a route used when the regular route is closed to traffic. ◆*v.* to go or send by a detour.

de·vice (di vīs′) *n.* something made or invented for some special use; tool, machine, etc. [A windmill is a *device* for putting wind power to work.]

di·ag·nose (dī əg nōs′) *v.* to make a diagnosis of. —**di·ag·nosed′, di·ag·nos′ing**

di·ag·no·sis (dī′əg nō′sis) *n.* **1** the act or practice of examining a patient and studying the symptoms to find out what disease the patient has. **2** a careful examination of all the facts in a situation to find out how it has been brought about [a *diagnosis* of the last election]. —*pl.* **di·ag·no·ses** (dī′əg nō′sēz)

di·a·logue or **di·a·log** (dī′ə lôg) *n.* **1** a talking together, especially an open exchange of ideas, as in an effort to understand each other's views. **2** the parts of a play, novel, radio or television program, etc. that are conversation.

di·a·mond (dī′mənd *or* dī′ə mənd) *n.* **1** a very precious stone, usually colorless, formed of nearly pure carbon. It is the hardest known mineral and is used as a gem, as the tip of a phonograph needle, and in the cutting edge of tools. **2** a figure shaped like this: ◇.

☆**di·e·ti·tian** or **di·e·ti·cian** (dī′ə tish′ən) *n.* a person whose work is planning diets that will give people the kinds and amounts of food that they need.

di·lap·i·dat·ed (di lap′ə dāt′id) *adj.* falling to pieces; broken down; shabby and neglected [a *dilapidated* barn].

di·lem·ma (di lem′ə) *n.* a situation in which one must choose between things that are equally unpleasant or dangerous; difficult choice.

di·min·ish (də min′ish) *v.* to make or become smaller in size or less in force, importance, etc. [Overpopulation *diminishes* the world food supply. Danger of frost *diminishes* in April.]

dis·ad·van·tage (dis′əd van′tij) *n.* **1** anything that stands in the way of success; handicap; drawback [A trick knee is a *disadvantage* to a baseball player.] **2** loss or harm [This decision will work to your *disadvantage*.] —**dis·ad·van·ta·geous** (dis ad′vən tā′jəs) *adj.*

dis·as·ter (di zas′tər) *n.* a happening that causes much damage or suffering, as a flood or earthquake; catastrophe. —**dis·as′trous** *adj.*

dis·mal (diz′m'l) *adj.* **1** causing gloom or misery; sad [a *dismal* story]. **2** dark and gloomy [a *dismal* room]. —**dis′mal·ly** *adv.*

Dismal comes from two Latin words meaning "evil days." In the Middle Ages certain days of the year were thought to be unlucky or evil. These "evil days" made people sad. In time, anything that made people sad could be called dismal.

dis·pen·sa·ry (dis pen′sə rē) *n.* a room or place, as in a school, where a person can get medicines or first-aid treatment. —*pl.* **dis·pen′sa·ries**

dis·perse (dis pʉrs′) *v.* to break up and scatter; spread in all directions [The crowd began to *disperse* after the game was over. The wind *dispersed* the clouds.] —**dis·persed′, dis·pers′ing** —**dis·per′sal** or **dis·per′sion** *n.*

dis·pute (dis pyŏŏt′) *v.* **1** to argue or discuss a question; debate or quarrel. **2** to question or deny the truth of [The U.S. *disputed* Spain's claim to Cuba.] —**dis·put′ed, dis·put′ing** ◆*n.* a disputing; argument, debate, etc.

dis·re·spect (dis′ri spekt′) *n.* lack of respect or politeness; rudeness. —**dis′re·spect′ful** *adj.* —**dis′re·spect′ful·ly** *adv.*

dis·rupt (dis rupt′) *v.* **1** to break apart. **2** to disturb the orderly course of [A few noisy members *disrupted* the meeting.] —**dis·rup′tion** *n.*

dis·sat·is·fac·tion (dis sat′is fak′shən) *n.* the condition of being dissatisfied; discontent.

dis·sim·i·lar (di sim′ə lər) *adj.* not alike; different. —**dis·sim·i·lar·i·ty** (di sim′ə lar′ə tē) *n.*

dis·solve (di zälv′) *v.* **1** to make or become liquid, as by melting in a liquid [to *dissolve* sugar in coffee]. **2** to break up and disappear or make disappear [Our courage *dissolved* in the face of danger.] **3** to bring or come to an end; finish [They *dissolved* their partnership.] —**dis·solved′, dis·solv′ing**

a	ask, fat
ā	ape, date
ä	car, lot
e	elf, ten
er	berry, care
ē	even, meet
i	is, hit
ir	mirror, here
ī	ice, fire
ō	open, go
ô	law, horn
oi	oil, point
ŏŏ	look, pull
ōō	ooze, tool
yŏŏ	unite, cure
yōō	cute, few
ou	out, crowd
u	up, cut
ʉr	fur, fern
ə	a in ago
	e in agent
	e in father
	i in unity
	o in collect
	u in focus
ch	chin, arch
ng	ring, singer
sh	she, dash
th	thin, truth
th	then, father
zh	s in pleasure
′	as in (ā′b'l)

dis·tort (dis tôrt') **v. 1** to twist out of its usual shape or look [The old mirror gave a *distorted* reflection.] **2** to change so as to give a false idea [The facts were *distorted*.] **3** to make a sound or signal sound different when reproduced [The sound of music is *distorted* on my new radio.] —**dis·tor′tion** *n.*

dis·tri·bu·tion (dis′trə byoo′shən) *n.* the act or way of distributing something [a *distribution* of funds; a fair *distribution*]. —**dis·trib·u·tive** (dis trib′yoo tiv) *adj.*

di·ver·si·ty (də vʉr′sə tē) *n.* **1** the condition of being different or varied; difference [The male and female cardinal show a *diversity* in plumage.] **2** variety [a *diversity* of opinions]. —*pl.* **di·ver′si·ties**

doc·u·men·ta·ry (däk′yə men′tə rē) *adj.* **1** made up of documents [You must show *documentary* proof of age.] **2** that shows or presents news events, social conditions, etc. in a story based mainly on facts [a *documentary* film]. ◆*n.* a documentary film, TV show, etc. —*pl.* **doc′u·men′ta·ries**

dom·i·nate (däm′ə nāt) *v.* **1** to control or rule; be most important or powerful [A desire to win *dominates* all her actions. The colonies were *dominated* by the mother country.] **2** to tower over; rise high above [These tall buildings *dominate* the city.] —**dom′i·nat·ed, dom′i·nat·ing** —**dom′i·na′tion** *n.*

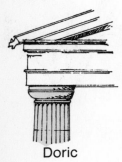

Doric

Dominate comes from the Latin word for "master," *dominus,* and so do the words **domineer** and **dominion.**

do·min·ion (də min′yən) *n.* **1** the power of governing; rule. **2** a territory or country ruled over.

Dor·ic (dôr′ik) *adj.* describing the oldest and plainest style of Greek architecture. The columns have no fancy carving at the top.

drap·er·y (drā′pər ē) *n.* a curtain or other cloth hanging in loose folds. —*pl.* **drap′er·ies**

drapery

driz·zle (driz′'l) *v.* to rain lightly in fine drops. —**driz′zled, driz′zling** —**driz′zly** *adj.*

du·et (doo et′ *or* dyoo et′) *n.* **1** a piece of music for two voices or two instruments. **2** the two people who sing or play it.

du·plex (doo′pleks *or* dyoo′pleks) *adj.* having two parts or units; double [a *duplex* house]. ◆☆*n. a shorter form of* **duplex house.**

du·pli·cate (doo′plə kit *or* dyoo′plə kit) *adj.* **1** exactly like another or like each other [*duplicate* keys]. **2** double. ◆*n.* a thing exactly like another; an exact copy [The typist made a *duplicate* of the letter.] ◆*v.* (doo′plə kāt *or* dyoo′plə kāt) to make an exact copy or copies of. —**du′pli·cat·ed, du′pli·cat·ing**—**du′pli·ca′tion** *n.*

dy·nam·ic (dī nam′ik) *adj.* **1** having to do with energy or force in action. **2** full of energy or power; forceful; vigorous [a *dynamic* person]. —**dy·nam′i·cal·ly** *adv.*

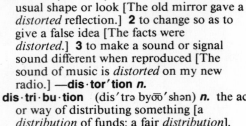

Ee

ec·cen·tric (ik sen′trik) *adj.* not usual or normal in the way one behaves; odd or queer [an *eccentric* old hermit].◆*n.* an eccentric person. —**ec·cen′tri·cal·ly** *adv.*

e·clipse (i klips′) *n.* **1** a hiding of all or part of the sun by the moon when it passes between the sun and the earth (called a **solar eclipse**); also, a hiding of the moon by the earth's shadow (called a **lunar eclipse**). **2** a becoming dim or less brilliant [Her fame went into an *eclipse*.] ◆*v.* to cause an eclipse of; darken. —**e·clipsed′, e·clips′ing**

e·co·nom·i·cal (ē′kə näm′i k'l *or* ek′ə näm′i k'l) *adj.* not wasting money, time, material, etc.; thrifty [an *economical* person; an *economical* car]. —**e′co·nom′i·cal·ly** *adv.*

e·con·o·mize (i kän′ə mīz) *v.* to be economical or to cut down on expenses. [She *economized* by riding a bus to work.] —**e·con′o·mized, e·con′o·miz·ing**

ed·i·to·ri·al (ed′ə tôr′ē əl) *adj.* of or by an editor [*editorial* offices]. ◆☆*n.* an article in a newspaper or magazine, or a talk on radio or TV, that openly gives the opinion of the editor, publisher, or owner. —**ed′i·to′ri·al·ly** *adv.*

e·las·tic (i las′tik) *adj.* **1** able to spring back into shape or position after being stretched or squeezed; springy [an *elastic* rubber ball]. **2** that can easily be changed to fit conditions; adaptable [*elastic* rules]. ◆*n.* any cloth or tape with rubber or rubberlike threads running through it to make it elastic. —**e·las′ti·cal·ly** *adv.*

☆**e·lec·tri·cian** (i lek′trish′ən) *n.* a person whose work is setting up or fixing electrical equipment.

The word **electrician** was made up by Benjamin Franklin, who was one of the first people to study and experiment with electricity.

e·lec·tro·mag·net (i lek′trō mag′nit) *n.* a piece of soft iron with a coil of wire around it, that becomes a magnet when an electric current passes through the wire. —**e·lec·tro·mag·net·ic** (i lek′trō mag net′ik) *adj.*

el·i·gi·ble (el′i jə b'l) *adj.* having the qualities or conditions that are required; qualified [Is the caretaker *eligible* for a pension?] —**el′i·gi·bil′i·ty** *n.*

el·o·quent (el′ə kwənt) *adj.* **1** having eloquence; stirring people's feelings or having an effect on how they think [an *eloquent* plea to a jury]. **2** showing much feeling [an *eloquent* sigh of relief]. —**el′o·quent·ly** *adv.*

El Sal·va·dor (el sal′və dôr) a country in western Central America.

em·bry·o (em′brē ō) *n.* **1** an animal in the first stages of its growth, while it is in the egg or in the uterus. **2** the part of a seed from which a plant develops. —*pl.* **em′bry·os**

em·i·nent (em′ə nənt) *adj.* standing above most others in rank, worth, fame, etc.; very famous [an *eminent* scientist]. —**em′i·nent·ly** *adv.*

em·phat·ic (im fat′ik) *adj.* **1** said or done with emphasis, or special force [She agreed with an *emphatic* nod.] **2** without doubt; definite [an *emphatic* defeat]. —**em·phat′i·cal·ly** *adv.*

en·cap·su·late (in kap′sə lāt *or* in kap′syoo lāt) *v.* to enclose in a capsule or in something like a capsule. —**en·cap′su·lat·ed, en·cap′su·lat·ing**

en·dive (en′dīv *or* än′dēv) *n.* a plant with ragged, curly leaves that are used in salads.

en·ter·prise (en′tər prīz) *n.* **1** any business or undertaking, especially one that takes daring and energy. **2** willingness to undertake new or risky projects [They succeeded because of their *enterprise*.]

en·thu·si·asm (in thoo′zē az'm) *n.* a strong liking or interest [an *enthusiasm* for baseball].

Enthusiasm comes from a Greek word meaning "inspired by a god." Poets and prophets long ago were thought to be inspired by a god. The earliest meaning of *enthusiasm* was "the inspiration of a poet or prophet."

en·tire (in tīr′) *adj.* **1** including all the parts; whole; complete [I've read the *entire* book.] **2** not broken, not weakened, not lessened, etc. [We have his *entire* support.] —**en·tire′ly** *adv.*

e·nun·ci·ate (i nun′sē āt) *v.* **1** to speak or pronounce words [A telephone operator must *enunciate* clearly.] **2** to state clearly; announce [to *enunciate* a theory]. —**e·nun′ci·at·ed, e·nun′ci·at·ing** —**e·nun·ci·a′tion** *n.*

en·zyme (en′zīm) *n.* a substance produced in plant and animal cells that causes a chemical change in other substances but is not changed itself [Pepsin is an *enzyme* in the stomach that helps to digest food.]

ep·i·der·mis (ep′ə dur′mis) *n.* the outer layer of the skin of animals. It has no blood vessels.

ep·i·gram (ep′ə gram) *n.* a short saying that makes its point in a witty or clever way ["Experience is the name everyone gives to his mistakes" is an *epigram*.] —**ep·i·gram·mat·ic** (ep′i grə mat′ik) *adj.*

ep·i·logue *or* **ep·i·log** (ep′ə lôg) *n.* a part added at the end of a play, novel, etc., in which the author makes some comment; especially, a closing speech to the audience by one of the actors in a play.

ep·i·sode (ep′ə sōd) *n.* any happening or incident that forms part of a whole story, life, history, etc. [The surrender at Appomattox was the last *episode* of the Civil War.]

e·pis·tle (i pis′'l) *n.* **1** a letter: *now used in a joking way.* **2** **Epistle,** any of the letters written by the Apostles and included as books of the New Testament.

ep·i·taph (ep′ə taf) *n.* words carved on a tomb in memory of the person buried there.

ep·i·thet (ep′ə thet) *n.* a word or phrase that describes a person or thing by naming some quality or feature, as America *the Beautiful.*

Epithet comes from a Greek word meaning "something that is put on, or added." An epithet is a description that is added to the regular name.

e·qual (ē′kwəl) *adj.* **1** of the same amount, size, or value [The horses were of *equal* height.] **2** having the same rights, ability, or position [All persons are *equal* in a court of law in a just society.] ◆*n.* any person or thing that is equal [As a sculptor, she has few *equals*.] ◆*v.* **1** to be equal to; match [His long jump *equaled* the school record. Six minus two *equals* four.] **2** to do or make something equal to [You can *equal* my score easily.] —**e′qualed** *or* **e′qualled, e′qual·ing** *or* **e′qual·ling** —**e′qual·ly** *adv.*

e·quiv·a·lent (i kwiv′ə lənt) *adj.* equal or the same in amount, value, meaning, etc. ◆*n.* something that is equal or the same [Three teaspoonfuls are the *equivalent* of one tablespoonful.] —**e·quiv′a·lence** *n.*

e·ro·sion (i rō′zhən) *n.* an eroding or wearing away [the *erosion* of soil by water and wind].

es·ca·pade (es′kə pād) *n.* a daring or reckless adventure or prank.

es·pe·cial·ly (ə spesh′əl ē) *adv.* mainly; in particular; specially [I like all fruit, but I am *especially* fond of pears.]

et·i·quette (et′i kət *or* et′i ket) *n.* rules that society has set up for the proper way to behave in dealing with other people; good manners [The best *etiquette* is based on being kind and polite to other people.]

Etiquette is a French word that actually means "ticket," "label," or "list." It was first used of the lists of rules that were posted in a court or army camp. We might also say that **etiquette** can be a "ticket" that allows a person to enter polite society.

eu·lo·gy (yoo′lə jē) *n.* a speech or writing praising a person or thing; often, a formal speech praising a person who has just died. —*pl.* **eu′lo·gies**

endive

a	ask, fat
ā	ape, date
ä	car, lot
e	elf, ten
er	berry, care
ē	even, meet
i	is, hit
ir	mirror, here
ī	ice, fire
ō	open, go
ô	law, horn
oi	oil, point
oo	look, pull
oo	ooze, tool
yoo	unite, cure
yoo	cute, few
ou	out, crowd
u	up, cut
ur	fur, fern
ə	a in ago
	e in agent
	e in father
	i in unity
	o in collect
	u in focus
ch	chin, arch
ng	ring, singer
sh	she, dash
th	thin, truth
th	then, father
zh	s in pleasure
'	as in (ā′b'l)

eu·phe·mism (yōō′fə miz′m) *n.* **1** a word or phrase that is used in place of another that is thought to be too strong or unpleasant ["Remains" is a *euphemism* for "corpse."] **2** the use of such words or phrases. —**eu′phe·mis′tic** *adj.*

eu·pho·ri·a (yōō fôr′ ē ə) *n.* an exaggerated feeling of well-being and high spirits having no obvious cause.

e·ven·tu·al·i·ty (i ven′chōō wal′ə tē) *n.* a possible happening [Be prepared for any *eventuality.*] —*pl.* **e·ven′tu·al′i·ties**

ex·cess (ik ses′ *or* ek′ses) *n.* **1** more than what is needed or proper; too much [Eating an *excess* of candy will harm the teeth.] **2** the amount by which one quantity is greater than another [After paying all my bills, I had an *excess* of $50 last month.] ◆*adj.* (*usually* ek′ses) more than the usual limit; extra [Airlines charge for *excess* luggage.]

ex·cit·a·ble (ik sīt′ə b'l) *adj.* easily excited. —**ex·cit′a·bil′i·ty** *n.*

ex·cla·ma·tion (eks′klə mā′shən) *n.* **1** the act of exclaiming. **2** a word or phrase that is exclaimed to show strong feeling; interjection ["Oh!" and "Help!" are *exclamations.*]

ex·clude (iks klōōd′) *v.* to keep out or shut out; refuse to let in, think about, include, etc.; bar [They *excluded* John from their club. Don't *exclude* the possibility of defeat.] —**ex·clud′ed, ex·clud′ing**

ex·clu·sive (iks klōō′siv) *adj.* **1** given or belonging to no other; not shared; sole [That store has the *exclusive* right to sell this Swedish glassware.] **2** keeping out certain people, especially those who are not wealthy or against whom there is prejudice; not open to the public [an *exclusive* club]. **3** shutting out all other interests, thoughts, activities, etc. [an *exclusive* interest in sports]. —**ex·clu′sive·ly** *adv.*

ex·hib·it (ig zib′it) *v.* **1** to show or display to the public [to *exhibit* stamp collections]. **2** to show or reveal [Such an act *exhibits* great courage.] ◆*n.* **1** something exhibited to the public [an art *exhibit*]. **2** something shown as evidence in a court of law.

ex·hil·a·rate (ig zil′ə rāt) *v.* to make feel cheerful and lively [I was *exhilarated* by the fresh air.] —**ex·hil′a·rat·ed, ex·hil′a·rat·ing** —**ex·hil′a·ra′tion** *n.*

ex·or·bi·tant (ig zôr′bə tənt) *adj.* too much or too great; not reasonable or not fair [an *exorbitant* price]. —**ex·or′bi·tance** *n.*

ex·pec·ta·tion (ek′spek tā′shən) *n.* **1** the act of expecting, or looking forward to something [He sat on the edge of his seat in *expectation.*] **2** *often* **expectations,** *pl.* something expected, or looked forward to, especially with good reason [She has *expectations* of being promoted to a better job.]

ex·pel (ik spel′) *v.* **1** to drive out or throw out with force; eject [a tea kettle *expelling* steam through its spout]. **2** to send away or make leave as a punishment [Paul was *expelled* from the club because he failed to pay his dues.] —**ex·pelled′, ex·pel′ling**

ex·pense (ik spens′) *n.* **1** the act of spending money, time, etc. **2** *also* **expenses,** *pl.* the amount of money spent; often, money spent or needed for carrying out a job [Many salespersons are paid a salary, plus traveling *expenses.*] **3** something that causes spending [Owning a car is a great *expense.*] **4** loss or sacrifice [The battle was won at terrible *expense.*]

ex·per·i·men·tal (ik sper′ə men′t'l) *adj.* **1** based on or having to do with experiment [an *experimental* science]. **2** being an experiment; testing; trial [a baby's first, *experimental* steps]. —**ex·per′i·men′tal·ly** *adv.*

ex·pire (ik spīr′) *v.* **1** to come to an end; stop [The lease *expires* next month.] **2** to die. **3** to breathe out. —**ex·pired′, ex·pir′ing**

ex·po·si·tion (eks′pə zish′ən) *n.* **1** a large show or fair that is open to the public [Chicago held a great *exposition* in 1893.] **2** explanation, or some writing or speaking that explains something [Your *exposition* of the play was helpful.]

ex·po·sure (ik spō′zhər) *n.* **1** the act of exposing [the *exposure* of a plot]. **2** the fact of being exposed [tanned by *exposure* to the sun]. **3** the position of a house, etc., described by the direction from which it is exposed to sun and wind [Our kitchen has a southern *exposure.*] **4** the time during which film in a camera is exposed to light; also, a section of film that can be made into one picture [Give this film a short *exposure.* There are twelve *exposures* on this film.]

ex·ter·mi·nate (ik stur′mə nāt) *v.* to kill or destroy completely; wipe out [That company's work is *exterminating* rats.] —**ex·ter′mi·nat·ed, ex·ter′mi·nat·ing** —**ex·ter′mi·na′tion** *n.* —**ex·ter′mi·na·tor** *n.*

ex·traor·di·nar·y (ik strôr′d'n er′ē) *adj.* much different from the ordinary; very unusual; remarkable [*extraordinary* skill]. —**ex·traor′di·nar′i·ly** *adv.*

fab·ri·cate (fab′rə kāt) **v. 1** to make or build by putting parts together; manufacture. **2** to make up; invent [He *fabricated* an excuse for being late. In other words, he told a lie.] —**fab′ri·cat·ed, fab′ri·cat·ing** —**fab′ri·ca′tion** *n.* —**fab′ri·ca′tor** *n.*

fa·çade or **fa·cade** (fə sä′) *n.* **1** the front of a building. **2** a grand or fine front that is meant to conceal something not at all grand.

fac·et (fas′it) *n.* **1** any of the many polished sides of a cut gem, as a diamond. **2** any of the various sides or appearances [the many *facets* of someone's personality].

fa·cil·i·ty (fə sil′ə tē) *n.* **1** ease or skill in working or acting [She reads French with great *facility*.] **2** usually **facilities**, *pl.* a thing that helps one do something [The apartment has its own laundry *facilities*.] **3** a building or room for some activity [This added wing is a new *facility* for the nursery school.] —*pl.* **fa·cil′i·ties**

fac·tion (fak′shən) *n.* **1** a group of people inside a political party, club, government, etc. working together against other such groups for its own ideas or goals. **2** an arguing or quarreling among the members of a group [bitter *faction* in the Senate over taxes]. —**fac′tion·al** *adj.*

fal·la·cy (fal′ə sē) *n.* **1** a false or mistaken idea, opinion, etc. **2** false reasoning. —*pl.* **fal′la·cies**

fas·ci·nate (fas′ə nāt) *v.* to hold the attention of by being interesting or delightful; charm [The puppet show *fascinated* the children.] —**fas′ci·nat·ed, fas′ci·nat·ing** —**fas′ci·na′tion** *n.*

fer·til·ize (fur′t'l īz) *v.* **1** to make fertile, especially by adding fertilizer to [*Fertilize* your lawn in the spring.] **2** to bring a male germ cell to a female egg cell so as to cause a new animal or plant to develop [Bees *fertilize* flowers by carrying pollen from one to another.] —**fer′til·ized, fer′til·iz·ing** —**fer′til·i·za′tion** *n.*

fe·tus (fēt′əs) *n.* a human being or an animal in the later stages of its growth inside the uterus or egg. —*pl.* **fe′tus·es**

fi·an·cée (fē′än sā′) *n.* the woman who is engaged to marry a certain man.

fic·tion (fik′shən) *n.* **1** a piece of writing about imaginary people and happenings, as a novel, play, or story; also, such writings as a group. **2** something made up or imagined [What she said about her uncle is just a *fiction*.] —**fic′tion·al** *adj.*

fi·nesse (fi nes′) *n.* **1** skill in taking care of difficult or touchy problems without causing anger [to show *finesse* in dealing with customers]. **2** delicate or skillful work [the *finesse* with which the artist drew a portrait].

fi·nite (fī′nīt) *adj.* having definite limits; that can be measured [*finite* distances].

fis·cal (fis′kəl) *adj.* having to do with money matters; financial. —**fis′cal·ly** *adv.*

flex·i·ble (flek′sə b'l) *adj.* **1** that bends easily without breaking [a *flexible* rubber hose]. **2** easily changed or managed [Our doctor has *flexible* office hours.] —**flex′i·bil′i·ty** *n.*

for·bid (fər bid′) *v.* to order that something not be done; not allow; prohibit [The law *forbids* you to park your car there. Talking out loud is *forbidden* in the library.] —**for·bade′** or **for·bad′, for·bid′den, for·bid′ding**

for·mal·i·ty (fôr mal′ə tē) *n.* **1** the condition of being formal; especially, the following of rules or customs in an exact way. **2** a formal act or ceremony [the *formalities* of graduation exercises]. —*pl.* **for·mal′i·ties**

frag·ment (frag′mənt) *n.* **1** a piece of something that has broken; a part broken away [*fragments* of a broken cup]. **2** a part taken from a whole [a *fragment* of a song].

franc (fraŋk) *n.* the basic unit of money in France, and also in Belgium, Switzerland, etc.

fran·chise (fran′chīz) *n.* **1** a special right or permission given by a government [One must get a *franchise* from the Federal government to operate a TV station.] **2** the right given to a dealer to sell the products of a certain company.

fra·ter·nal (frə tur′n'l) *adj.* of or like brothers; brotherly.

fra·ter·ni·ty (frə tur′nə tē) *n.* **1** the close tie among brothers; brotherly feeling. **2** a club of men or boys, especially a social club, as in a college. Fraternities usually have letters of the Greek alphabet for their name. **3** a group of people with the same work, interests, beliefs, etc. [Doctors are often called the medical *fraternity*.] —*pl.* **fra·ter′ni·ties**

fre·quen·cy (frē′kwən sē) *n.* **1** the fact of being frequent, or happening often. **2** the number of times something is repeated in a certain period [a *frequency* of 1,000 vibrations per second]. The frequency of radio waves is measured in hertz. —*pl.* **fre′quen·cies**

fric·tion (frik′shən) *n.* **1** a rubbing of one thing against another. **2** arguments or quarrels caused by differences of opinions. **3** the force that slows down the motion of surfaces that touch [Ball bearings lessen *friction* in machines.]

a	ask, fat
ā	ape, date
ä	car, lot
e	elf, ten
er	berry, care
ē	even, meet
i	is, hit
ir	mirror, here
ī	ice, fire
ō	open, go
ô	law, horn
oi	oil, point
o͝o	look, pull
o͞o	ooze, tool
yo͞o	unite, cure
yo͞o	cute, few
ou	out, crowd
u	up, cut
ur	fur, fern
ə	a in ago
	e in agent
	e in father
	i in unity
	o in collect
	u in focus
ch	chin, arch
ŋ	ring, singer
sh	she, dash
th	thin, truth
th	then, father
zh	s in pleasure
′	as in (ā′b'l)

frieze

frieze (frēz) *n.* a band of designs, drawings, or carvings used as a decoration along a wall or around a room.

ful·fill or **ful·fil** (fool fil′) *v.* to make happen; carry out, perform, do, complete, etc. [to *fulfill* a promise, a duty, a purpose, a mission]. —**ful·filled′, ful·fill′ing** —**ful·fill′ment** or **ful·fil′ment** *n.*

fun·gus (fuŋ′gəs) *n.* a plant that has no leaves, flowers, or green color. Mildews, molds, mushrooms, and toadstools are forms of fungus. —*pl.* **fun·gi** (fun′jī or fuŋ′gī) or **fun′gus·es**

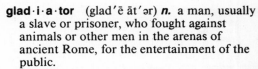

gar·goyle (gär′goil) *n.* a decoration on a building in the form of a strange, imaginary creature. It usually has a channel to let rain water run off through its mouth.

☆**gas·o·line** or **gas·o·lene** (gas ə lēn′ or gas′ə lēn) *n.* a pale liquid that burns very easily and is used mainly as a motor fuel. It is made from petroleum.

gen·er·os·i·ty (jen′ə räs′ə tē) *n.* **1** the quality of being generous. **2** a generous or unselfish act. —*pl.* **gen′er·os′i·ties**

ge·net·ics (jə net′iks) *n.pl.* the study of the way animals and plants pass on to their offspring such characteristics as size, color, etc.; science of heredity: *used with a singular verb.* —**ge·net′ic** *adj.*

ge·o·des·ic (jē′ə des′ik or jē′ə dē′sik) *adj.* ☆having a strong surface made of short, straight bars joined together in a framework [a *geodesic* dome].

ge·o·graph·i·cal (jē′ə graf′i k′l) or **ge·o·graph·ic** (jē′ə graf′ik) *adj.* having to do with geography —**ge·o·graph′i·cal·ly** *adv.*

ge·o·log·ic (jē′ə läj′ik) or **ge·o·log·i·cal** (jē′ə läj′i k′l) *adj.* having to do with geology —**ge·o·olog·′i·cal·ly** *adv.*

ge·om·e·tric (jē′ə met′rik) or **ge·o·met·ri·cal** *adj.* **1** having to do with geometry. **2** formed of straight lines, triangles, circles, etc. [a *geometric* pattern].

ger·und (jer′ənd) *n.* a verb ending in *-ing* that is used as a noun. A gerund can take an object [In "Playing golf is my only exercise," the word "playing" is a *gerund*.]

gey·ser (gī′zər) *n.* a spring that shoots streams of boiling water and steam up into the air from time to time.

gla·cier (glā′shər) *n.* a large mass of ice and snow that moves very slowly down a mountain or across land until it melts. Icebergs are pieces of a glacier that have broken away into the sea.

gargoyle

glad·i·a·tor (glad′ē āt′ər) *n.* a man, usually a slave or prisoner, who fought against animals or other men in the arenas of ancient Rome, for the entertainment of the public.

glos·sa·ry (gläs′ə rē or glôs′ə rē) *n.* a list of hard words with their meanings, often printed at the end of a book. —*pl.* **glos′sa·ries**

> **Glossary** comes from a Greek word meaning "tongue." And since the tongue is so important in forming words when we speak, it is easy to see the connection between that old Greek word and our modern term for a list of words.

gram·mar (gram′ər) *n.* **1** the study of the forms of words and of the way they are arranged in phrases and sentences. **2** a system of rules for speaking and writing a particular language. **3** a book containing such rules. **4** the way a person speaks or writes, as judged by these rules [His *grammar* is poor.]

grat·i·tude (grat′ə tōōd or grat′ə tyōōd) *n.* the condition of being grateful for some favor; thankfulness.

guard·i·an (gär′dē ən) *n.* **1** a person chosen by a court to take charge of a child or of someone else who cannot take care of his or her own affairs. **2** a person who guards or protects; custodian [A sexton is a *guardian* of church property.] —**guard′i·an·ship′** *n.*

Gua·te·ma·la (gwä′tə mä′lə) a country in Central America, south and east of Mexico.

guild (gild) *n.* **1** in the Middle Ages, a union of men in the same craft or trade to keep the quality of work high and to protect the members. **2** any group of people joined together in some work or for some purpose [The Ladies' *Guild* of the church is planning a supper.]

guil·der (gil′dər) *n.* the basic unit of money in the Netherlands.

gur·ney (gur′nē) *n.* a stretcher or cot on wheels, used in hospitals to move people who are sick or hurt. —*pl.* **gur′neys**

hand·i·cap (han′dē kap) *n.* **1** a race or other contest in which things are made harder for some or easier for others so that all have an equal chance. **2** something that holds a person back or makes things harder; hindrance [Lack of education can be a great *handicap*.] ◆*v.* to be or give a handicap; make things harder for. —**hand′i·capped, hand′i·cap·ping**

hydrant

har·mo·nize (här′mə nīz) **v. 1** to be, sing, or play in harmony [Those colors *harmonize* well.   The voices *harmonized* in a quartet.] **2** to bring into harmony [to *harmonize* the colors in a room; to *harmonize* a melody]. —**har′mo·nized, har′mo·niz·ing**

har·row·ing (har′ō ing) **adj.** causing pain, fear, or discomfort [The fire was a *harrowing* experience.]

he·red·i·ty (hə red′ə tē) **n. 1** the passing on of certain characteristics from parent to offspring by means of genes in the chromosomes [The color of one's hair is determined by *heredity*.] **2** all the characteristics passed on in this way [Their good health is due to their *heredity*.]

hom·o·nym (häm′ə nim) **n.** a word that is pronounced like another word but that has a different meaning and is usually spelled differently ["Bore" and "boar" are *homonyms*.]

hor·ti·cul·ture (hôr′tə kul′chər) **n.** the science of growing flowers, fruits, and vegetables. —**hor′ti·cul′tur·al adj.** —**hor′ti·cul′tur·ist n.**

hos·pice (häs′pis) **n. 1** a kind of inn where travelers can stop for rest and food, especially one run by monks. **2** a place with a homelike feeling where patients who are dying of some disease are taken care of and made comfortable.

hos·pi·tal·i·ty (häs′pə tal′ə tē) **n.** a friendly and generous way of treating guests.

hos·pi·tal·ize (häs′pi t'l īz′) **v.** to put in a hospital [I was *hospitalized* for a week when I broke my leg.] —**hos′pi·tal·ized′, hos′pi·tal·iz′ing**

hos·tage (häs′tij) **n.** a person given to or taken by an enemy and held prisoner until certain things are done.

hos·tel (häs′t'l) **n.** an inn or other place for staying overnight; now often, a shelter for use by hikers.

hos·tile (häs′t'l) **adj. 1** of or like an enemy; warlike [*hostile* tribes]. **2** having or showing hate or dislike; unfriendly [a *hostile* look]. —**hos′tile·ly adv.**

☆**hy·drant** (hī′drənt) **n.** a closed pipe at a street curb, with a spout that can be opened up so as to draw water from a main waterline; fireplug.

hy·drau·lic (hī drô′lik) **adj. 1** worked by the force of a moving liquid [*hydraulic* brakes]. **2** hardening under water [*hydraulic* cement]. **3** having to do with hydraulics. —**hy·drau′li·cal·ly adv.**

hy·dro·plane (hī′drə plān) **n. 1** a small motorboat that skims along on the back of its hull at high speeds. **2** *another name for* **seaplane.**

hy·gi·en·ist (hī′jē ə nist *or* hī jē′nist) **n.** an expert in hygiene, or the rules of health.

hy·per·ten·sion (hī′pər ten′shən) **n.** blood pressure that is much higher than normal.

hys·ter·i·cal (his ter′i k'l) **adj. 1** of or like hysteria. **2** having or likely to have wild fits of laughing, crying, etc. **3** very funny or comical.   *Also* **hys·ter′ic.** —**hys·ter′i·cal·ly adv.**

i·den·ti·cal (ī den′ti k'l) **adj. 1** the very same [This is the *identical* house where I was born.] **2** exactly alike [These two pictures are *identical*.] —**i·den′ti·cal·ly adv.**

id·i·om (id′ē əm) **n. 1** a phrase or expression that has a meaning different from what the words suggest in their usual meaning ["To catch one's eye," meaning "to get one's attention," is an *idiom*.] **2** the way in which a certain people, writer, group, etc. puts words together to express meaning [the Italian *idiom*; the *idiom* of Shakespeare]. —**id·i·o·mat′ic** (id′ē ə mat′ik) **adj.** —**id′i·o·mat′i·cal·ly adv.**

ig·ne·ous (ig′nē əs) **adj.** formed by fire or great heat, especially by the action of volcanoes [Granite is an *igneous* rock.]

im·mac·u·late (i mak′yə lit) **adj. 1** perfectly clean; spotless [an *immaculate* kitchen]. **2** without sin; pure [the *immaculate* life of a saint]. —**im·mac′u·late·ly adv.**

im·mense (i mens′) **adj.** very large; huge; vast [an *immense* territory]. —**im·mense′ly adv.**

im·mi·grate (im′ə grāt) **v.** to come into a foreign country to make one's home [Over 15 million persons *immigrated* into the United States from 1900 to 1955.] —**im′mi·grat·ed, im′mi·grat·ing** —**im′mi·gra′tion n.**

im·mo·bi·lize (i mō′bə līz) **v.** to make immobile; keep from moving. —**im·mo′bi·lized, im·mo′bi·liz·ing**

im·pa·tient (im pā′shənt) **adj. 1** not patient; not willing to put up with delay, annoyance, etc. [Some parents become *impatient* when their children cry.] **2** eager to do something or for something to happen [Rita is *impatient* to go swimming.] —**im·pa′tient·ly adv.**

im·pend (im pend′) **v.** to be about to happen; threaten [Disaster seemed to be *impending*.]

im·per·son·ate (im pur′sə nāt) **v. 1** to imitate or mimic in fun [The students *impersonated* their teachers in the school play.] **2** to pretend to be in order to cheat or trick [He was arrested for *impersonating* a police officer.] —**im·per′son·at·ed, im·per′son·at·ing** —**im·per′son·a′tion n.** —**im·per′son·a′tor n.**

a	ask, fat
ā	ape, date
ä	car, lot
e	elf, ten
er	berry, care
ē	even, meet
i	is, hit
ir	mirror, here
ī	ice, fire
ō	open, go
ô	law, horn
oi	oil, point
͞oo	look, pull
͞oo	ooze, tool
yoo	unite, cure
yoo	cute, few
ou	out, crowd
u	up, cut
ur	fur, fern
ə	a in ago
	e in agent
	e in father
	i in unity
	o in collect
	u in focus
ch	chin, arch
ng	ring, singer
sh	she, dash
th	thin, truth
th	then, father
zh	s in pleasure
′	as in (ā′b'l)

im·ple·ment (im′plə mənt) *n.* something used in doing some work; tool or instrument [A plow is a farm *implement*.] ◆*v.* (im′plə ment) to carry out; put into effect [to *implement* a plan.]

im·pli·cate (im′plə kāt) *v.* to show that someone has had a part, especially in something bad; involve [Her confession *implicated* Gordon in the crime.] —**im′pli·cat·ed, im′pli·cat·ing**

im·pos·tor (im päs′tər) *n.* a person who cheats or tricks people, especially by pretending to be someone else or a different sort of person.

im·promp·tu (im prämp′tōō *or* im prämp′tyōō) *adj., adv.* without preparation or thought ahead of time; offhand [After winning the prize, she gave an *impromptu* speech.]

im·pru·dent (im prōōd′′nt) *adj.* not prudent or careful; rash or indiscreet. —**im·pru′dence** *n.* —**im·pru′dent·ly** *adv.*

im·pu·ri·ty (im pyoor′ə tē) *n.* **1** the condition of being impure [a high level of *impurity*]. **2** something mixed in that makes another thing impure [Strain the oil to remove *impurities*.] —*pl.* **im·pu′ri·ties**

in·ac·cu·rate (in ak′yər it) *adj.* not accurate or exact; in error; wrong [an *inaccurate* clock]. —**in·ac′cu·rate·ly** *adv.*

in·ac·tive (in ak′tiv) *adj.* not active; idle. —**in·ac′tive·ly** *adv.* —**in′ac·tiv′i·ty** *n.*

in·au·di·ble (in ô′də b'l) *adj.* not audible; that cannot be heard. —**in·au′di·bly** *adv.*

in·cin·er·a·tor (in sin′ə rāt′ər) *n.* a furnace for burning trash.

in·clude (in klōōd′) *v.* to have or take in as part of a whole; contain [Prices *include* taxes.] —**in·clud′ed, in·clud′ing**

in·cog·ni·to (in′käg nēt′ō *or* in käg′ni tō′) *adv., adj.* using a false name [The king traveled *incognito*.]

in·cu·ba·tor (ing′kyə bāt′ər) *n.* **1** a container that is kept warm for hatching eggs. **2** a container in which babies who are born too soon are kept warm and protected for a time.

in·cur (in kʉr′) *v.* to bring something bad or unpleasant upon oneself [He *incurred* debts when he was out of work.] —**in·curred′, in·cur′ring**

in·de·ci·sive (in′di sī′siv) *adj.* **1** not able to decide or make up one's mind; hesitating. **2** not deciding or settling anything [an *indecisive* reply]. —**in′de·ci′sive·ly** *adv.*

in·de·pend·ent (in′di pen′dənt) *adj.* **1** not ruled or controlled by another; self-governing [Many colonies became *independent* countries after World War II.] **2** not connected with others; separate [an *independent* grocer]. **3** not influenced by others; thinking for oneself [an *independent* voter]. ◆*n.* an independent person; especially, ☆a voter who is not a member of any political party. —**in′de·pend′ent·ly** *adv.*

in·dict (in dīt′) *v.* to accuse of having committed a crime; especially, to order that a suspect be put on trial after being charged with some crime [A grand jury can *indict* a person if it decides there is enough evidence to do so.] —**in·dict′ment** *n.*

in·di·ges·tion (in′di jes′chən) *n.* **1** difficulty in digesting food. **2** the discomfort caused by this.

in·di·vid·u·al·i·ty (in′di vij′oo wal′ə tē) *n.* **1** the qualities that make a person different from all others [Her unusual use of color shows her *individuality* as an artist.] **2** the condition of being different from others [Houses in the suburbs often have no *individuality*.] —*pl.* **in′di·vid′u·al′i·ties**

In·do·ne·sia (in′də nē′zhə) a country in the Malay Archipelago made up of Java, Sumatra, most of Borneo, and other islands.

in·er·tia (in ʉr′shə) *n.* **1** the natural force in matter that makes it stay at rest or keep on moving in a fixed direction unless it is acted on by an outside force. **2** a feeling that keeps one from wanting to do things, make changes, etc. [*Inertia* kept her from looking for a new job.]

Inertia comes from a Latin word meaning "having no skill" or "idle." A person who does not know how to do a certain thing tends to be idle and not do anything. Inertia keeps such a person from moving or acting.

in·ex·pli·ca·ble (in eks′pli kə b'l *or* in′ik splik′ə b'l) *adj.* that cannot be explained or understood. —**in·ex′pli·ca·bly** *adv.*

in·fe·ri·or·i·ty (in fir′ē ôr′ə tē) *n.* the condition of being inferior.

in·fin·i·tive (in fin′ə tiv) *n.* a form of a verb that does not show person, number, or tense, and is usually used with "to" [In "I need to eat" and "I must eat," "eat" is an *infinitive*.]

in·fir·ma·ry (in fʉr′mə rē) *n.* a room or building where people who are sick or injured are cared for, especially at a school or other institution. —*pl.* **in·fir′ma·ries**

in·fla·tion (in flā′shən) *n.* **1** an inflating or being inflated. ☆**2** an increase in the amount of money in circulation. It makes the money less valuable and brings prices up.

in·sec·ti·cide (in sek′tə sīd) *n.* any poison used to kill insects.

in·spect (in spekt′) **v. 1** to look at carefully; examine [You should *inspect* the bicycle before you buy it.] **2** to examine officially; review [The major will *inspect* Company B.] —**in·spec′tion** *n.*

in·spi·ra·tion (in′spə rā′shən) *n.* **1** an inspiring or being inspired [Our cheers gave *inspiration* to the team.] **2** something that inspires thought or action [The ocean was an *inspiration* to the artist.] **3** an inspired idea, action, etc. [Your bringing the camera was an *inspiration*.] **4** a breathing in; inhaling. —**in′spi·ra′tion·al** *adj.*

in·stall (in stôl′) **v. 1** to place in an office or position with a ceremony [We saw the new governor *installed*.] **2** to fix in position for use [to *install* a gas stove.] **3** to put or settle in a place [The cat *installed* itself in the big chair.] —**in·stal·la·tion** (in′stə lā′shən) *n.*

in·struc·tion (in struk′shən) *n.* **1** the act of teaching; education [The philosopher spent a lifetime in the *instruction* of others.] **2** something taught; lesson [swimming *instruction*]. **3 instructions**, *pl.* orders or directions [*instructions* for a test].

in·te·gral (in′tə grəl) *adj.* **1** necessary to something to make it complete; essential [Wheels are *integral* parts of automobiles.] **2** having to do with integers.

in·ter·jec·tion (in′tər jek′shən) *n.* **1** the act of interjecting. **2** a word or phrase that is exclaimed to show strong feeling; exclamation ["Oh!" and "Good grief!" are *interjections*.] **3** a remark, question, etc. interjected.

in·ter·rog·a·tive (in′tə räg′ə tiv) *adj.* that asks a question [an *interrogative* sentence].

in·ter·rupt (in tə rupt′) **v. 1** to break in on talk, action, etc. or on a person who is talking, working, etc. [We *interrupt* this program with a news bulletin. Don't *interrupt* me!] **2** to make a break in; cut off [A strike *interrupted* steel production.]

in·ter·scho·las·tic (in′tər skə las′tik) *adj.* between or among schools [*interscholastic* sports].

in·to·na·tion (in′tə nā′shən) *n.* **1** the way of singing or playing notes with regard to correct pitch. **2** the way the voice of a person who is talking rises and falls in pitch.

in·tra·mur·al (in′trə myoor′əl) *adj.* between or among members of the same school, college, etc. [*intramural* sports].

in·tra·ve·nous (in′trə vē′nəs) *adj.* directly into a vein [an *intravenous* injection].

in·trep·id (in trep′id) *adj.* very brave; fearless; bold. —**in·trep′id·ly** *adv.*

in·tro·duc·to·ry (in′trə duk′tər ē) *adj.* that introduces or begins something; preliminary [an *introductory* course in science].

in·va·lid[1] (in′və lid) *n.* a person who is sick or injured, especially one who is likely to be so for some time. ◆*adj.* **1** not well; weak and sick [caring for an *invalid* parent]. **2** of or for invalids [an *invalid* home].

in·val·id[2] (in val′id) *adj.* not valid; having no force or value [A check with no signature is *invalid*.]

in·vest (in vest′) **v. 1** to use or lend money for some business, property, stock, etc. in order to get a profit. **2** to spend in order to get something in return [to *invest* much time in a search for a cure]. **3** to cause to have; furnish with [The law *invests* a governor with many powers.] —**in·ves′tor** *n.*

in·ves·ti·gate (in ves′tə gāt) **v.** to search into so as to learn the facts; examine in detail [to *investigate* an accident]. —**in·ves′ti·gat·ed, in·ves′ti·gat·ing** —**in·ves′ti·ga′tion** *n.* —**in·ves′ti·ga′tor** *n.*

> The Latin word from which we took our word **investigate** means "to search out by following the footprints of." Detectives, including a famous one in stories, Sherlock Holmes, have often followed tracks when investigating a crime.

i·o·dine (ī′ə dīn *or* ī′ə din) *n.* a mineral that is a chemical element. It is in the form of dark crystals which can be dissolved in alcohol and used as an antiseptic.

I·on·ic (ī än′ik) *adj.* describing a style of Greek architecture in which the columns have decorations like scrolls at the top.

☆**i·tem·ize** (īt′əm īz) **v.** to list the items of, one by one [Please *itemize* my purchases.] —**i′tem·ized, i′tem·iz·ing**

Ionic

Jj

jar·gon (jär′gən) *n.* **1** the special words and phrases used by people in the same kind of work [Sportswriters have a *jargon* of their own, and so do scientists.] **2** talk that makes no sense; gibberish.

> **Jargon** comes from an old French word that meant "the sound of chattering by birds." From this it came to mean the kind of talk that one cannot understand any better than one can understand the sounds that birds make.

jeop·ard·y (jep′ər dē) *n.* great danger or risk [A firefighter's life is often in *jeopardy*.]

jour·nal·ism (jur′nəl iz′m) *n.* the work of gathering, writing, or editing the news for publication in newspapers or magazines or for broadcasting on radio or television.

ju·bi·lant (joo′b'l ənt) *adj.* joyful and proud; rejoicing [*Jubilant* crowds celebrated the victory.] —**ju′bi·lant·ly** *adv.*

a	ask, fat
ā	ape, date
ä	car, lot
e	elf, ten
er	berry, care
ē	even, meet
i	is, hit
ir	mirror, here
ī	ice, fire
ō	open, go
ô	law, horn
oi	oil, point
oo	look, pull
ōō	ooze, tool
yoo	unite, cure
yōō	cute, few
ou	out, crowd
u	up, cut
ur	fur, fern
ə	a in ago
	e in agent
	e in father
	i in unity
	o in collect
	u in focus
ch	chin, arch
ng	ring, singer
sh	she, dash
th	thin, truth
th	then, father
zh	s in pleasure
′	as in (ā′b'l)

judg·ment (juj′mənt) **n. 1** a judging or deciding. **2** a decision given by a judge or a law court [The *judgment* was for the defendant.] **3** criticism or blame [to pass *judgment* on another]. **4** a being able to decide what is right, good, practical, etc.; good sense [a person of clear *judgment*]. *Sometimes spelled* **judgement**.

ju·di·cial (jōō dish′əl) **adj. 1** of judges, law courts, or their duties [*judicial* robes; *judicial* duties]. **2** ordered or allowed by a court [a *judicial* decree]. **3** careful in forming opinions or making decisions; fair [a *judicial* mind]. —**ju·di′cial·ly adv.**

jun·ior (jōōn′yər) **adj. 1** the younger: a word written after the name of a son who has exactly the same name as his father: abbreviated **Jr. 2** lower in position or rank [a *junior* executive]. ☆**3** of juniors in a high school or college [the *junior* class]. ◆**n. 1** a person who is younger or has a lower rank than another [Her sister is her *junior* by three years.] ☆**2** a student in the next to last year of a high school or college.

ju·ven·ile (jōō′və n′l *or* jōō′və nīl) **adj. 1** young or youthful. **2** of, like, or for children or young people [*juvenile* ideas; *juvenile* books]. ◆**n. 1** a child or young person. ☆**2** a book for children.

kil·o·li·ter (kil′ə lēt′ər) **n.** a unit of volume, equal to 1,000 liters or one cubic meter.

kil·o·watt (kil′ə wät) **n.** a unit of electrical power, equal to 1,000 watts.

lacrosse

lab·o·ra·to·ry (lab′rə tôr′ē *or* lab′ər ə tôr′ē) **n.** a room or building where scientific work or tests are carried on, or where chemicals, drugs, etc. are prepared. —*pl.* **lab′o·ra·to′ries**

☆**la·crosse** (lə krôs′) **n.** a ball game played by two teams on a field with a goal at each end. The players use webbed rackets with long handles.

lar·ynx (lar′iŋks) **n.** the upper end of the windpipe, that contains the vocal cords.

lat·er·al (lat′ər əl) **adj.** of, at, from, or toward the side; sideways [*lateral* movement]. —**lat′er·al·ly adv.**

lathe (lāth) **n.** a machine for shaping a piece of wood, metal, etc. by holding and turning it rapidly against the edge of a cutting tool.

laud·a·ble (lôd′ə b′l) **adj.** deserving praise [a *laudable* performance]. —**laud′a·bly adv.**

le·gal·i·ty (li gal′ə tē) **n.** the condition of being legal or lawful.

leg·end·ar·y (lej′ən der′ē) **adj.** of, in, or like a legend [a *legendary* heroine].

length·wise (leŋkth′wīz) **adj., adv.** in the direction of the length [Carry the box in *lengthwise*.]

li·a·bil·i·ty (lī′ə bil′ə tē) **n. 1** the condition of being liable [*liability* to error; *liability* for damages]. **2 liabilities,** *pl.* money owed; debts. **3** a condition that acts against one; disadvantage [Small hands can be a *liability* to a pianist.] —*pl.* **li′a·bil′i·ties**

li·a·ble (lī′ə b′l) **adj.** obliged by law to pay; responsible [We caused the accident and are *liable* for the damage done.]

li·bel (lī′b′l) **n. 1** anything written or printed that harms a person's reputation in an unfair way. **2** the act or crime of publishing such a thing. ◆**v.** to publish a libel against. —**li′beled** or **li′belled, li′bel·ing** or **li′bel·ling** —**li′bel·er** or **li′bel·ler n.**

li·bel·ous or **li·bel·lous** (lī′b′l əs) **adj.** containing or making a libel against someone.

lib·er·al (lib′ər əl) **adj. 1** giving freely; generous [a *liberal* contributor to charity]. **2** open to new ideas; broad-minded; tolerant. **3** broad in range; not limited to one subject or field of study [a *liberal* education]. **4** in favor of reform or progress in politics, religion, etc. ◆**n.** a person who is in favor of reform and progress. —**lib′er·al·ly adv.**

lib·er·ate (lib′ə rāt) **v.** to free as from slavery [to *liberate* prisoners of war]. —**lib′er·at·ed, lib′er·at·ing** —**lib′er·a·tor n.**

li·brar·i·an (lī brer′ē ən) **n. 1** a person who is in charge of a library. **2** a person who has had special training in order to work in a library.

lin·e·ar (lin′ē ər) **adj. 1** of, made of, or using a line or lines [*linear* boundaries]. **2** of length [*linear* measure].

liq·ui·date (lik′wə dāt) **v. 1** to settle the affairs of a business that is closing, usually because it is bankrupt. **2** to pay a debt in full. **3** to get rid of, as by killing [The dictator *liquidated* enemies.] —**liq′ui·dat·ed, liq′ui·dat·ing** —**liq′ui·da′tion n.**

li·ra (lir′ə) **n.** the basic unit of money in Italy and Turkey. —*pl.* **li·re** (lir′ā) or **li′ras**

lit·er·al (lit′ər əl) **adj. 1** following the original, word for word [a *literal* translation of a French poem]. **2** based on the actual words in their usual meaning; not allowing for idiom or exaggeration [The *literal* meaning of "lend an ear" is to let another borrow one's ear.] —**lit′er·al·ly adv.**

lit·er·a·ture (lit′ər ə chər) *n.* **1** all the writings of a certain time, country, etc.; especially, those that have lasting value because of their beauty, imagination, etc., as fine novels, plays, and poems. **2** the work or profession of writing such things; also, the study of such writings.

li·thog·ra·phy (li thäg′rə fē) *n.* the process of printing from a flat stone or metal plate whose surface is treated so that only the parts having the design will hold ink. —**li·thog′ra·pher** *n.*

log·a·rithm (lôg′ə ri*th*′m) *n.* the figure that tells to what power a certain fixed number, as ten, must be raised to equal a given number [The *logarithm* of 100 is 2, when 10 is taken as the fixed number ($10^2 = 100$).] Such numbers are listed in tables to shorten the working of problems in mathematics.

log·i·cal (läj′i k′l) *adj.* **1** based on logic or using logic [a *logical* explanation]. **2** that is to be expected because of what has gone before [the *logical* result of one's actions]. —**log′i·cal·ly** *adv.*

lu·mi·nous (lo͞o′mə nəs) *adj.* **1** giving off light; bright [the *luminous* rays of the sun]. **2** filled with light [a *luminous* room]. **3** glowing in the dark [*luminous* paint]. —**lu·mi·nos·i·ty** (lo͞o′mə näs′ə tē) *n.*

Mm

mag·is·trate (maj′is trāt) *n.* **1** an official with the power to put laws into effect, as the president of a republic. **2** a minor official, as a judge in a police court.

mag·net·ic (mag net′ik) *adj.* **1** working like a magnet [a *magnetic* needle]. **2** that can be magnetized. **3** that attracts strongly [*magnetic* eyes].

ma·hog·a·ny (mə häg′ə nē *or* mə hôg′ə nē) *n.* **1** the hard, reddish-brown wood of a tropical American tree, used in making furniture. **2** this tree. **3** reddish brown. —*pl.* **ma·hog′a·nies**

mal·ad·just·ed (mal′ə jus′tid) *adj.* badly adjusted; especially, not able to fit happily into the life around one. —**mal′ad·just′ment** *n.*

ma·lev·o·lent (mə lev′ə lənt) *adj.* wishing harm or evil to others; malicious. —**ma·lev′o·lence** *n.* —**ma·lev′o·lent·ly** *adv.*

mal·func·tion (mal fuŋk′shən) *v.* to fail to work as it should. ◆*n.* an instance of such failure [The launch was delayed by the *malfunction* of a rocket.]

mal·ice (mal′is) *n.* a feeling of wanting to hurt or harm someone; ill will; spite.

man·date (man′dāt) *n.* **1** an order or command, especially one in writing. **2** the will of the people as made known by their votes in elections. **3** control over a territory as formerly given by the League of Nations to one of its member nations; also, the territory so controlled.

man·da·to·ry (man′də tôr′ē) *adj.* ordered or demanded by someone in power; required.

man·i·cure (man′ə kyo͝or) *n.* the care of the hands; especially, the trimming and cleaning of the fingernails. ◆*v.* to give a manicure to. —**man′i·cured, man′i·cur·ing** —**man′i·cur′ist** *n.*

mar·i·o·nette (mar′ē ə net′) *n.* a puppet or small jointed doll moved by strings or wires and used in putting on shows on a small stage.

mark (märk) *n.* **1** the basic unit of money in East Germany. **2** the basic unit of money in West Germany: *the full name is* **deut·sche mark** (doi′che märk).

mar·riage (mar′ij) *n.* **1** the state of being married; married life. **2** the act or ceremony of marrying; wedding.

ma·ter·nal (mə tur′n′l) *adj.* **1** of or like a mother; motherly. **2** related to one on one's mother's side [my *maternal* aunt]. —**ma·ter′nal·ly** *adv.*

ma·ter·ni·ty (mə tur′nə tē) *n.* the condition or character of being a mother; motherhood or motherliness. ◆*adj.* for women who are about to become mothers or women who have just had babies [a *maternity* dress; a *maternity* ward in a hospital].

math·e·ma·ti·cian (math′ə mə tish′ən) *n.* an expert in mathematics.

mat·ri·mo·ny (mat′rə mō′nē) *n.* the condition of being married; marriage. —**mat′ri·mo′ni·al** *adj.*

ma·tron (mā′trən) *n.* **1** a wife or a widow, especially one who is not young. **2** a woman who has charge of others, as in a prison.

max·i·mum (mak′sə məm) *n.* **1** the greatest amount or number that is possible or allowed [Forty pounds of luggage is the *maximum* you can take.] **2** the highest degree or point reached [Today's *maximum* was 35°C.] —*pl.* **max·i·mums** or **max·i·ma** (mak′sə mə) ◆*adj.* greatest possible or allowed [*maximum* speed].

me·chan·i·cal (mə kan′i k′l) *adj.* **1** having to do with machinery, or having skill in its use. **2** made or run by machinery [a *mechanical* toy]. —**me·chan′i·cal·ly** *adv.*

marionette

a	ask, fat
ā	ape, date
ä	car, lot
e	elf, ten
er	berry, care
ē	even, meet
i	is, hit
ir	mirror, here
ī	ice, fire
ō	open, go
ô	law, horn
oi	oil, point
o͝o	look, pull
o͞o	ooze, tool
yo͞o	unite, cure
yo͞o	cute, few
ou	out, crowd
u	up, cut
ur	fur, fern
ə	a in ago
	e in agent
	e in father
	i in unity
	o in collect
	u in focus
ch	chin, arch
ng	ring, singer
sh	she, dash
th	thin, truth
th	then, father
zh	s in pleasure
′	as in (ā′b′l)

mel·o·dra·ma (mel′ə drä′mə *or* mel′ə dram′ə) *n.* **1** a play in which there is much suspense and strong feeling, and a great exaggeration of good and evil in the characters. **2** any exciting action or talk like that in such a play.

Melodrama comes from a Greek word meaning "song" and the French word for "drama." In the original melodramas there were songs sung at various points in the action of the play.

mem·oir (mem′wär) *n.* **1 memoirs,** *pl.* the story of one's life written by oneself; autobiography; also, a written record based on the writer's own experience and knowledge. **2** a written story of someone's life; biography.

men·u (men′yōō) *n.* a list of the foods served at a meal [a restaurant's dinner *menu*].

mer·can·tile (mur′kən til *or* mur′kən tīl) *adj.* having to do with merchants, trade, or commerce.

☆**me·sa** (mā′sə) *n.* a large, high rock having steep walls and a flat top.

mesa

Mesa is a Spanish word that came from a Latin word meaning "table." Some mesas looked like tables to the Spanish explorers in what is now the southwestern United States.

me·tab·o·lism (mə tab′ə liz′m) *n.* the process in all plants and animals by which food is changed into energy, new cells, waste products, etc. —**met·a·bol·ic** (met′ə bäl′ik) *adj.*

met·al·lur·gy (met′'l ur′jē) *n.* the science of getting metals from their ores and making them ready for use, by smelting, refining, etc. —**met·al·lur′gi·cal** *adj.* —**met′al·lur′gist** *n.*

met·a·mor·pho·sis (met′ə môr′fə sis) *n.* **1** a change in form; especially, the change that some animals go through in developing, as of tadpole to frog or larva to moth. **2** a complete change in the way someone or something looks or acts. —*pl.* **met·a·mor·pho·ses** (met′ə môr′fə sēz)

met·a·phor (met′ə fôr) *n.* the use of a word or phrase in a way that is different from its usual use, to show a likeness to something else ["The curtain of night" is a *metaphor* that likens night to a curtain that hides something.]

me·te·or·ol·o·gy (mēt′ē ə räl′ə jē) *n.* the science that studies weather, climate, and the earth's atmosphere. —**me′te·or·ol′o·gist** *n.*

me·trop·o·lis (mə träp′'l is) *n.* **1** the main city of a state, country, or region. **2** any large or important city. —*pl.* **me·trop′o·lis·es**

Metropolis comes from the ancient Greek words for "mother" and "city." For the ancient Greeks a metropolis was the mother city of a colony.

met·ro·pol·i·tan (met′rə päl′ə t'n) *adj.* **1** of a metropolis [a *metropolitan* park]. ☆**2** making up a metropolis [*Metropolitan* Chicago includes the central city and its suburbs.] ◆*n.* a person who lives in, or is at home in, a big city.

mi·cro·or·gan·ism (mī′krō ôr′gə niz′m) *n.* any living thing too tiny to be seen without a microscope; especially, any of the bacteria, viruses, protozoans, etc.

mil·li·gram (mil′ə gram) *n.* a unit of weight, equal to one thousandth of a gram.

mil·li·li·ter (mil′ə lēt′ər) *n.* a unit of volume, equal to one thousandth of a liter.

mim·ic·ry (mim′ik rē) *n.* **1** the art of imitating, or an example of this. **2** the way in which some living thing looks like another or like some natural object. —*pl.* **mim′ic·ries**

min·i·a·ture (min′ē ə chər *or* min′i chər) *n.* **1** a very small copy or model [a *miniature* of the Liberty Bell]. **2** a very small painting, especially a portrait. ◆*adj.* that is a miniature [a *miniature* car].

mis·de·mean·or (mis′di mēn′ər) *n.* a breaking of the law that is less serious than a felony and brings a lesser penalty [It is a *misdemeanor* to throw litter in the streets.]

mo·bile (mō′b'l *or* mō′bīl *or* mō′bēl) *adj.* **1** that can be moved quickly and easily [a *mobile* army]. **2** that can change rapidly or easily in response to different moods, conditions, needs, etc. [*mobile* features; *mobile* policies]. ◆*n.* (mō′bēl) a kind of sculpture made of flat pieces, rods, etc. that hang balanced from wires so as to move easily in air currents. —**mo·bil·i·ty** (mō bil′ə tē) *n.*

mod·er·a·tor (mäd′ə rāt′ər) *n.* a person who is in charge of conducting a discussion or debate.

mod·i·fy (mäd′ə fī) *v.* **1** to make a small or partial change in [Exploration has *modified* our maps of Antarctica.] **2** to make less harsh, strong, etc. [to *modify* a jail term]. **3** to limit the meaning of; describe or qualify [In the phrase "old man" the adjective "old" *modifies* the noun "man."] —**mod′i·fied, mod′i·fy·ing** —**mod′i·fi·ca′tion** *n.* —**mod′i·fi′er** *n.*

mod·ule (mäj′ōōl) *n.* ☆**1** any of a set of units, as wall cabinets, that can be arranged together in various ways. ☆**2** a section of a machine or device that can be detached for some special use [the landing *module* of a spacecraft]. —**mod·u·lar** (mäj′ə lər) *adj.*

mol·e·cule (mäl′ə kyōōl) *n.* **1** the smallest particle of a substance that can exist alone without losing its chemical form. A molecule consists of one or more atoms. —**mo·lec·u·lar** (mə lek′yə lər) *adj.*

mo·men·tum (mō men′təm) *n.* **1** the force with which a body moves, equal to its mass multiplied by its speed [His sled gained *momentum* as it coasted downhill.] **2** strength or force that keeps growing [The peace movement gained *momentum*.]

mon·arch (män′ərk) *n.* **1** a ruler, as a king, queen, or emperor. **2** a large North American butterfly, with reddish-brown wings with black edges.

mon·e·tar·y (män′ə ter′ē) *adj.* **1** in money; pecuniary [That old car has little *monetary* value.] **2** of the money used in a country [The *monetary* unit of France is the franc.]

mon·o·lith (män′ə lith) *n.* a large block of stone, or a statue, monument, etc. carved from a single, large stone. **—mon′o·lith′ic** *adj.*

mon·o·logue or **mon·o·log** (män′ə lôg) *n.* **1** a long speech by one person during a conversation. **2** a poem, part of a play, etc. in which one person speaks alone. **3** a play, skit, etc. performed by one actor.

mo·nop·o·ly (mə näp′ə lē) *n.* **1** complete control of a product or service in some place by a single person or group. A company with a monopoly has no competition and can set prices as it wishes. **2** such control given and regulated by a government [The city gave the bus company a *monopoly* for ten years.] **3** the condition of having something all to oneself [No one has a *monopoly* on brains.] *—pl.* **mo·nop′o·lies**

mon·o·tone (män′ə tōn) *n.* **1** a keeping of the same tone or pitch without change, as in talking or singing. **2** a person who sings with few if any changes of tone. **3** sameness of color, style, etc. [The room was decorated in gray *monotones*.]

Mo·roc·co (mə rä′kō) a country in northwestern Africa. **—Mo·roc′can** *adj., n.*

mor·tal (môr′t'l) *adj.* **1** that must die at some time [All men are *mortal*.] **2** of people as beings who must die; human [a *mortal* weakness]. **3** causing death of the body or soul [a *mortal* wound; *mortal* sin]. **4** lasting until death [*mortal* combat; *mortal* enemies]. ◆*n.* a human being.

mort·gage (môr′gij) *n.* **1** an agreement in which a person borrowing money gives the lender a claim to property as a pledge that the debt will be paid [The bank holds a *mortgage* of $15,000 on our house.] **2** the legal paper by which such a claim is given. ◆*v.* **1** to pledge by a mortgage in order to borrow money [to *mortgage* a home]. **2** to put a claim on; make risky [He *mortgaged* his future by piling up debts.] **—mort′gaged, mort′gag·ing**

Mortgage comes from two words in old French *mort* and *gage* that meant "dead" and "pledge." The pledge would be "dead" to the lender if the borrower paid the debt and kept the property that had been pledged. And the pledge would be "dead" to the borrower if he or she failed to pay the debt and lost the property.

☆**mor·ti·cian** (môr tish′ən) *n. another name for* **funeral director**.

mor·tu·ar·y (môr′choo wer′ē) *n.* a place where dead bodies are kept before the funeral. *—pl.* **mor′tu·ar′ies** ◆*adj.* of death or funerals.

muck·rake (muk′rāk) *v.* ☆to search out dishonest acts of public officials, business people, etc. and make them known, as in newspapers. **—muck′raked, muck′rak·ing** —☆**muck′rak·er** *n.*

mu·nic·i·pal·i·ty (myoo nis′ə pal′ə tē) *n.* a city or town that has self-government in local matters. *—pl.* **mu·nic′i·pal′i·ties**

mur·mur (mur′mər) *n.* **1** a low, steady sound, as of voices far away. **2** a complaint made in a very low voice. ◆*v.* **1** to make a low, steady sound [The wind *murmured* through the trees.] **2** to speak or complain in a very low voice.

mu·si·cian (myoo zish′ən) *n.* a person skilled in music, as a composer or one who plays a musical instrument or sings, especially for a living.

myr·i·ad (mir′ē əd) *n.* **1** ten thousand: *used mostly in old stories.* **2** any very large number [a *myriad* of locusts]. ◆*adj.* of a very large number; countless.

monolith

Nn

nar·ra·tive (nar′ə tiv) *n.* **1** a story; a report of happenings; tale. **2** the telling of stories or events; narration. ◆*adj.* in the form of a story [a *narrative* history of the United States].

neb·u·la (neb′yə lə) *n.* a cloudlike patch seen in the sky at night. It is either a large mass of thin gas or a group of stars too far away to be seen clearly. *—pl.* **neb·u·lae** (neb′yə lē) or **neb′u·las** **—neb′u·lar** *adj.*

nec·es·sar·y (nes′ə ser′ē) *adj.* **1** that is needed or must be done; required; essential [Do only the *necessary* repairs.] **2** that cannot be avoided; inevitable [The accident was a *necessary* result of the driver's carelessness.] ◆*n.* something necessary. *—pl.* **nec′es·sar′ies**

a	ask, fat
ā	ape, date
ä	car, lot
e	elf, ten
er	berry, care
ē	even, meet
i	is, hit
ir	mirror, here
ī	ice, fire
ō	open, go
ô	law, horn
oi	oil, point
σο	look, pull
σσ	ooze, tool
yσο	unite, cure
yσσ	cute, few
ou	out, crowd
u	up, cut
ur	fur, fern
ə	a in ago
	e in agent
	e in father
	i in unity
	o in collect
	u in focus
ch	chin, arch
ng	ring, singer
sh	she, dash
th	thin, truth
th	then, father
zh	s in pleasure
′	as in (ā′b'l)

ne·ces·si·ty (nə ses′ə tē) *n.* **1** that which is necessary or needed or cannot be done without [Food and shelter are *necessities*.] **2** great need [Call only in case of *necessity*.] **3** poverty; want [to live in great *necessity*]. —*pl.* **ne·ces′si·ties**

neg·a·tive (neg′ə tiv) *adj.* **1** saying that something is not so or refusing; answering "no" [a *negative* reply]. **2** that does not help, improve, etc. [*negative* criticism]. **3** opposite to or lacking something that is positive [He always takes a *negative* attitude and expects the worst.] **4** showing that a certain disease, condition, etc. is not present [The reaction to her allergy test was *negative*.] **5** describing a quantity less than zero or one that is to be subtracted. ◆*n.* **1** a word, phrase, or action showing that one does not approve or agree ["No" and "not" are *negatives*.] **2** the film or plate from which a finished photograph is printed. The negative shows the light areas of the original subject as dark and the dark areas as light. —**neg′a·tive·ly** *adv.*

neon

neg·lect (ni glekt′) *v.* **1** to fail to do what one should do, as because of carelessness [In her hurry, Sharon *neglected* to lock the door.] **2** to fail to take care of as one should; give too little attention to [He became so busy with work that he began to *neglect* his family.] ◆*n.* the act of neglecting or the condition of being neglected [The old house suffered from *neglect*.]

neg·li·gent (neg′li jənt) *adj.* in the habit of neglecting things; not being careful; careless. —**neg′li·gence** *n.* —**neg′li·gent·ly** *adv.*

ne·go·ti·ate (ni gō′shē āt) *v.* **1** to talk over a problem, business deal, dispute, etc. in the hope of reaching an agreement [to *negotiate* a contract]. **2** to succeed in crossing, climbing, etc. [to *negotiate* a deep river]. —**ne·go′ti·at·ed, ne·go′ti·at·ing** —**ne·go′ti·a′tion** *n.* —**ne·go′ti·a′tor** *n.*

ne·on (nē′än) *n.* a chemical element that is a gas without color or smell. It is found in the air in very small amounts.

neu·tron (no͞o′trän *or* nyo͞o′trän) *n.* one of the particles that make up the nucleus of an atom. A neutron has no electrical charge.

nic·o·tine (nik′ə tēn) *n.* a poisonous, oily liquid found in tobacco leaves. It is used to kill insects.

nom·i·na·tive (näm′ə nə tiv) *adj.* showing the subject of a verb or the words that agree with the subject. ◆*n.* the case in grammar that shows this.

In Latin and some other languages, nouns, pronouns, and adjectives have special endings to show that they are in the **nominative** case. In English, only a few pronouns, such as *I*, *she*, *he*, and *who* are in the nominative case.

non·cha·lant (nän shə länt′ *or* nän′shə lənt) *adj.* not caring; not showing concern; casual [He is *nonchalant* about his debts.] —**non·cha·lance′** *n.* —**non·cha·lant′ly** *adv.*

Nonchalant is a word borrowed from French and comes from two Latin words meaning "to be not warm." A person who is nonchalant does not get warm or passionate about things, but seems always to be cool or lukewarm.

non·ex·ist·ent (nän′ig zis′tənt) *adj.* not existing; not real [to worry over *nonexistent* dangers]. —**non′ex·ist′ence** *n.*

☆**no·ta·rize** (nōt′ə rīz) *v.* to sign a legal paper and stamp it with one's seal as a notary public. —**no′ta·rized, no′ta·riz·ing**

nu·mer·i·cal (no͞o mer′i k'l *or* nyo͞o mer′i k'l) *adj.* **1** of or having to do with a number or numbers; by numbers [to arrange in *numerical* order]. **2** shown as a number, not as a letter [In the equation $x + y = 10$, 10 is the only *numerical* quantity.] —**nu·mer′i·cal·ly** *adv.*

Oo

o·bit·u·ar·y (ō bich′o͞o wer′ē) *n.* an announcement, as in a newspaper, that someone has died, usually with a brief story of the person's life. —*pl.* **o·bit′u·ar′ies**

In talking about unpleasant things, people often try to use softer, or less harsh, words or phrases. Just as we sometimes say of someone who has died that the person "has passed on," the ancient Romans would use the verb *obit*, meaning "has gone forward." From this verb we get **obituary**.

ob·jec·tive (əb jek′tiv) *adj.* **1** not having or showing a strong opinion for or against something; without bias [A judge must remain *objective*.] **2** that shows the object of a verb or of a preposition [In "I gave them to her," "them" and "her" are in the *objective* case.] ◆*n.* **1** something that one tries to reach; goal; purpose [What are your *objectives* in this job?] **2** the objective case. —**ob·jec′tive·ly** *adv.* —**ob·jec·tiv·i·ty** (äb′jek tiv′ə tē) *n.*

ob·serv·ant (əb zʉr′vənt) *adj.* **1** strict in observing, or keeping, a law, custom, etc. [*observant* of the rules of etiquette]. **2** paying careful attention; alert [An *observant* student noticed the wrong spelling.] —**ob·serv′ant·ly** *adv.*

ob·serv·a·to·ry (əb zʉr′və tôr′ē) *n.* a building with telescopes and other equipment in it for studying the stars, weather conditions, etc. —*pl.* **ob·serv′a·to′ries**

ob·sid·i·an (əb sid′ē ən) *n.* a dark, glassy rock formed from the lava of volcanoes.

ob·so·lete (äb sə lēt′ *or* äb′sə lēt) *adj.* no longer in use or fashion; out-of-date [an *obsolete* word; an *obsolete* airplane].

ob·sta·cle (äb′sti k'l) *n.* anything that gets in the way or keeps one from going ahead; obstruction [Lack of an education was the main *obstacle* to his success.]

oc·ca·sion·al·ly (ə kā′zhən 'l ē) *adv.* now and then; once in a while.

oc·cur (ə kʉr′) *v.* **1** to come into one's mind [The idea never *occurred* to me.] **2** to happen; take place [That event *occurred* years ago.] —**oc·curred′, oc·cur′ring**

oc·ta·gon (äk′tə gän) *n.* a flat figure having eight angles and eight sides.

o·mit (ō mit′) *v.* to leave out [You may *omit* the raisins.] —**o·mit′ted, o·mit′ting**

o·paque (ō pāk′) *adj.* **1** that cannot be seen through; not letting light through; not transparent [an *opaque* screen]. **2** not shiny; dull [The desk had an *opaque* surface.] **3** hard to understand [an *opaque* remark].

op·por·tu·ni·ty (äp′ər tōō′nə tē *or* äp′ər tyōō′nə tē) *n.* a time or occasion that is right for doing something; good chance [You will have an *opportunity* to ask questions after the talk.] —*pl.* **op′por·tu′ni·ties**

op·pose (ə pōz′) *v.* **1** to act or be against; fight or resist [The mayor *opposes* raising taxes.] **2** to put opposite or in contrast; set against [To each of his arguments the lawyer *opposed* one of her own.] —**op·posed′, op·pos′ing**

op·press (ə pres′) *v.* **1** to trouble the mind of; worry; weigh down [*oppressed* by a feeling of fear]. **2** to keep down by the cruel use of power; rule in a very harsh way [Pharaoh *oppressed* the Israelite slaves.] —**op·pres′sor** *n.*

op·ti·cian (äp tish′ən) *n.* a person who makes or sells eyeglasses and other optical supplies.

op·ti·mism (äp′tə miz'm) *n.* **1** a bright and hopeful feeling about life, in which one expects things to turn out all right. **2** the belief that there is more good than evil in life. —**op′ti·mis′tic** *adj.* —**op′ti·mis′ti·cal·ly** *adv.*

op·tion (äp′shən) *n.* **1** the act of choosing; choice [I had no *option* but to go.] **2** the right of choosing [They have the *option* of taking a vacation now or in the winter.]

op·u·lent (äp′yə lənt) *adj.* **1** wealthy; rich [an *opulent* nation]. **2** in great amounts; abundant [an *opulent* growth of hair]. —**op·u·lence** (äp′yə ləns) *n.*

or·di·nance (ôr′d'n əns) *n.* **1** an order, command, or rule. ☆**2** a law, especially one made by a city government [an *ordinance* forbidding jaywalking].

or·na·ment (ôr′nə mənt) *n.* **1** anything added or put on to make something look better; decoration [Christmas-tree *ornaments*]. **2** a person whose character or talent makes the whole group seem better [That teacher is an *ornament* to the profession.] ◆*v.* (ôr′nə ment′) to add ornaments to; decorate.

Ot·to·man (ät′ə mən) *n.* **1** *another name for* **Turk.** —*pl.* **Ot′to·mans 2** ottoman, a low seat without back or arms; also, a padded footstool. ◆*adj. another word for* **Turkish.**

o·ver·lap (ō vər lap′) *v.* to lap over part of something or part of each other [The scales on a fish *overlap* one another. The two events *overlapped* in time.] —**o·ver·lapped′, o·ver·lap′ping** ◆*n.* (ō′vər lap) **1** the act of overlapping. **2** a part that overlaps.

octagon

Pp

pag·eant (paj′ənt) *n.* **1** a large, elaborate public show, parade, etc. **2** an elaborate play based on events in history, often performed outdoors.

Pa·ki·stan (pä′ki stän′ *or* pak′i stan′) a country in southern Asia, on the Arabian Sea.

par·a·ble (par′ə b'l) *n.* a short, simple story that teaches a moral lesson, as in the Bible.

par·a·dox (par′ə däks) *n.* **1** a statement that seems to contradict itself or seems false, but that may be true in fact. Example: "Water, water, everywhere, and not a drop to drink." **2** a statement that contradicts itself and is false. Example: The sun was so hot we nearly froze. **3** a person or thing that seems full of contradictions. —**par′a·dox′i·cal** *adj.*

par·al·lel (par′ə lel) *adj.* **1** moving out in the same direction and always the same distance apart so as to never meet, as the tracks of a sled in the snow. **2** similar or alike [Their lives followed *parallel* courses.] ◆*n.* **1** a parallel line, plane, etc. **2** something similar to or like something else [Your experience is a *parallel* to mine.] **3** a comparison showing how things are alike [The teacher drew a *parallel* between the two books.] **4** any of the imaginary circles around the earth parallel to the equator that mark degrees of latitude [New Orleans is on the 30th *parallel* north of the equator.] ◆*v.* to be in a *parallel* line or plane with [The road *parallels* the river.] —**par′al·leled** or **par′al·lelled, par′al·lel·ing** or **par′al·lel·ling**

a	ask, fat
ā	ape, date
ä	car, lot
e	elf, ten
er	berry, care
ē	even, meet
i	is, hit
ir	mirror, here
ī	ice, fire
ō	open, go
ô	law, horn
oi	oil, point
ơơ	look, pull
ōō	ooze, tool
yōō	unite, cure
yōō	cute, few
ou	out, crowd
u	up, cut
ʉr	fur, fern
ə	a in ago
	e in agent
	e in father
	i in unity
	o in collect
	u in focus
ch	chin, arch
ng	ring, singer
sh	she, dash
th	thin, truth
th	then, father
zh	s in pleasure
'	as in (ā′b'l)

pa·ral·y·sis (pə ral′ə sis) *n.* **1** a loss of the power to move or feel in any part of the body, as because of injury to the brain or spinal cord. **2** a condition of being powerless or helpless to act [a *paralysis* of industry].

☆**par·a·med·ic** (par′ə med′ik) *n.* a person doing paramedical work.

☆**par·a·med·i·cal** (par′ə med′i k'l) *adj.* being or having to do with persons whose work is helping doctors and nurses. Paramedical workers, such as midwives or nurses' aides, get special training.

par·a·phrase (par′ə frāz) *n.* a putting of something spoken or written into different words having the same meaning. ◆*v.* to write or say in a paraphrase. —**par′a·phrased, par′a·phras·ing**

par·a·site (par′ə sīt) *n.* **1** a plant or animal that lives on or in another plant or animal and gets food from it [Mistletoe and fleas are *parasites*.] **2** a person who lives at another's expense without paying that person back in any way.

pa·ren·the·sis (pə ren′thə sis) *n.* **1** a word, phrase, etc. put into a complete sentence as an added note or explanation and set off, as between curved lines, from the rest of the sentence. **2** either or both of the curved lines ( ) used to set off such a word, phrase, etc. —*pl.* **pa·ren·the·ses** (pə ren′thə sēz)

Parenthesis comes from a Greek word meaning "to put beside." Words in parentheses are put beside other words to explain them.

par·o·dy (par′ə dē) *n.* a piece of writing or music that imitates another in such a way as to make fun of it. —*pl.* **par′o·dies** ◆*v.* to make fun of by imitating. —**par′o·died, par′o·dy·ing**

par·quet (pär kā′) *n.* **1** a flooring made of pieces of wood fitted together to form a pattern. **2** the main floor of a theater; orchestra.

par·tic·i·pate (pär tis′ə pāt) *v.* to take part with others; have a share [Sue *participated* in the school play.] —**par·tic′i·pat·ed, par·tic′i·pat·ing** —**par·tic′i·pa′tion** *n.* —**par·tic′i·pa′tor** *n.*

par·ti·ci·ple (pär′tə sip′'l) *n.* a form of a verb used as both a verb and an adjective. Participles have tense and voice, and can take an object [In "He is humming a tune," "humming" is a present *participle* used as a verb. In "a man dressed in grey," "dressed" is a past *participle* used as an adjective.]

par·tic·u·lar (pər tik′yə lər) *adj.* **1** of only one person, group, part, or thing; not general; individual [What is your *particular* opinion?] **2** apart from any other; specific [Do you have a *particular* color in mind?] **3** more than ordinary; unusual; special [Pay *particular* attention.] **4** hard to please; very careful [They are *particular* about what movies they see.] ◆*n.* a detail; fact; item [Give full *particulars* about the robbery to the police.]

pa·trol (pə trōl′) *v.* to make regular trips around a place in order to guard it. —**pa·trolled′, pa·trol′ling** ◆*n.* **1** a patrolling. **2** a person or group that patrols. **3** a group of soldiers, ships, or airplanes used to guard an area or to get information about the enemy.

pe·cul·iar (pi kyōol′yər) *adj.* **1** odd; strange; queer [Things look *peculiar* through these dark glasses.] **2** of a particular person, thing, or group; special; distinctive [These markings are *peculiar* to this bird.] —**pe·cul′iar·ly** *adv.*

ped·es·tal (ped′is t'l) *n.* **1** the piece at the bottom that holds up a statue, column, lamp, etc. **2** any base, especially a high one.

pe·di·at·rics (pē′dē at′riks) *n.pl.* the branch of medicine that has to do with the care and treatment of babies and children: *used with a singular verb.* —**pe′di·at′ric** *adj.*

pend·ant (pen′dənt) *n.* an ornament that hangs down, as a locket or earring.

pen·du·lum (pen′jōo ləm *or* pen′d'l əm) *n.* a weight hung so that it swings freely back and forth, often used to control a clock's movement.

per·en·ni·al (pə ren′ē əl) *adj.* **1** that lives for more than two years: said of certain plants. **2** returning or becoming active again and again [Raising money for new sports equipment is a *perennial* problem.] **3** lasting or going on for a long time [to seek *perennial* youth]. ◆*n.* a plant that lives for more than two years. —**per·en′ni·al·ly** *adv.*

per·ma·nent (pur′mə nənt) *adj.* lasting or meant to last for a very long time [One's *permanent* teeth should last as long as one lives.] ◆*n.* a hair wave put in by means of chemicals and lasting for months: *the full name is* **permanent wave.** —**per′ma·nence** *or* **per′ma·nen·cy** *n.* —**per′ma·nent·ly** *adv.*

per·mit (pər mit′) *v.* **1** to give consent to; let; allow [Will you *permit* me to help you?] **2** to give a chance [We'll fly if the weather *permits*.] —**per·mit′ted, per·mit′ting** ◆*n.* (pur′mit) a paper, card, etc. showing permission; license [a *permit* to carry a gun].

pedestal

pendant

per·pen·dic·u·lar (pur′pən dik′yə lər) **adj.**
1 at right angles [The wall should be
perpendicular to the floor.] **2** straight up
and down; exactly upright [a *perpendicular*
flagpole]. ◆**n.** a line that is at right angles
to the horizon, or to another line or plane [The
Leaning Tower of Pisa leans away from the
perpendicular.]

per·pet·u·al (pər pech′oo wəl) **adj. 1** lasting
forever or for a long time. **2** continuing;
constant [a *perpetual* bore]. —**per·pet′u·
al·ly adv.**

per·plex (pər pleks′) **v.** to make unsure of
what to do; fill with doubt; confuse or
puzzle [Your silence *perplexes* me.]

per·son·al·i·ty (pur′sə nal′ə tē) **n. 1** all the
special qualities which make a person
different from other people. **2** personal
qualities that attract others to one; charm,
energy, cleverness, etc. [Your friend is
smart, but has no *personality*.] **3** a person;
especially, a very unusual or famous person.
—**pl. per′son·al′i·ties**

per·son·i·fy (pər sän′ə fī) **v. 1** to think of
or show some idea or thing as a person [A
ship is *personified* when it is referred to as
"she."] **2** to be a good example of some
quality, idea, etc. [Tom Sawyer *personifies*
the spirit of boyhood.] —**per·son′i·fied,
per·son′i·fy·ing** —**per·son′i·fi·ca′tion n.**

per·spec·tive (pər spek′tiv) **n. 1** the way
things look from a given point according to
their size, shape, distance, etc. [*Perspective*
makes things far away look small.] **2** the art
of picturing things so that they seem close or
far away, big or small, etc., just as they look
to the eye when viewed from a given
point. **3** a certain point of view in
understanding or judging things or
happenings, especially one that shows them
in their true relations to one another
[Working in a factory will give you a new
perspective on labor problems.]

pe·so (pā′sō) **n.** the basic unit of money in
Argentina, Colombia, Cuba, Mexico, etc.
—**pl. pe′sos**

pe·ti·tion (pə tish′ən) **n. 1** a strong, serious
request, as a prayer. **2** a formal, written
request to someone in authority, signed by a
number of people. ◆**v.** to make a petition to
or a request for [The mayor of our town has
petitioned the governor for flood relief.]
—**pe·ti′tion·er n.**

phar·ma·cist (fär′mə sist) **n.** a person who
is trained to prepare and sell drugs and
medicine according to the orders of a
doctor; druggist.

phar·ma·cy (fär′mə sē) **n. 1** the work of
preparing drugs and medicines according to
a doctor's orders. **2** a place where this is
done; drugstore. —**pl. phar′ma·cies**

phil·har·mon·ic (fil′här män′ik) **adj.**
loving music [a *philharmonic* society]. ◆**n.**
a society that supports a symphony
orchestra; also, such an orchestra.

physical therapy the treatment of disease or
injury by physical means rather than with
drugs, as by exercise, massage, heat, baths,
etc. —**physical therapist**

phys·ics (fiz′iks) **n.pl.** the science that deals
with energy and matter, and studies the
ways that things are moved and work is
done: *used with a singular verb* [*Physics*
includes the study of light, heat, sound,
electricity, and mechanics.]

plan·e·tar·i·um (plan′ə ter′ē əm) **n.** a
room with a large dome ceiling on which
images of the heavens are cast by a special
projector. The natural movements of the
sun, moon, planets, and stars can be shown
in these images.

plaque (plak) **n. 1** a thin, flat piece of metal,
wood, etc. with decoration or lettering on
it. Plaques are hung on walls, set in
monuments, etc. **2** a thin film that forms on
the teeth. It hardens into tartar if it is not
removed.

pleas·ant (plez′'nt) **adj. 1** that gives
pleasure; bringing happiness; enjoyable [a
pleasant day in the park]. **2** having a look
or manner that gives pleasure; likable [a
pleasant person]. —**pleas′ant·ly adv.**
—**pleas′ant·ness n.**

po·et·ic (pō et′ik) **adj. 1** of, like, or fit for a
poet or poetry [*poetic* talent; *poetic*
language]. **2** written in verse [*poetic* drama].
Also sometimes **po·et′i·cal.** —**po·et′i·cal·
ly adv.**

pol·i·tics (päl′ə tiks) **n.pl. 1** the science of
government; political science. **2** the act of
taking part in political affairs, often as a
profession. **3** the use of schemes to get what
one wants, especially power [office *politics*].
*This word is used with a singular verb in
meanings* 1, 2, *and* 3.

pol·len (päl′ən) **n.** the yellow powder found
on the stamens of flowers. It is made up of
male cells which fertilize another flower
when carried to its pistil, as by bees or the
wind.

por·ce·lain (pôr′s'l in) **n.** a fine, white, hard
earthenware used in making bathtubs, sinks,
tiles, etc. Porcelain used for dishes is called
china.

Por·tu·gal (pôr′chə gəl) a country in
southwestern Europe, west of Spain. It
includes the Azores and the Madeira
Islands.

pos·ses·sion (pə zesh′ən) **n. 1** the fact of
possessing, holding, or owning; ownership
[to have *possession* of secret information]. **2**
something that one owns [This vase is my
most prized *possession*.] **3** territory ruled by
an outside country [Guam is a *possession* of
the U.S.]

Portugal

a	ask, fat
ā	ape, date
ä	car, lot
e	elf, ten
er	berry, care
ē	even, meet
i	is, hit
ir	mirror, here
ī	ice, fire
ō	open, go
ô	law, horn
oi	oil, point
oo	look, pull
o͞o	ooze, tool
yoo	unite, cure
yo͞o	cute, few
ou	out, crowd
u	up, cut
ur	fur, fern
ə	a in ago
	e in agent
	e in father
	i in unity
	o in collect
	u in focus
ch	chin, arch
ng	ring, singer
sh	she, dash
th	thin, truth
th	then, father
zh	s in pleasure
′	as in (ā′b'l)

pos·ses·sive (pə zes′iv) *adj.* **1** having or showing a strong feeling for owning or keeping things [a *possessive* person]. **2** in grammar, describing the case of words that shows ownership, origin, etc. [The *possessive* case of English nouns is formed by adding 's or ' (the neighbor's dog; Jesus' teachings). "My," "mine," "your," "yours," "its," etc. are *possessive* pronouns.] ◆*n.* **1** the possessive case. **2** a word in this case. —**pos·ses′sive·ly** *adv.* —**pos·ses′sive·ness** *n.*

pound (pound) *n.* **1** a unit of weight, equal to 16 ounces in avoirdupois weight or 12 ounces in troy weight. One pound avoirdupois equals 453.59 grams. **2** the basic unit of money in the United Kingdom, equal to 100 pennies; also, the basic unit of money in certain other countries, as Ireland, Israel, Sudan, etc. £ is the symbol for this unit of money.

prac·ti·cal (prak′ti k'l) *adj.* **1** that can be put to use; useful and sensible [a *practical* idea; *practical* shoes]. **2** dealing with things in a sensible and realistic way [Wouldn't it be more *practical* to paint it yourself than pay to have it painted?] **3** learned through practice or experience [*practical* nursing]. —**prac′ti·cal′i·ty** (-kal′ ə tē) *n.*

pre·am·ble (prē′am′b'l) *n.* the part at the beginning of a document such as a constitution or law that tells its reason and purpose.

pre·cinct (prē′siŋkt) *n.* ☆**1** any of the districts into which a ward or city is divided [a voting *precinct*; a police *precinct*]. **2** *usually* **precincts**, *pl.* the grounds inside the limits of a church, school, etc. **3** a boundary or limit.

pre·clude (pri klood′) *v.* to make impossible; shut out; prevent [His care *precluded* any chance of failure.] —**pre·clud′ed, pre·clud′ing**

pred·i·cate (pred′ə kit) *n.* the word or words that say something about the subject of a sentence or clause. A predicate may be a verb, a verb and adverb, a verb and its object, etc. (The wind *blows*. The wind *blows hard*. The wind *blows the leaves down*.) ◆*adj.* of or in a predicate [In the sentence "Julie is ill," "ill" is a *predicate* adjective.] ◆*v.* (pred′ə kāt) to base upon certain facts, conditions, etc. [The decisions of the courts are *predicated* upon the Constitution.] —**pred′i·cat·ed, pred′i·cat·ing**

pre·fer (pri fur′) *v.* **1** to like better; choose first [He *prefers* baseball to football.] **2** to bring before a law court [She *preferred* charges against the thief who stole her car.] —**pre·ferred′, pre·fer′ring**

preg·nan·cy (preg′nən sē) *n.* the condition of being pregnant. —*pl.* **preg′nan·cies**

preg·nant (preg′nənt) *adj.* having an unborn child or offspring growing in the uterus; with young.

prej·u·dice (prej′ə dis) *n.* **1** an opinion formed without knowing the facts or by ignoring the facts; unfair or unreasonable opinion [Some people have a *prejudice* against modern art.] **2** dislike or distrust of people just because they are of another race, religion, country, etc. ◆*v.* to fill with prejudice [Joan *prejudiced* her sister against their uncle.] —**prej′u·diced, prej′u·dic·ing**

pre·lim·i·nar·y (pri lim′ə ner′ē) *adj.* leading up to the main action; introductory [the *preliminary* matches before the main bout]. ◆*n.* something that is done first; preliminary step [When the *preliminaries* were over, the meeting began.] —*pl.* **pre·lim′i·nar′ies**

prel·ude (prel′yood *or* prē′lood) *n.* **1** a part that comes before or leads up to what follows [The calm was a *prelude* to the storm.] **2** a part at the beginning of a piece of music, as of a fugue; also, a short, romantic piece of music.

pre·ma·ture (prē mə toor′ *or* prē mə choor′) *adj.* before the usual or proper time; too early or too hasty. —**pre·ma·ture′ly** *adv.*

pre·mier (pri mir′) *n.* a chief official; especially, a prime minister. ◆*adj.* first in importance or position; chief.

pre·mo·ni·tion (prē′mə nish′ən) *n.* a feeling that something bad will happen; forewarning.

prep·o·si·tion (prep′ə zish′ən) *n.* a word that connects a noun or pronoun to something else in the sentence, as to a verb (we went *to* the store), to a noun (the sound *of* music), or to an adjective (good *for* you).

pre·sup·pose (prē sə pōz′) *v.* **1** to suppose beforehand; take for granted [Her questions *presuppose* that we have read the book.] **2** to need or show as a reason [A healthy body *presupposes* a proper diet.] —**pre·sup·posed′, pre·sup·pos′ing** —**pre·sup·po·si·tion** (prē′sup ə zish′ən) *n.*

prev·a·lent (prev′ə lənt) *adj.* that exists, happens, etc. over a wide area; common; general [a *prevalent* belief]. —**prev′a·lence** *n.*

pri·ma·ry (prī′mer′ē *or* prī′mər ē) *adj.* **1** first in time or order [the *primary* grades in school]. **2** from which others are taken or made; basic [Red, yellow, and blue are the *primary* colors in painting.] **3** first in importance; chief [a matter of *primary* interest]. ◆*n.* **1** something first in order, importance, etc. ☆**2** an election in which candidates are chosen for a later election. —*pl.* **pri′ma′ries**

prim·i·tive (prim′ə tiv) *adj.* **1** of or living in earliest times; ancient [Some *primitive* peoples worshiped the sun.] **2** like that of earliest times; crude; simple [*primitive* art]. ◆*n.* a primitive person or thing. —**prim′i·tive·ly** *adv.*

pro·ce·dure (prə sē′jər) *n.* a way or method of doing something [the correct *procedure* to follow during a fire drill].

pro·ces·sion (prə sesh′ən) *n.* 1 a number of persons or things moving forward in an orderly way. 2 the act of moving in this way.

pro·duc·tion (prə duk′shən) *n.* 1 the act of producing [The new steel plant began *production* last week.] 2 the amount produced [The new machinery increased *production*.] 3 something that is produced, as a play that is staged for the public.

pro·fes·sor (prə fes′ər) *n.* a teacher; especially, a college teacher of the highest rank. —**pro·fes·so·ri·al** (prō′fə sôr′ē əl) *adj.* —**pro·fes′sor·ship** *n.*

pro·logue (prō′lôg) *n.* 1 an introduction to a poem, play, etc.; especially, lines spoken by an actor before a play begins. 2 any action or happening that serves as an introduction to another, more important happening.

pro·pel·ler *n.* a device made up of blades mounted on a shaft, which is turned by an engine for driving an airplane, ship, etc.

prop·er·ty (präp′ər tē) *n.* 1 something owned, especially land or real estate [There is much loss of *property* because of fire. We have a fence around our *property*.] 2 any of the special qualities by which a thing is known; characteristic [Oxygen has the *properties* of being colorless, odorless, and tasteless.] —*pl.* **prop′er·ties**

proph·et (präf′it) *n.* 1 a religious leader who is believed to speak for God or a god, as in giving messages or warnings [Isaiah was a *prophet*. The Greek oracles were *prophets*.] 2 a person who claims to tell what will happen in the future.

pro·pos·al (prə pō′z'l) *n.* 1 the act of suggesting or offering. 2 something proposed, as a plan or scheme [The council approved the mayor's *proposal*.] 3 an offer of marriage.

pro·pri·e·tar·y (prə prī′ə ter′ē) *adj.* 1 owned by a person or company, as under a patent, trademark, or copyright [A *proprietary* medicine is patented.] 2 owning property [the *proprietary* classes]. 3 of ownership [*proprietary* rights].

pro·pri·e·tor (prə prī′ə tər) *n.* a person who owns and sometimes also operates a store or business. —**pro·pri′e·tor·ship′** *n.*

pro·pul·sion (prə pul′shən) *n.* 1 a propelling, or driving forward. 2 a force that propels.

prose (prōz) *n.* speech or writing that is not poetry; ordinary language.

Prose comes from a Latin phrase meaning "direct speech." Prose is the form of language we ordinarily speak and write to each other. It does not have a formal pattern of rhyme or meter, as poetry usually does.

pro·té·gé (prōt′ə zhā) *n.* a person who is helped and guided in his or her career by another.

pro·to·col (prōt′ə kôl) *n.* the manners and forms that are accepted as proper and polite in official dealings, as between the ministers of different countries.

Protocol comes from the Greek words for "first" and "glue," and originally meant the first leaf glued to a document, describing what was in it. From this it came to mean the document telling of points of agreement reached by countries making a treaty. Later it also came to mean the code of behavior in ceremonies and dealings between high officials.

pro·trude (prō trōōd′) *v.* to stick out; project; extend [*protruding* front teeth]. —**pro·trud′ed, pro·trud′ing** —**pro·tru·sion** (prō trōō′zhən) *n.*

prov·erb (präv′ərb) *n.* an old and familiar saying that tells something wise ["A stitch in time saves nine" is a *proverb*.]

prov·ince (präv′ins) *n.* 1 a region in or belonging to a country, having its own local government; especially, any of the ten divisions of Canada that are like the States. 2 **provinces,** *pl.* the parts of a country away from the large cities. 3 range of duties or work [Enforcing laws falls within the *province* of a police department.]

pro·voke (prə vōk′) *v.* 1 to annoy or make angry [It *provoked* me to see litter on the lawn.] 2 to arouse or call forth [The clown's antics *provoked* laughter from the crowd.] —**pro·voked′, pro·vok′ing**

Provoke comes from Latin words that mean "to call forth." One might say that to provoke someone is to call forth some kind of reaction, so that the person becomes curious, angry, amused, etc.

prox·y (präk′sē) *n.* 1 a person who is given the power to act for another, as in voting; agent. 2 a statement in writing giving such power. 3 the action of a proxy [to vote by *proxy*]. —*pl.* **prox′ies**

pru·dent (prōōd′ənt) *adj.* careful or cautious in a sensible way; not taking chances; wise. —**pru′dence** *n.* —**pru′dent·ly** *adv.*

pseu·do·nym (sōō′də nim *or* syōō′də nim) *n.* a name used by a writer or other person in place of the real name [O. Henry is the *pseudonym* of William Sydney Porter.]

psy·chi·a·trist (sə kī′ə trist *or* sī kī′ə trist) *n.* a doctor who takes care of people who are mentally ill.

psy·chol·o·gy (sī käl′ə jē) *n.* 1 the science that studies the mind and the reasons for the ways that people think and act. 2 the ways of thinking and acting of a person or group [the *psychology* of the child; mob *psychology*]. —*pl.* **psy·chol′o·gies** —**psy·chol′o·gist** *n.*

propeller

a	ask, fat
ā	ape, date
ä	car, lot
e	elf, ten
er	berry, care
ē	even, meet
i	is, hit
ir	mirror, here
ī	ice, fire
ō	open, go
ô	law, horn
oi	oil, point
oo	look, pull
ōō	ooze, tool
yoo	unite, cure
yōō	cute, few
ou	out, crowd
u	up, cut
ur	fur, fern
ə	a in ago
	e in agent
	e in father
	i in unity
	o in collect
	u in focus
ch	chin, arch
ng	ring, singer
sh	she, dash
th	thin, truth
th	then, father
zh	s in pleasure
′	as in (ā′b'l)

179

pub·lic·i·ty (pə blis′ə tē) *n.* ☆**1** information that brings a person, place, or thing to the attention of the public [The newspapers gave much *publicity* to our play.] **2** the attention of the public [A politician seeks *publicity*.] **3** things done or the business of doing things to get public attention [An agent handles the rock star's *publicity*.]

punc·tu·al (puŋk′choo wəl) *adj.* coming, or doing something, at the right time; prompt. **—punc′tu·al′i·ty** *n.* **—punc′tu·al·ly** *adv.*

quad·ri·lat·er·al (kwäd′rə lat′ər əl) *adj.* having four sides. ◆*n.* a flat figure with four sides and four angles.

quar·an·tine (kwôr′ən tēn) *n.* **1** the act of keeping a diseased person, animal, or plant away from others so that the disease will not spread. **2** a place where such persons, animals, or plants are kept. **3** the time during which a ship is kept in port while the passengers, cargo, etc. are inspected for some disease. ◆*v.* **1** to put in a place of quarantine. **2** to cut off, as a country, from dealings with another or others. **—quar′an· tined, quar′an·tin·ing**

quadrilateral

Quarantine comes from an Italian word meaning "forty days." Originally a ship was kept in port for forty days when it was suspected of carrying a disease.

rack·et (rak′it) *n.* a light bat for tennis, badminton, etc., having a network as of catgut or nylon strung in a frame attached to a handle.

This word **racket** comes from an Arabic word meaning "palm of the hand." The first "racket" used in games was certainly the palm of the hand, and it is still the one used in the game of handball.

rac·quet (rak′it) *n. another spelling of* **racket**.

☆**rac·quet·ball** (rak′it bôl′) *n.* a game like handball, but played with a short-handled racket.

ra·di·ol·o·gy (rā′dē äl′ə jē) *n.* the use of X-rays, radioactive drugs, etc. to discover and treat diseases. **—ra′di·ol′o·gist** *n.*

ra·tion·al·ize (rash′ən ə līz′) *v.* to give a reasonable explanation without seeming to know that it is not the real one [We *rationalized* the small audience by blaming it on the weather.] **—ra′tion·al·ized′, ra′tion·al·iz′ing —ra′tion·al·i·za′tion** *n.*

re·cit·al (ri sīt′'l) *n.* **1** the act of reciting or telling with many details [a long *recital* of his troubles]. **2** the story or report told in this way. **3** a program of music or dances given by a soloist or soloists.

re·dun·dant (ri dun′dənt) *adj.* **1** more than enough; not needed. **2** using more words than are necessary to the meaning [It is *redundant* to say "Take daily doses every day."] **—re·dun′dant·ly** *adv.*

Redundant comes from a Latin word that means "to overflow." A redundant expression can be said to overflow with too many words.

re·flec·tor (ri flek′tər) *n.* a surface or part that reflects light, heat, sound, etc. [a *reflector* on a lamp].

re·frac·tion (ri frak′shən) *n.* the bending of a ray of light, etc. as it passes on a slant into a medium of a different density, as from air into water

re·gime or **ré·gime** (rə zhēm′ *or* rā zhēm′) *n.* a system of rule or government [a democratic *regime*].

re·ha·bil·i·tate (rē′hə bil′ə tāt) *v.* **1** to bring back to a normal or good condition [to *rehabilitate* a slum area]. **2** to bring back to a former rank or reputation. **—re′ha· bil′i·tat·ed, re′ha·bil′i·tat·ing —re′ha· bil′i·ta′tion** *n.*

rel·a·tiv·i·ty (rel′ə tiv′ə tē) *n.* **1** the condition of being relative. **2** a theory of the universe developed by Albert Einstein, dealing with the relationship of matter, energy, space, and time.

rel·e·vant (rel′ə vənt) *adj.* having to do with the matter at hand; to the point [a *relevant* remark]. **—rel′e·vance** or **rel′e· van·cy** *n.*

rep·re·sent·a·tive (rep′rə zen′tə tiv) *adj.* **1** representing; standing for [a sculptured figure *representative* of Justice]. **2** based on representation of the people by delegates [*representative* government]. **3** being an example; typical [This building is *representative* of modern architecture.] ◆*n.* **1** a typical example. **2** a person chosen to act or speak for others [Judy is our *representative* on the student council.] ☆**3 Representative**, a member of the lower house of Congress or of a State legislature.

re·pro·duc·tion (rē′prə duk′shən) *n.* **1** a reproducing or being reproduced. **2** a copy or imitation [a *reproduction* of an ancient statue]. **3** the process by which animals and plants produce others of their kind. **—re′pro·duc′tive** *adj.*

re·pub·li·can (ri pub′li kən) *adj.* **1** of or having to do with a republic [a *republican* form of government]. ☆**2 Republican**, of or belonging to the Republican Party. ◆*n.* **1** a person who believes in and supports a republic. ☆**2 Republican**, a member of the Republican Party.

re·search (ri surch′ *or* rē′surch) *n.* careful, patient study in order to find out facts and principles about some subject [to carry on *research* into the causes of cancer]. ◆*v.* to do research.

res·i·den·tial (rez′ə den′shəl) *adj.* **1** used for residences, or homes, not businesses [a *residential* area]. **2** of or having to do with residence [a *residential* requirement for voting].

res·pi·ra·tion (res′pə rā′shən) *n.* **1** the act or process of breathing. **2** the process by which a living thing takes in oxygen from the air or water and gives off carbon dioxide, etc.

ré·su·mé (rez′oo mā′ *or* rā′zoo mā′) *n.* **1** a brief report that tells the main points. ☆**2** a record of the work experience and education of a person applying for a job. *Also written* **resumé**.

res·ur·rect (rez′ə rekt′) *v.* **1** to bring back to life. **2** to bring back into use [to *resurrect* an old custom].

ret·i·cent (ret′ə s′nt) *adj.* not saying much, especially about one's thoughts. —**ret′i·cence** *n.*

re·ver·ber·ate (ri vur′bə rāt) *v.* to bounce back, as sound; echo [The guide's call *reverberated* in the cave.] —**re·ver′ber·at·ed, re·ver′ber·at·ing** —**re·ver′ber·a′tion** *n.*

re·viv·al (ri vī′v'l) *n.* **1** the act of bringing or coming back into use, being, etc. [the *revival* of an old custom]. **2** a meeting at which there is excited preaching for the purpose of stirring up religious feeling.

re·voke (ri vōk′) *v.* to put an end to, as a law, permit, license, etc.; cancel; repeal. —**re·voked′, re·vok′ing**

rev·o·lu·tion·ar·y (rev′ə loo′shən er′ē) *adj.* **1** of, in favor of, or causing a revolution, especially in a government. **2** bringing about very great change [a *revolutionary* new way to make glass]. **3** revolving or rotating. ◆*n.* another name for **revolutionist.** —*pl.* **rev′o·lu′tion·ar′ies**

rhet·o·ric (ret′ər ik) *n.* **1** the art of using words skillfully in speaking or writing. **2** a book about this. **3** a showy way of writing or speaking, especially when used to say something that is not important. —**rhe·tor·i·cal** (ri tôr′i k'l) *adj.* —**rhe·tor′i·cal·ly** *adv.*

ru·ble (roo′b'l) *n.* the basic unit of money in the U.S.S.R.

Rug·by (rug′bē) a private school for boys in England. ◆*n.* a kind of football first played at this school.

ru·pee (roo pē′) *n.* the basic unit of money in India, and also in Pakistan.

ru·ral (roor′əl) *adj.* having to do with the country or with people who live there, as on farms.

Ss

sanc·tu·ar·y (saŋk′choo wer′ē) *n.* **1** a place set aside for religious worship, as a church or temple. **2** a place where one can find safety and shelter; also, the safety found there [The criminals found *sanctuary* in a church.] **3** a place where birds and animals are protected from hunters [a wildlife *sanctuary*.] —*pl.* **san′tu·ar′ies**

sap·phire (saf′ir) *n].* **1** a clear, deep-blue, costly jewel. **2** deep blue.

sar·casm (sär′kaz'm) *n.* **1** a mocking or sneering remark meant to hurt or to make someone seem foolish. **2** the making of such remarks ["I only explained it five times," she replied in *sarcasm.*]

Sarcasm comes from the Greek word that means "to tear flesh the way dogs do." Sarcastic words are sometimes spoken of as biting words, for they are intended to bite into feelings and hurt, as a dog's teeth would hurt flesh.

sat·el·lite (sat′'l īt) *n.* **1** a heavenly body that revolves around another, larger one [The moon is a *satellite* of the earth.] **2** an artificial object put into orbit around the earth, the moon, or some other heavenly body. **3** a country that depends on and is controlled by a larger, more powerful one.

sat·is·fac·to·ry (sat′is fak′tə rē) *adj.* good enough to satisfy, or meet the need or wish. —**sat′is·fac′to·ri·ly** *adv.*

sat·u·rate (sach′ə rāt) *v.* **1** to soak through and through [The baby's bib was *saturated* with milk.] **2** to fill so completely or dissolve so much of something that no more can be taken up [to *saturate* water with salt]. —**sat′u·rat·ed, sat′u·rat·ing** —**sat′u·ra′tion** *n.*

sau·té (sō tā′) *v.* to fry quickly in a pan with a little fat. **sau·téed** (sō tād′), **sau·té·ing** (sō tā′iŋ) ◆*adj.* fried in this way [chicken livers *sauté*].

sa·vor·y¹ (sā′vər ē) *adj.* pleasing to the taste or smell [a *savory* stew].

sa·vor·y² (sā′vər ē) *n.* a kind of herb with a mint flavor. used in cooking.

satellite

a	ask, fat
ā	ape, date
ä	car, lot
e	elf, ten
er	berry, care
ē	even, meet
i	is, hit
ir	mirror, here
ī	ice, fire
ō	open, go
ô	law, horn
oi	oil, point
oo	look, pull
ōō	ooze, tool
yoo	unite, cure
yōō	cute, few
ou	out, crowd
u	up, cut
ur	fur, fern
ə	a in ago
	e in agent
	e in father
	i in unity
	o in collect
	u in focus
ch	chin, arch
ng	ring, singer
sh	she, dash
th	thin, truth
th	then, father
zh	s in pleasure
′	as in (ā′b'l)

181

scal·lop (skäl′əp *or* skal′əp) *n.* **1** a water animal with a soft body enclosed in two hard, ribbed shells hinged together. It has a large muscle, used as food. **2** any of a series of curves that form a fancy edge on cloth, lace, etc. ◆*v.* **1** tó bake with a milk sauce and bread crumbs [*scalloped* potatoes]. **2** to cut in scallops [a *scalloped* neckline].

scallop

scar·ci·ty (sker′sə tē) *n.* the condition of being scarce; lack, rareness, etc. —*pl.* **scar′ci·ties**

scav·eng·er (skav′in jər) *n.* **1** an animal that feeds on rotting meat and garbage [Vultures and hyenas are *scavengers*.] **2** a person who gathers things that others have thrown away.

sce·nar·i·o (si ner′ē ō) *n.* ☆**1** the written script from which a movie is made. **2** an outline for the way something might happen or is planned to happen. —*pl.* **sce·nar′i·os**

sched·ule (skej′ool) *n.* ☆**1** a list of the times at which certain things are to happen; timetable [a *schedule* of the sailings of an ocean liner]. ☆**2** a timed plan for a project [The work is ahead of *schedule*.] **3** a list of details [a *schedule* of postal rates]. ◆*v.* **1** to make a schedule of [to *schedule* one's hours of work]. ☆**2** to plan for a certain time [to *schedule* a game for 3:00 P.M.] —**sched′uled, sched′ul·ing**

scheme (skēm) *n.* **1** a plan or system in which things are carefully put together [the color *scheme* of a painting]. **2** a plan or program, often a secret or dishonest one [a *scheme* for getting rich quick]. ◆*v.* to make secret or dishonest plans; plot [Lee is always *scheming* to get out of work.] —**schemed, schem′ing** —**schem′er** *n.*

schooner

☆**schoon·er** (skoo′nər) *n.* a ship with two or more masts and sails that are set lengthwise.

se·clu·sion (si kloo′zhən) *n.* a secluding or being secluded; isolation; privacy [to live in *seclusion*].

sec·re·tar·y (sek′rə ter′ē) *n.* **1** a person whose work is keeping records, writing letters, etc. for a person, organization, etc. **2** the head of a department of government [the *Secretary* of State]. **3** a writing desk, especially one with a bookcase built at the top. —*pl.* **sec′re·tar′ies** —**sec·re·tar·i·al** (sek′rə ter′ē əl) *adj.*

se·cu·ri·ty (si kyoor′ə tē) *n.* **1** the condition or feeling of being safe or sure; freedom from danger, fear, doubt, etc. **2** something that protects [Insurance is a *security* against loss.] **3** something given or pledged as a guarantee [A car may be used as *security* for a loan.] **4 securities,** *pl.* stocks and bonds. —*pl.* **se·cu′ri·ties**

sed·i·men·ta·ry (sed′ə men′tər ē) *adj.* of, containing, or formed from sediment [*sedimentary* rock].

sem·i·an·nu·al (sem′i an′yoo wəl) *adj.* happening, coming, etc. twice a year [*semiannual* payment of taxes]. —**sem′i·an′nu·al·ly** *adv.*

sem·i·pre·cious (sem′i presh′əs) *adj.* describing gems, as the garnet or turquoise, that are of less value than the precious gems.

sen·sa·tion·al (sen sā′shən 'l) *adj.* more stirring up strong feeling or great excitement [a *sensational* new theory]. **2** meant to shock, thrill, excite, etc. [a *sensational* novel]. **3** very good: *used only in everyday talk*. —**sen·sa′tion·al·ism** *n.* —**sen·sa′tion·al·ly** *adv.*

sev·er·al (sev′ər əl *or* sev′rəl) *adj.* more than two but not many; a few [*Several* people called while you were out.] ◆*pron., n.* not many; a small number [Most of them left, but *several* stayed. *Several* of the windows were broken.]

shek·el (shek′'l) *n.* a gold or silver coin of the ancient Hebrews.

Si·er·ra Le·one (sē er′ə lē ōn) a country on the western coast of Africa.

sig·nif·i·cant (sig nif′ə kənt) *adj.* **1** important; full of meaning [The President gave a *significant* speech.] **2** having a meaning, especially a hidden one [She gave him a *significant* wink.] —**sig·nif′i·cant·ly** *adv.*

sim·i·lar·i·ty (sim′ə lar′ə tē) *n.* **1** the state of being similar; likeness. **2** a similar point or feature. —*pl.* **sim′i·lar′i·ties**

sim·i·le (sim′ə lē) *n.* a figure of speech in which two things that are different in most ways are said to be alike, by using either the word *as* or *like* ["He's as thin as a rail" and "She sings like a bird" are *similes*.] —*pl.* **sim′i·les**

sim·u·late (sim′yoo lāt) *v.* **1** to pretend to have or feel [to *simulate* anger]. **2** to look or act like; imitate [The insect *simulated* a twig.] —**sim′u·lat·ed, sim′u·lat·ing** —**sim′u·la′tion** *n.*

si·mul·ta·ne·ous (sī′m'l tā′nē əs) *adj.* done or happening together or at the same time. —**si′mul·ta′ne·ous·ly** *adv.*

sin·gu·lar (sing′gyə lər) *adj.* **1** being the only one of its kind; unique [a *singular* specimen]. **2** showing that only one is meant [The *singular* form of "geese" is "goose."] ◆*n.* the singular form of a word in grammar. —**sin·gu·lar·i·ty** (sing′gyə lar′ə tē) *n.* —**sin′gu·lar·ly** *adv.*

sit·u·a·tion (sich′oo wā′shən) *n.* **1** a place or position; location; site. **2** condition or state, as caused by things that have happened [Her election as mayor has created an interesting *situation*.]

ski (skē) *n.* one of a pair of long, wooden runners fastened to the shoes for gliding over snow. ◆*v.* to glide on skis, as down snow-covered hills. —**skied** (skēd), **ski′ing** —**ski′er** *n.*

slang (slaŋ) *n.* words and phrases that are used in everyday talk but are out of place in fine or serious speech or writing.

Slang words are usually popular for only a short time. A few slang words and meanings that have been in use for a longer time are included in this dictionary. "Crummy" is slang, and so are "rocky" when used to mean "weak or dizzy" and "grub" when used to mean "food."

so·journ (sō'jurn) *n.* a short stay; visit. ◆*v.* (*also* só jurn') to stay for a while, as on a visit [We *sojourned* in Italy.] —**so'journ·er** *n.*

Sojourn comes from a Latin word that means "under a day." Originally a sojourn was a short visit or trip that would take less than a day. **Sojourn**, **journal**, and **journey** all come to us from the same Latin word for "day."

so·lil·o·quy (sə lil'ə kwē) *n.* **1** the act of talking to oneself. **2** a speech in a play in which a character tells his or her thoughts to the audience by talking aloud, as if to himself or herself. —*pl.* **so·lil'o·quies**

so·lo (sō'lō) *n.* a piece of music that is sung or played by one person. —*pl.* **so'los** ◆*adj.* **1** for or by one singer or one instrument. **2** made or done by one person [a *solo* flight in an airplane]. ◆*adv.* without another or others; alone [She flew *solo*.] ◆*v.* **1** to fly an airplane alone. **2** to play or sing a musical solo. —**so'loed, so'lo·ing** —**so'lo·ist** *n.*

so·lu·tion (sə lōō'shən) *n.* **1** the solving of a problem. **2** an answer or explanation [to find the *solution* to a mystery]. **3** the dissolving of something in a liquid. **4** a mixture formed in this way [Make a *solution* of sugar and vinegar.]

son·net (sän'it) *n.* a poem of fourteen lines that rhyme in a certain pattern.

soph·o·more (säf'ə môr) *n.* a student in the tenth grade or in the second year of college.

so·ror·i·ty (sə rôr'ə tē) *n.* a club of women or girls, especially a social club, as in a college. —*pl.* **so·ror'i·ties**

souf·flé (sōō flā') *n.* a baked food made light and fluffy by adding beaten egg whites before baking [a cheese *soufflé*].

source (sôrs) *n.* **1** a spring or fountain that is the starting point of a stream. **2** a thing or place from which something comes or is got [The sun is our *source* of energy. This book is the *source* of my information.]

sou·ve·nir (sōō və nir') *n.* an object kept to remind one of something; memento [We save our programs as *souvenirs* of plays we've seen.]

spec·i·fi·ca·tion (spes'ə fi kā'shən) *n.* **1** the act of specifying; detailed mention. **2** something specified; a specific item. **3** *usually* **specifications**, *pl.* a statement or a description of all the necessary details, as of sizes, materials, etc. [the *specifications* for a new building].

spec·ta·cle (spek'tə k'l) *n.* **1** something to look at, especially an unusual sight or a grand public show [The fireworks display was a *spectacle*.] **2** spectacles, *pl.* a pair of eyeglasses: *an old-fashioned meaning.*

Spectacle, spectacular, spectator, specter, spectroscope, and spectrum all come from the Latin word *spectare*, meaning "to behold." All of these words have to do with someone seeing or with something seen or used in seeing.

spec·u·late (spek'yə lāt) *v.* **1** to think about or make guesses; ponder; meditate [Scientists *speculate* on the kinds of life there may be on distant planets.] **2** to make risky business deals with the hope of making large profits. —**spec'u·lat·ed, spec'u·lat·ing** —**spec'u·la'tion** *n.* —**spec'u·la'tor** *n.*

spir·it·u·al (spir'i chōō wəl) *adj.* **1** of the spirit or soul as apart from the body or material things. **2** having to do with religion or the church; sacred. ◆*n.* ☆a religious folk song of the kind created by black Americans. —**spir·it·u·al·i·ty** (spir'i chōō wal'ə tē) *n.* —**spir'it·u·al·ly** *adv.*

stage·coach (stāj'kōch) *n.* a coach pulled by horses that traveled a regular route, carrying passengers, mail, etc.

stan·za (stan'zə) *n.* a group of lines forming one of the sections of a poem or song; verse.

Stanza is an Italian word for "stopping place." A poem or song stops between the stanzas, each of which has a further thought about the poem's subject.

sta·tis·ti·cal (stə tis'ti k'l) *adj.* having to do with statistics. —**sta·tis'ti·cal·ly** *adv.*

staunch (stônch *or* stänch) *v.* to stop or slow down the flow of blood from a wound. ◆*adj.* **1** strong, firm, loyal, etc. [*staunch* friendship]. **2** watertight [a *staunch* ship]. —**staunch'ly** *adv.*

stim·u·lant (stim'yə lənt) *n.* something that stimulates or excites one, as coffee or any of certain drugs.

stri·dent (strīd''nt) *adj.* harsh in sound; shrill or grating [a *strident* voice]. —**stri'dent·ly** *adv.*

struc·tur·al (struk'chər əl) *adj.* **1** used in building [*structural* steel]. **2** of structure [*structural* design]. —**struc'tur·al·ly** *adv.*

sub·poe·na (sə pē'nə) *n.* an official paper ordering a person to appear in a court of law. ◆*v.* to order with such a paper. —**sub·poe'naed, sub·poe'na·ing** Also spelled **sub·pe'na.**

sub·sid·i·ar·y (səb sid'ē er'ē) *adj.* **1** helping or useful, especially in a lesser way. **2** of less importance; secondary. ◆*n.* **1** a person or thing that helps or gives aid. **2** a company that is controlled by another company [The bus company's *subsidiary* operates the lunchrooms in the stations.] —*pl.* **sub·sid'i·ar'ies**

stagecoach

a	ask, fat
ā	ape, date
ä	car, lot
e	elf, ten
er	berry, care
ē	even, meet
i	is, hit
ir	mirror, here
ī	ice, fire
ō	open, go
ô	law, horn
oi	oil, point
͝oo	look, pull
͞oo	ooze, tool
yͤoo	unite, cure
y͞oo	cute, few
ou	out, crowd
u	up, cut
ur	fur, fern
ə	a in ago
	e in agent
	e in father
	i in unity
	o in collect
	u in focus
ch	chin, arch
ng	ring, singer
sh	she, dash
th	thin, truth
th	then, father
zh	s in pleasure
'	as in (ā'b'l)

sub·urb (sub′ərb) **n.** a district, town, etc. on the outskirts of a city.

The word for city in ancient Rome was *urbs.* The *sub-* in **suburb** means "near," so the word itself means literally "near the city."

sub·ur·ban (sə bur′bən) **adj. 1** of or living in a suburb. **2** typical of suburbs or of those who live in them [a *suburban* style of living].

suc·ces·sive (sək ses′iv) **adj.** coming in regular order without a break; consecutive [I won six *successive* games.] —**suc·ces′sive·ly adv.**

suc·cu·lent (suk′yoo lənt) **adj.** full of juice; juicy [a *succulent* peach]. —**suc′cu·lence n.**

sum·mon (sum′ən) **v. 1** to call together; call or send for [The President *summoned* the Cabinet.] **2** to call forth; rouse; gather [*Summon* up your strength.] **3** to order to appear in a court of law.

su·per·flu·ous (soo pur′floo wəs) **adj.** more than is needed; unnecessary [*superfluous* motions; a *superfluous* remark]. —**su·per′flu·ous·ly adv.**

su·per·in·tend·ent (soo′pər in ten′dənt) **n. 1** a person in charge of an institution, school system, etc. **2** the manager of a building; custodian.

su·pe·ri·or (sə pir′ē ər) **adj. 1** higher in rank, position, etc. [Soldiers salute their *superior* officers.] **2** above average in quality, value, skill, etc.; excellent [a *superior* grade of cotton]. **3** showing a feeling of being better than others; haughty. ◆**n. 1** a person of higher rank, greater skill, etc. **2** the head of a monastery or convent. —**su·pe·ri·or·i·ty** (sə pir′ē ôr′ə tē) **n.**

su·per·vi·sor (soo′pər vi′zər) **n.** a person who supervises; director. —**su′per·vi′so·ry adj.**

sup·ple·ment (sup′lə mənt) **n. 1** something added, as to make up for something missing [Vitamin pills are a *supplement* to a poor diet.] **2** a section added to a book or newspaper, to give extra or more up-to-date information, special articles, etc. ◆**v.** (sup′lə ment) to be or give a supplement to; add to. —**sup′ple·men′tal adj.**

sup·press (sə pres′) **v. 1** to put down by force or power; crush [The ship's captain acted quickly to *suppress* the mutiny.] **2** to keep back; hide; conceal [to *suppress* a laugh; to *suppress* the truth; to *suppress* a news story]. —**sup·pres·sion** (sə presh′ə n) **n.**

sur·geon (sur′jən) **n.** a doctor who specializes in surgery.

sur·ger·y (sur′jər ē) **n. 1** the treating of disease or injury by operations with the hands or tools, as in setting broken bones, cutting out tonsils, etc. **2** an operation of this kind. **3** the room in a hospital where doctors do such operations. —*pl.* **sur′ger·ies**

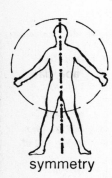

symmetry

Surgery comes from a Greek word meaning "a working with the hands." The doctor who does surgery must be skillful in using the hands to treat patients.

sur·viv·al (sər vī′v'l) **n. 1** the act or fact of surviving, or continuing to exist [Nuclear war threatens the *survival* of all nations.] **2** something surviving from an earlier time, as a custom.

sus·pend (sə spend′) **v. 1** to hang by a support from above [The keys were *suspended* by a chain from his belt.] **2** to keep out for a while as a punishment [She was *suspended* from school for misbehaving.] **3** to stop from operating for a time [to *suspend* bus service; to *suspend* a rule]. **4** to hold back or put off [The judge *suspended* her sentence.]

sus·pense (sə spens′) **n. 1** the condition of being anxious and uncertain [We waited in *suspense* for the jury's verdict.] **2** the growing excitement felt as a story, play, etc. builds to a high point or climax [a movie full of *suspense*].

syl·la·ble (sil′ə b'l) **n. 1** a word or part of a word spoken with a single sounding of the voice ["Moon" is a word of one *syllable.* "Moonlight" is a word of two *syllables.*] **2** any of the parts into which a written word is divided to show where it may be broken at the end of a line [The *syllables* of the entry words in this dictionary are divided by tiny dots.]

Syllable comes from a Greek word that means "to put or hold together." Syllables are put together to form words.

syl·la·bus (sil′ə bəs) **n.** an outline or summary, especially of a course of study. —*pl.* **syl′la·bus·es** or **syl·la·bi** (sil′ə bī)

sym·bol·ize (sim′b'l īz) **v. 1** to be a symbol of; stand for [A heart *symbolizes* love.] **2** to represent by a symbol [This artist *symbolizes* the human spirit by means of figures with wings.] —**sym′bol·ized, sym′bol·iz·ing**

sym·me·try (sim′ə trē) **n. 1** an arrangement in which the parts on opposite sides of a center line are alike in size, shape, and position [The human body has *symmetry.*] **2** balance or harmony that comes from such an arrangement.

sym·pho·ny (sim′fə nē) **n. 1** a long piece of music for a full orchestra, usually divided into four movements with different rhythms and themes. **2** a large orchestra for playing such works: *its full name is* **symphony orchestra. 3** harmony, as of sounds, color, etc. [The dance was a *symphony* in motion.] —*pl.* **sym′pho·nies** —**sym·phon·ic** (sim fän′ik) **adj.** —**sym·phon′i·cal·ly adv.**

sym·po·si·um (sim pō′zē əm) **n. 1** a meeting for discussing some subject. **2** a group of writings or opinions on a particular subject. —*pl.* **sym·po′si·ums** or **sym·po·si·a** (sim pō′zē ə)

symp·tom (simp′təm) *n.* something showing that something else exists; sign [Spots on the skin may be a *symptom* of chicken pox.] —**symp·to·mat·ic** (simp′tə mat′ik) *adj.*

syn·a·gogue (sin′ə gäg *or* sin′ə gôg) *n.* a building where Jews gather for worship and religious study.

syn·chro·nize (siŋ′krə nīz) *v.* **1** to move or happen at the same time or speed [The gears must *synchronize* when you shift.] **2** to make agree in time or rate of speed [Let's *synchronize* our watches. The movie film should be *synchronized* with the sound track.] —**syn′chro·nized, syn′chro·niz·ing**

Synchronize comes from two Greek words that mean "to be together in time." The shutter and flashbulb of a camera are synchronized so that they will both operate at the same time.

syn·co·pate (siŋ′kə pāt) *v.* in music, to shift the accent by putting the beat at a place that would normally not be accented and holding it into the next accented beat [Much jazz is *syncopated*.] —**syn′co·pat·ed, syn′co·pat·ing** —**syn′co·pa′tion** *n.*

syn·di·cate (sin′də kit) *n.* **1** a group of bankers, large companies, etc. formed to carry out some project that needs much money. ☆**2** an organization that sells articles, stories, comic strips, etc. to a number of newspapers. ◆*v.* (sin′di kāt) **1** to form into a syndicate. **2** to publish through a syndicate in a number of newspapers. —**syn′di·cat·ed, syn′di·cat·ing** —**syn′di·ca′tion** *n.*

syn·on·y·mous (si nän′ə məs) *adj.* of the same or almost the same meaning.

syn·tax (sin′taks) *n.* the way words are put together and related to one another in sentences; sentence structure. —**syn·tac′ti·cal** or **syn·tac′tic** *adj.*

syn·the·sis (sin′thə sis) *n.* the putting together of parts or elements so as to make a whole [Plastics are made by chemical *synthesis*.] —*pl.* **syn·the·ses** (sin′thə sēz)

sy·ringe (sə rinj′ *or* sir′inj) *n.* a device made up of a narrow tube with a rubber bulb or a plunger at one end, for drawing in a liquid and then pushing it out in a stream. Syringes are used to inject fluids into the body, to wash out wounds, etc. ◆*v.* to wash out with a syringe. —**sy·ringed′, sy·ring′ing**

Tt

tac·i·turn (tas′ə tɜrn) *adj.* not liking to talk; usually silent. —**tac′i·tur′ni·ty** *n.*

tech·ni·cal·i·ty (tek′nə kal′ə tē) *n.* **1** a technical point, detail, etc. [the *technicalities* of radio repair]. **2** a small point or detail related to a main issue [She was found guilty on a legal *technicality*.] —*pl.* **tech′ni·cal′i·ties**

tech·ni·cian (tek nish′ən) *n.* a person who has skill in the technique of some art or science.

tech·nol·o·gy (tek näl′ə jē) *n.* **1** the study of the industrial arts or applied sciences, as engineering, mechanics, etc. **2** science as it is put to use in practical work [medical *technology*]. **3** a method or process for dealing with a technical problem. —**tech·no·log·i·cal** (tek′nə läj′i k′l) *adj.* —**tech′no·log′i·cal·ly** *adv.* —**tech·nol′o·gist** *n.*

tel·e·cast (tel′ə kast) *v.* to broadcast by television. ◆*n.* a television broadcast. —**tel′e·cast** or **tel′e·cast·ed, tel′e·cast·ing** —**tel′e·cast·er** *n.*

tel·e·vise (tel′ə vīz) *v.* to send pictures of by television [to *televise* a baseball game]. —**tel′e·vised, tel′e·vis·ing**

tend·en·cy (ten′dən sē) *n.* the fact of being likely or apt to move or act in a certain way [There is a *tendency* for prices to go up. Pat has a *tendency* to complain.] —*pl.* **tend′en·cies**

ter·mi·nal (tɜr′mə n′l) *adj.* of, at, or forming the end [a *terminal* bud on a branch; the *terminal* payment of a loan]. ◆*n.* **1** an end or end part. **2** a main station of a railroad, bus line, or airline, where many trips begin or end. **3** a machine like a typewriter, but with a kind of TV screen, for feeding information to, or getting it from, a computer.

ter·race (ter′əs) *n.* **1** a flat platform of earth with sloping banks; also, any of a series of such platforms, rising one above the other, as on a hillside. **2** a paved area near a house, that overlooks a lawn or garden; patio. **3** a small, roofed balcony outside an apartment. ◆*v.* to form into a terrace or terraces. —**ter′raced, ter′rac·ing**

ter·rain (tə rān′) *n.* ground or an area of land [a farm with hilly *terrain*].

ter·ri·to·ry (ter′ə tôr′ē) *n.* **1** the land ruled by a nation or state. **2 Territory**, a large division of a country or empire, that does not have the full rights of a province or state, as in Canada or Australia [the Northwest *Territories*]. **3** any large stretch of land; region. **4** the particular area chosen as its own by an animal or group of animals. —*pl.* **ter′ri·to′ries**

the·ol·o·gy (thē äl′ə jē) *n.* **1** the study of God and of religious beliefs. **2** a system of religious beliefs. —*pl.* **the·ol′o·gies** —**the·o·lo·gian** (thē′ə lō′jən) *n.*

ther·a·peu·tic (ther′ə pyōōt′ik) *adj.* having to do with or used in treating or curing diseases. —**ther′a·peu′ti·cal·ly** *adv.*

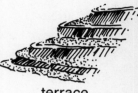

terrace

a	ask, fat
ā	ape, date
ä	car, lot
e	elf, ten
er	berry, care
ē	even, meet
i	is, hit
ir	mirror, here
ī	ice, fire
ō	open, go
ô	law, horn
oi	oil, point
ŏŏ	look, pull
ōō	ooze, tool
yŏŏ	unite, cure
yōō	cute, few
ou	out, crowd
u	up, cut
ʉr	fur, fern
ə	a in ago
	e in agent
	e in father
	i in unity
	o in collect
	u in focus
ch	chin, arch
ŋ	ring, singer
sh	she, dash
th	thin, truth
th	then, father
zh	s in pleasure
′	as in (ā′b'l)

thermos

ther·a·py (ther′ə pē) **n.** any method of treating disease [drug *therapy*; heat *therapy*]. —*pl.* **ther′a·pies** —☆**ther′a·pist n.**

ther·mos (thur′məs) **n.** a container for keeping liquids at almost the same temperature for several hours: *the full name is* **thermos bottle.**

ther·mo·stat (thur′mə stat) **n.** a device for keeping temperature even, especially one that automatically controls a furnace, etc. —**ther′mo·stat′ic adj.**

tim·bre (tim′bər *or* tam′bər) **n.** the quality of sound, apart from pitch or loudness, that makes one's voice or musical instrument different from others.

tol·er·ance (täl′ər əns) **n. 1** a willingness to let others have their own beliefs, ways, etc., even though these are not like one's own. **2** the power of the body to keep a drug or poison from working [My body has built up a *tolerance* for penicillin, so that it can no longer help me.]

to·pog·ra·phy (tə päg′rə fē) **n. 1** the surface features of a region, as hills, rivers, roads, etc. **2** the science of showing these on maps and charts. —**to·pog′ra·pher n.** —**top·o·graph·i·cal** (täp′ə graf′i k'l) **adj.**

tour·na·ment (toor′nə mənt) **n. 1** a contest in which knights on horseback tried to knock each other off the horses with lances. **2** a series of contests in some sport or game in which a number of people or teams take part, trying to win the championship.

tran·quil (traŋ′kwəl) **adj.** calm, quiet, peaceful, etc. [*tranquil* waters; a *tranquil* mood]. —**tran·quil′li·ty** or **tran·quil′i·ty n.** —**tran′quil·ly adv.**

☆**trans·con·ti·nen·tal** (trans′kän tə nen′t'l) **adj.** that goes from one side of a continent to the other [a *transcontinental* airplane flight].

trans·fuse (trans fyōōz′) **v. 1** to pass blood, blood plasma, etc. that has been taken from one person into a vein of another. **2** to pour in or spread through; instill [Victory *transfused* courage into the team.] —**trans·fused′, trans·fus′ing** —**trans·fu′sion n.**

tran·si·tive (tran′sə tiv) **adj.** describing a verb that takes a direct object [In the sentence "He saved money for a car," "saved" is a *transitive* verb.]

trans·mit (trans mit′) **v. 1** to send from one person or place to another; pass on; transfer [to *transmit* a disease; to *transmit* a letter; to *transmit* power from an engine by means of gears]. **2** to pass or let pass, as light, heat, etc. [Water *transmits* sound.] **3** to send out radio or TV signals. —**trans·mit′ted, trans·mit′ting**

trans·mit·ter (trans mit′ər) **n. 1** a person or thing that transmits. **2** the part of a telegraph or telephone that sends out sounds or signals. **3** the apparatus for sending out electric waves in radio and TV.

tweezers

tran·spire (tran spīr′) **v. 1** to give off vapor, moisture, etc., as through pores. **2** to become known. ☆**3** to take place; happen: *thought of by some people as a loose or incorrect meaning* [What *transpired* while I was gone?] —**tran·spired′, tran·spir′ing**

treach·er·ous (trech′ər əs) **adj. 1** not loyal or faithful; betraying or likely to betray. **2** seeming safe, reliable, etc. but not really so [*treacherous* rocks]. —**treach′er·ous·ly adv.**

treas·ur·er (trezh′ər ər) **n.** a person in charge of a treasury, as of a government, company, club, etc.

tres·pass (tres′pəs *or* tres′pas) **v. 1** to go on another's property without permission or right ["No *trespassing*" means "keep out."] **2** to break in on; intrude [Don't *trespass* on my privacy.] **3** to do wrong; sin. ◆**n. 1** the act of trespassing. **2** a sin or wrong. —**tres′pass·er n.**

trib·u·tar·y (trib′yōō ter′ē) **n. 1** a stream or river that flows into a larger one. **2** a nation that pays tribute or is under the power of another nation. —*pl.* **trib′u·tar′ies** ◆**adj. 1** flowing into a larger one [a *tributary* stream]. **2** paying tribute to another, or under another's power [a *tributary* nation].

trig·o·nom·e·try (trig′ə näm′ə trē) **n.** the branch of mathematics dealing with the relations between the sides and angles of triangles.

trite (trīt) **adj.** used so much that it is no longer fresh or new; stale ["Happy as a lark" is a *trite* expression.] —**trit′er, trit′est** —**trite′ly adv.**

Trite comes from a Latin word that means "to wear out." A trite phrase or saying has been used so much that it is worn out.

trop·i·cal (träp′i k'l) **adj.** of, in, or like the tropics [heavy *tropical* rains; *tropical* heat].

☆**troupe** (trōōp) **n.** a band or company, especially of actors, singers, etc. —**troup′er n.**

tur·bine (tur′bin *or* tur′bīn) **n.** an engine in which the driving shaft is made to turn by the pressure of steam, water, or air against the vanes of a wheel fixed to it.

tur·quoise (tur′koiz *or* tur′kwoiz) **n. 1** a greenish-blue stone used as a jewel. **2** a greenish blue.

Turquoise comes from an old French word meaning "Turkish." The first turquoise stones were brought to western Europe through Turkey and were thus thought to be Turkish although they really had come from Persia.

tweez·ers (twē′zərz) **n.pl.** small pincers for plucking out hairs, handling small things, etc.

Tweezers comes from an old French word, now no longer used, that means a set of surgical instruments. That word came in turn from *etuis*, plural of a word for a small case used to hold needles or other small implements.

tyr·an·ny (tir′ə nē) *n.* **1** the government or power of a tyrant; harsh and unjust government. **2** very cruel and unjust use of power. **3** a tyrannical act. —*pl.* **tyr′an·nies**

Uu

um·bil·i·cal cord (um bil′i k′l) the cord that connects a pregnant woman with her unborn baby. Through it the baby gets nourishment, and at the point where it is cut at birth the baby's navel is formed.

um·brel·la (um brel′ə) *n.* cloth, plastic, etc. stretched over a folding frame at the top of a stick, used to protect one from the rain or sun.

un·doubt·ed·ly (un dout′id lē) *adv.* without doubt; certainly [It is *undoubtedly* a ruby.]

un·for·get·ta·ble (un′fər get′ə b′l) *adj.* so important, beautiful, shocking, etc. that it cannot be forgotten.

u·ni·lat·er·al (yo͞o′nə lat′ər əl) *adj.* having to do with or done by only one of several persons, nations, etc. [a *unilateral* decision].

un·scathed (un skā*th*d′) *adj.* not hurt; unharmed [We got out of the accident *unscathed.*]

up·heav·al (up hē′v′l) *n.* **1** a forceful lifting up from beneath [the *upheaval* of ground in an earthquake]. **2** a sudden, violent change [the *upheaval* begun by the French Revolution.]

up·hol·ster·y (up hōl′stər ē *or* ə pōl′stər ē) *n.* the work of upholstering or materials used for this.

ur·ban (ur′bən) *adj.* of, living in, or having to do with cities or towns [*urban* dwellers].

Vv

vac·ci·nate (vak′sə nāt) *v.* to inject a vaccine into, in order to keep from getting a certain disease, as smallpox. —**vac′ci·nat·ed, vac′ci·nat·ing**

vag·a·bond (vag′ə bänd) *n.* **1** a person who moves from place to place. **2** *another name for* **tramp.** ◆*adj.* **1** wandering from place to place [a *vagabond* tribe]. **2** of or having to do with a drifting, carefree life [*vagabond* habits].

va·grant (vā′grənt) *n.* a person who wanders from place to place, doing odd jobs or begging; tramp. ◆*adj.* wandering from place to place, or living the life of a vagrant.

vague (vāg) *adj.* not clear, definite, or distinct, as in form, meaning, or purpose [*vague* figures in the fog; a *vague* answer]. —**va′guer, va′guest** —**vague′ly** *adv.* —**vague′ness** *n.*

var·i·a·tion (ver′ē ā′shən) *n.* **1** the act of varying, changing, or differing [a *variation* in style]. **2** the amount of a change [a *variation* of ten feet]. **3** the repeating of a tune or musical theme, with changes as in rhythm or key.

va·ri·e·ty (və rī′ə tē) *n.* **1** change; lack of sameness [I like *variety* in my meals.] **2** any of the various forms of something; sort; kind [many *varieties* of cloth; a cat of the striped *variety*]. **3** a number of different kinds [a *variety* of fruits at the market]. —*pl.* **va·ri′e·ties**

var·i·ous (ver′ē əs) *adj.* **1** of several different kinds [We planted *various* seeds.] **2** several or many [*Various* people have said so.] —**var′i·ous·ly** *adv.*

vaude·ville (vôd′vil *or* vôd′vil) *n.* ☆a stage show made up of different kinds of acts, as comic skits, songs, dances, etc.

The word **vaudeville** was French to begin with. It comes to us from *Vau-de-Vire*, the name of a valley in Normandy, France. The people of the valley have been famous for their light, merry songs.

ven·dor *or* **vend·er** (ven′dər) *n.* a person who sells; seller [She is a *vendor* of drinks at baseball games.]

ve·neer (və nir′) *v.* to cover a common material with a thin layer of fine wood or costly material [piano keys *veneered* with ivory]. ◆*n.* **1** a thin layer of fine wood or costly material put over a common material [a walnut *veneer* on a pine chest]. **2** an outward look or show that hides what is below [a coarse person with a thin *veneer* of culture.]

ven·ti·la·tor (ven′t′l āt ər) *n.* an opening or device for bringing in fresh air and driving out stale air.

ver·bose (vər bōs′) *adj.* using too many words; wordy. —**ver·bos·i·ty** (vər bäs′ə tē) *n.*

ver·dict (vur′dikt) *n.* **1** the decision reached by a jury in a law case [a *verdict* of "not guilty"]. **2** any decision or opinion.

ver·min (vur′min) *n.* **1** small animals or insects, such as rats and flies, that cause harm or are troublesome to people. **2** a disgusting person. —*pl.* **ver′min**

ver·nac·u·lar (vər nak′yə lər) *n.* **1** the native language of a country or place. **2** the everyday language of ordinary people. **3** the special words and phrases used in a particular work, by a particular group, etc. [In the *vernacular* of sailors, "deck" is the word for "floor."] ◆*adj.* of, using, or based on the everyday speech of ordinary people in a certain country or place [James Whitcomb Riley was a *vernacular* poet.]

umbrella

a	ask, fat
ā	ape, date
ä	car, lot
e	elf, ten
er	berry, care
ē	even, meet
i	is, hit
ir	mirror, here
ī	ice, fire
ō	open, go
ô	law, horn
oi	oil, point
o͞o	look, pull
o͞o	ooze, tool
yo͞o	unite, cure
yo͞o	cute, few
ou	out, crowd
u	up, cut
ur	fur, fern
ə	a in ago
	e in agent
	e in father
	i in unity
	o in collect
	u in focus
ch	chin, arch
ŋ	ring, singer
sh	she, dash
th	thin, truth
th	then, father
zh	s in pleasure
′	as in (ā′b'l)

ves·sel (ves′′l) *n.* **1** anything hollow for holding something; container [Bowls, kettles, tubs, etc. are *vessels*.] **2** a ship or large boat. **3** any of the tubes in the body through which a fluid flows [a blood *vessel*].

vet·er·i·nar·i·an (vet′ər ə ner′ē ən) *n.* a doctor who treats the diseases and injuries of animals.

vi·bra·to (vi brät′ō) *n.* a slight throbbing in the sound of a singer's voice or of a musical instrument. It is produced by rapid, slight changes of the pitch back and forth.

vice-pres·i·dent (vīs′prez′i dənt) *n.* **1** an officer next in rank to a president, who takes the place of the president if the president should die, be absent, etc. ☆**2 Vice-President**, such an officer in the United States government, who is also president of the Senate: *usually written* **Vice President**.

vid·e·o·tape (vid′ē ō tāp′) *n.* a thin magnetic tape on which both the sound and picture signals of a TV program can be recorded by electronics.

vin·dic·tive (vin dik′tiv) *adj.* **1** wanting to get revenge; ready to do harm in return for harm [A *vindictive* person holds a grudge.] **2** said or done in revenge [*vindictive* punishment]. —**vin·dic′tive·ly** *adv.*

vin·e·gar (vin′i gər) *n.* a sour liquid made by fermenting cider, wine, etc., used to flavor or pickle foods.

vir·tu·o·so (vur′choo wō′sō) *n.* a person having great skill in the practice of some art, especially in playing music. —*pl.* **vir′tu·o′sos** or **vir·tu·o·si** (vur′choo wō′sē) —**vir·tu·os·i·ty** (vur′choo wäs′ə tē) *n.*

vis·i·bil·i·ty (viz′ə bil′ə tē) *n.* **1** the condition of being visible. **2** the distance within which things can be seen [Fog reduced the *visibility* to 500 feet.]

vo·cab·u·lar·y (vō kab′yə ler′ē) *n.* **1** all the words of a language, or all those used by a certain person or group [Jan's *vocabulary* is large. The word "fracture" is part of the medical *vocabulary*.] **2** a list of words, usually in alphabetical order with their meanings, as in a dictionary. —*pl.* **vo·cab′u·lar′ies**

vo·cal·ize (vō′k'l īz) *v.* to make sounds with the voice; speak or sing. —**vo′cal·ized, vo′cal·iz·ing**

vo·ca·tion (vō kā′shən) *n.* one's profession, occupation, trade, or career [He found his *vocation* in social work.] —**vo·ca′tion·al** *adj.*

A **vocation** is sometimes referred to as a "calling," and there is a connection between these words. The word **vocation** comes from a Latin word meaning "to call." People often feel as though they have been called upon to follow a certain kind of work.

vessel

wharf

vo·cif·er·ous (vō sif′ər əs) *adj.* loud and noisy in making one's feelings known; clamorous [a *vociferous* crowd; *vociferous* complaints].

☆**vol·ley·ball** (väl′ē bôl′) *n.* **1** a game played by two teams who hit a large, light ball back and forth over a high net with their hands. **2** the ball used in this game.

volt·age (vōl′tij) *n.* the force that produces electric current. It is measured in volts.

vol·un·tar·y (väl′ən ter′ē) *adj.* **1** acting, done, or given of one's own free will; by choice [*voluntary* workers; *voluntary* gifts]. **2** controlled by one's mind or will [*voluntary* muscles]. —**vol′un·tar′i·ly** *adv.*

vul·ner·a·ble (vul′nər ə b'l) *adj.* **1** that can be hurt, destroyed, attacked, etc. [The wolf looked for a *vulnerable* spot into which to sink its fangs.] **2** likely to be hurt; sensitive [A vain person is *vulnerable* to criticism.] —**vul′ner·a·bil′i·ty** *n.*

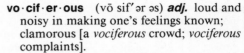

war·rant (wôr′ənt) *n.* **1** a good reason for something; justification [She has no *warrant* for such a belief.] **2** something that makes sure; guarantee [His wealth is no *warrant* of happiness.] **3** an official paper that gives the right to do something [The police must have a *warrant* to search a house.] ◆*v.* **1** to be a good reason for; justify [Her good work *warrants* our praise.] **2** to give the right to do something [His arrest was not *warranted*.] **3** to give a warranty for [This appliance is *warranted*.]

wharf (hwôrf) *n.* a long platform built out over water so that ships can dock beside it to load and unload. —*pl.* **wharves** (hwôrvz) or **wharfs**

whol·ly (hō′lē) *adv.* to the whole amount or degree; altogether; completely [You are *wholly* right. The building was *wholly* destroyed.]

win·some (win′səm) *adj.* attractive in a sweet, pleasant way; charming [a *winsome* girl].

with·hold (with hōld′) *v.* **1** to keep from giving or granting; refuse [She *withheld* her approval of the plan.] **2** to hold back; keep back; check [He *withheld* his anger.] —**with·held′, with·hold′ing**

zinnia

yeast (yēst) *n.* **1** a yellow, frothy substance made up of tiny fungi, used in baking to make dough rise. **2** this substance dried in flakes or tiny grains, or made up in small cakes.

yen (yen) *n.* the basic unit of money in Japan.

Yu·go·sla·vi·a (yōō′gō slä′vē ə) a country in southeastern Europe, on the Balkan Peninsula.

Zim·ba·bwe (zim bä′bwe) a country in southern Africa.

zinc (ziṇk) *n.* a bluish-white metal that is a chemical element. It is used to coat iron, and in making certain alloys, medicines, etc.

zin·ni·a (zin′ē ə) *n.* a garden plant with brightly colored flowers having many petals.

zo·ol·o·gy (zō äl′ə jē) *n.* the science that studies animals and animal life. —**zo·ol′o·gist** *n.*

a	ask, fat
ā	ape, date
ä	car, lot
e	elf, ten
er	berry, care
ē	even, meet
i	is, hit
ir	mirror, here
ī	ice, fire
ō	open, go
ô	law, horn
oi	oil, point
oo	look, pull
ōō	ooze, tool
yoo	unite, cure
yōō	cute, few
ou	out, crowd
u	up, cut
ʉr	fur, fern
ə	a in ago
	e in agent
	e in father
	i in unity
	o in collect
	u in focus
ch	chin, arch
ng	ring, singer
sh	she, dash
th	thin, truth
th	then, father
zh	s in pleasure
′	as in (ā′b'l)